A Genealogy of Puberty Science

A Genealogy of Puberty Science explores the modern invention of puberty as a scientific object. Drawing on Foucault's genealogical analytic, Pinto and Macleod trace the birth of puberty science in the early 1800s and follow its expansion and shifting discursive frameworks over the course of two centuries.

Offering a critical inquiry into the epistemological and political roots of our present pubertal complex, this book breaks the almost complete silence concerning puberty in critical theories and research about childhood and adolescence. Most strikingly, the book highlights the failure of ongoing medical debates on early puberty to address young people's sexual and reproductive embodiment and citizenships.

A Genealogy of Puberty Science will be of great interest to academics, researchers, and postgraduate students in the fields of child and adolescent health research, critical psychology, developmental psychology, health psychology, feminist and gender studies, medical history, science and technology studies, and sexualities and reproduction studies.

Pedro Pinto is an independent science and technology studies scholar from Lisbon. His previous research work focused on post-feminist discourse, embodiment, and the industrialisation of sexual and gender difference.

Catriona Ida Macleod is Distinguished Professor of Psychology, SARChI Chair of Critical Studies in Sexualities and Reproduction at Rhodes University, South Africa, and editor-in-chief of *Feminism & Psychology*.

Pinto and Macleod not only show the gaps in the scientific construction of 'early puberty' but also these instigate and rely upon ideological tropes of gender and racialized differences, both intersected by class. Not only is this a really important work of scholarship in its genealogical analysis of original historical documents, but the emerging critique convincingly highlights, through the attention to the so-called crisis in puberty, how science masks its own ambiguities at the expense of normalizing and pathologizing the pubertal child and her/his parents. The most supposedly natural and biological of developmental processes, puberty, is so rendered only by most unnatural knowledge generation practices. Pinto and Macleod take the specific example of puberty and brilliantly show how it exemplifies and illuminates wider axes and processes governing the management of young bodies and minds.

Erica Burman, Professor in the Manchester Institute of Education, The University of Manchester; author of *Deconstructing Developmental Psychology*

This book is a real tour de force – an eloquent, thought-provoking and detailed genealogical analysis of puberty science. It traces the way that medical science gradually got to grips with the phenomenon of puberty, and, especially the threats it was seen to pose to social and moral order. Its focus on 'precocious puberty' traces a historical story of the successive ways in which puberty has been problematized. It is elegantly drawn, and highly informative.

Wendy Stainton Rogers, Emeritus Professor, The Open University; author of *Stories of Childhood: Shifting Agendas of Child Concern*

Meticulously researched and written with much gusto, this book provides a gripping account of the history of pubertal science. Filling a major gap in Foucault's account of the history of modern sex, it demonstrates genealogy's enduring importance in addressing the significant questions of our age.

Celia Roberts, Professor in the ANU College of Arts and Social Sciences; author of *Puberty in Crisis: The Sociology of Early Sexual Development*

A Genealogy of Puberty Science

Monsters, Abnormals, and Everyone Else

Pedro Pinto and
Catriona Ida Macleod

Routledge
Taylor & Francis Group
LONDON AND NEW YORK

First published 2019
by Routledge
2 Park Square, Milton Park, Abingdon, Oxon OX14 4RN

and by Routledge
52 Vanderbilt Avenue, New York, NY 10017

First issued in paperback 2020

Routledge is an imprint of the Taylor & Francis Group, an informa business

British Library Cataloguing-in-Publication Data
A catalogue record for this book is available from the British Library

Library of Congress Cataloging-in-Publication Data
Names: Pinto, Pedro, author.
Title: A genealogy of puberty science: monsters, abnormals, and everyone else/Pedro Pinto and Catriona Ida Macleod.
Description: Milton Park, Abingdon, Oxon; New York, NY: Routledge, 2019.
Identifiers: LCCN 2018049131 (print) | LCCN 2018051564 (ebook) | ISBN 9781315142098 (E-book) | ISBN 9781138295391 (hbk) | ISBN 9781315142098 (ebk)
Subjects: LCSH: Puberty.
Classification: LCC QP84.4 (ebook) | LCC QP84.4 P5335 2019 (print) | DDC 612.6/54 — dc23
LC record available at https://lccn.loc.gov/2018049131

ISBN 13: 978-0-367-66143-4 (pbk)
ISBN 13: 978-1-138-29539-1 (hbk)

Typeset in Bembo
by Apex CoVantage, LLC

Contents

Preface and acknowledgements

This book is the result of my post-doctoral research, conducted under the auspices of the Critical Studies in Sexualities & Reproduction (CSSR) research programme, at Rhodes University. Over the four years it took me to complete the study, I had the enormous privilege to work together with Catriona Macleod, a truly inspirational woman and scholar, and the most determined academic activist I have ever met.

The book was drafted partly in Grahamstown (now Makhanda), partly in Lisbon, but the idea behind it actually emerged in the UK. In January 2010, I borrowed a pile of old psychology books from Wendy Stainton Rogers' private library (several of which I believe she and Rex Stainton Rogers had used in their critical work on child and sexual development). I also took Wendy's last copy of their *Stories of Childhood*, a book unknown to me at the time (and which I still have with a precious dedication from Wendy). In the following year, when I was thinking around post-feminist discourse and 'techno-puberty' for my PhD, I met Celia Roberts at a conference on 'sexualisation', in London, where I was lucky to share a session with her. Celia's presentation was my first important contact with the problematic of early puberty. This series of events was the starting point of the genealogical investigation showcased in this book. I am deeply grateful to Celia and Wendy as well as to Erica Burman for all their support in the past and feedback on the book manuscript.

While at the CSSR, I was fortunate to work in a stunning part of the campus – right next to an old colonial military panopticon prison, now converted to the Provost Café from where I fetched my daily coffees – and surrounded by an amazingly vibrant and welcoming community of students, scholars, and staff members. I want to thank Florence Faxa for having sweetened my workdays every time she came in to say hello: *enkosi mhlobo wam obekekileyo*. I also want to thank Rina Goosen, the director of the inter-library loan services of Rhodes University, who was relentless in locating and sending me the countless publications I requested for analysis.

Of the many fantastic people I have met in Makhanda, there is one with a special bond to the development of this book. To make a long story short, Ulandi du Plessis and I became close friends, then colleagues at the

CSSR, and suddenly part of each other's lives. I am eternally thankful to her for having proofread so many of my initial drafts, and for her incommensurable support throughout this journey.

In the beginning of 2014, before Catriona and I first met in South Africa, I told her about a project that had been slowly cooking in my mind for several years. Catriona promptly granted me the conditions to start shaping it. A few months later, I presented her the first research sketch. 'Do you know what you have here, Pedro? A book!' My gratitude for her continual encouragement and committed partnership cannot be put into words.

I would like to dedicate this book to my beautiful parents, Emília and Fausto Matoso, to whom my stories of childhood also belong.

Pedro Pinto,
Lisbon, 22 September 2018

Chapter 1

Introduction

Towards a history of the present

This book is about the modern invention of puberty as a scientific object and a health matter. Drawing on a Foucauldian genealogical analytic, or a 'history of the present', our research traces the birth of Western puberty science in the early 1800s, and follows its expansion and shifting discursive frameworks over the course of two centuries. We focus on the range of discourses and practices through which pubertal development was shaped and problematised in medical, psychiatric and paediatric literature, and historicise how, on the basis of those problematics, puberty has become a normalising technology of young people's bodies and souls. Our main aim, thus, is to expound upon the conditions of possibility of the ensemble of norms, anxieties, and modalities of intervention within which pubescent subjects are medically figured and managed around the world.

In the introduction, we set the scene with a snapshot of today's 'puberty'. Starting with a brief review of explanations and advice offered in medical online sources, we home in on the ongoing medical debates about 'precocious' development. After framing the main issues and puzzles currently facing puberty science, we proceed to outline the overarching theoretical and methodological standpoints of our research. Finally, we present an overview of how the book's central argument unfolds throughout the chapters.

Navigating 'puberty': from being *a crisis* to being *in crisis*

At present (April 2018), anyone searching for 'puberty' online will find several medical sites providing young people and adults with plenty of information. Similar definitions of puberty feature on the top pages:

> Puberty is when a child's body begins to develop and change as they become an adult. Girls develop breasts and start their periods, and boys develop a deeper voice and start to look like men.[1]
>
> Puberty is the time in life when a boy or girl becomes sexually mature. It is a process that usually happens between ages 10 and 14 for girls and ages 12 and 16 for boys.[2]

> Puberty (say: PYOO-ber-tee) is the name for the time when your body begins to develop and change as you move from kid to adult. We're talking about stuff like girls developing breasts and boys starting to look more like men.[3]

Alongside such physiological and chronological descriptions, several sites offer gentle reminders about the challenges that pubertal changes might pose and advice on how to handle them. While describing those issues, they reassure readers that it is natural to be concerned about this transitional time of life. Herewith some tips 'for Kids' provided by KidsHealth.org:

> During puberty, you might feel confused or have strong emotions that you've never had before. . . . You also may feel anxious about how your changing body looks.[4]
>
> Perhaps you've sprouted several inches above everyone else in class. Or maybe they all did the sprouting and you feel too short. . . . And now you're looking in the mirror, thinking only one thing: Am I normal? . . . First of all, what's normal? There's no *one* type of normal. Otherwise, the world would be full of a lot of abnormal people![5]
>
> Your doctor knows all about puberty and can help determine if you are developing normally. But just about everyone catches up eventually, and most differences between you and your friends will even out. Until then, hang in there. Puberty can be quite a wild ride![6]

The site simultaneously anticipates and appeases tweens' anxieties. In doing so, it conveys the familiar figure of a pubescent subject naturally uneasy with new desires and bodily changes, and prone to doubt the normality of their own development. In the site's encouraging words of advice, readers inescapably learn that going through puberty is not simply about growing up: it is about growing up either normally or abnormally. Incidentally, they learn that puberty can be a 'wild' transformation, a period marked by perplexing feelings, watchful expectations, and confusion about oneself – a time of 'crisis', as 19th-century doctors would say.

As for grown-ups, they also learn that a similar sense of confusion and some worrying uncertainties can reasonably be provoked by their children's pubescence:

> Puberty can be a confusing time for a tween, and for parents. As a child changes, so does his [sic] mood, body, interests, and even family dynamics can change. While you may prefer that your child remain little forever, puberty is coming, and that means you have to prepare.[7]
>
> While puberty is a normal condition and not an illness, many medical conditions and illnesses may first appear during puberty.[8]

In other words, puberty is said to be a critical period for parents in that they are confronted with their children becoming sexual, meaning that parents might find themselves grappling with a sense of loss, that is to say, their own children's loss of innocence. Just as children will have to adjust to their new bodies and selves, so parents have to adjust to these changes. Similar to the instructions given to young readers, parents are enjoined to keep in mind that pubescence is but 'a normal condition' while, at the same time, remaining vigilant about the health dangers inherent in this period.

As these quotes illustrate, today's medicalised discourses on puberty, either targeted at youngsters or their guardians, rest on a set of premises with peculiar internal tensions. First, puberty is a natural phenomenon which paradoxically leaves the limits between childhood and adulthood in doubt. Second, it is a 'normal condition' susceptible to the onset of abnormal and pathological states. These forces entangling around maturing young subjects – naturalness and dangerousness, normalness and abnormality/pathology – compose the overarching plot of our genealogy.

Our book is mainly about this 'normal condition', so naturally at risk of abnormalities, and about 'normal' and 'abnormal' pubescent people, who are neither children nor adults. We trace the confusion between maturity and immaturity within the pubescent body, as construed and continually reworked over the last two centuries in medical discourse. Through the following chapters, we show how this dilemma emerged in modern clinical practice to become one of the most important and disputed objects of today's sexual health sciences. But, for now, we shall continue exploring our present.

Pubertal timing: 'too late', 'too early'

As quoted above, MedlinePlus.gov, the site of the US National Library of Medicine, indicates that '[puberty] is a process that usually happens between ages 10 and 14 for girls and ages 12 and 16 for boys'. These are, roughly put, the age norms established at the end of the 1960s by the famous 20th-century growth scientist, J. M. Tanner, in collaboration with human biologist W. A. Marshall (Marshall and Tanner 1969, 1970). Their work laid the foundations of today's clinical standards of pubertal development, the Tanner Scale used to assess breast, pubic hair, and testicular and penile growth: from Stage 1 (prepubertal) to Stage 5 (mature).

Although these norms are currently adopted in international medical practice, their validity has been increasingly debated over the last two decades in paediatric circles worldwide. As we show a bit later, several experts have called for the lowering of the earliest age limits at which the onset of puberty is considered 'normal'. Unsurprisingly, thus, wider age ranges of pubertal development are more cautiously proposed in other medical sites, as found in the pages 'for Teens' by KidHealth.org: 'Puberty takes place over a number of years, and the age at which it starts and ends varies widely. It generally begins somewhere between the ages of 7 and 13 for girls, and somewhere between the ages of 9 and 15 for guys'.[9]

Regardless of the version adopted concerning the age ranges of 'normal' pubertal development, the physiological processes involved in the onset of puberty are agreed upon. KidsHealth.org explains as follows:

> When your body is ready to begin puberty, your pituitary (say: pih-TOO-uh-ter-ee) gland (a pea-shaped gland located at the bottom of your brain) releases special hormones. Depending on whether you're a boy or a girl, these hormones go to work on different parts of the body.[10]

More detailed physiological descriptions can be found in other health web resources, such as the site of the UK Society for Endocrinology, 'You and Your Hormones':

> In normal puberty, hormones from an area of the brain called the hypothalamus signal to the pituitary gland (a small gland situated underneath the brain) via a hormone called gonadotrophin-releasing hormone to produce hormones known as gonadotrophins (luteinising hormone and follicle stimulating hormone). These gonadotrophins in turn stimulate the sex glands (gonads: testicles in boys and ovaries in girls) to produce steroid hormones. These hormones are mainly testosterone in boys and oestrogen in girls and it is these steroid hormones that stimulate the development of the physical signs of puberty.[11]

As these sites indicate, a range of clinical issues may occur which will disturb the endocrinal mechanisms described above. Consequently, they can either hasten or delay the appearance of pubertal manifestations, namely breast development and testicular growth. 'In a few cases', as KidsHealth.org tells young readers, 'kids who are developing very early or who are very late in starting have a problem that may need to be checked or treated. If you are concerned about that possibility, talk with your parents and schedule a visit with your doctor'.[12]

Of course, parents might also reasonably wonder: when is the young body clinically deemed 'very early' and 'very late'?

> Precocious puberty is the abnormally early development of any secondary sexual characteristics: before the age of nine years in a boy and eight years of age in a girl.[13]
>
> Delayed puberty is defined as no secondary sexual maturation or any sign of puberty by the age of 13 years in girls and 14 years in boys.[14]

Delayed puberty is known, as indicated in these sites, to be caused by malnutrition or anorexia, excessive bodily exercise or stress, chronic illnesses (e.g. diabetes or cystic fibrosis), hormonal deficiency caused by disorders of the hypothalamus and the pituitary or thyroid glands, ovarian disease and testicular problems (e.g. cryptorchidism), and chromosomic disorders, namely Turner and Klinefelter syndromes.

But, in a vast majority of the cases, it turns out that teenagers are simply 'late bloomers', meaning there is no underlying condition causing the delay:

> Most often, it's simply a pattern of growth and development in a family. . . . This is called constitutional delay (or being a late bloomer), and it usually doesn't require any kind of treatment. These teens will eventually develop normally, just later than most of their peers.[15]
>
> In over 90% of cases, delayed puberty is due to what is known as a constitutional delay in growth and puberty. . . . Typically these children will have a short stature compared with other children of the same age and they are often thin and have a family history of delayed puberty.[16]

As to precocious puberty, it can also result from several clinical issues. Pituitary tumours and brain injuries or infections might trigger excessive levels of gonadotrophin production, in which case secondary sexual characters take form earlier, although assuming their 'normal' sequential pattern. This is nowadays called 'central' or 'true' precocious puberty. Also, gonadal and adrenal disorders causing alterations in steroid production can lead to breast budding with no other signs of sexual maturation (premature thelarche) or the appearance of pubic or axillary hair alone (premature pubarche or adrenarche). In such instances, the precocity is understood as 'peripheral'. Precocious pubescence is also one of the symptoms of the McCune-Albright syndrome, a very rare genetic disorder which, besides endocrine abnormalities, causes severe bone disease and a particular pattern of skin pigmentation.

However, the largest number of early developers are healthy girls with what is frequently called idiopathic true precocious puberty: their hypothalamus' nerve cells are activated so that gonadotrophin-releasing hormones are produced, just as occurs in any 'normal' pubescent body, only prematurely in their case. Until today, nobody has found the cause of this phenomenon – just as no scientist knows what exactly triggers puberty *tout court.*

> For the majority of girls, there's no medical problem at fault – they simply start puberty too early for no known reason. In boys, the condition is less common and more likely to be related to another medical problem.[17]
>
> The cause of precocious puberty related to early increases in activity of the hypothalamus is usually unknown although underlying causes are occasionally found in girls and in up to 50% of boys.[18]

In short, similar to what is said about delayed puberty, most cases of pubertal precocity are 'constitutional'. Unlike the average late bloomer, however, early pubescent children have rarely inherited their condition: 'Less than 1% of girls' and 'about 5% of boys'.[19]

Furthermore, the two conditions are said to follow quite distinctive epidemiologic patterns, as evidenced in the extracts below. First, there is a striking sex-differentiation as to their incidence: late bloomers are mostly male adolescents, and early developers, as seen above, mostly female children. Second, not only is precocious puberty suggested as more prevalent than 'late blooming', it is often framed in racial terms. Third, it seems that the age of puberty onset has continually declined over the decades among several world populations:

> Delayed puberty is roughly estimated to occur in about 3% of children, with 90% of these cases being caused by a constitutional delay. Constitutional delay is 10 times more common in boys than girls.[20]
>
> According to 1997 data, an estimated 4–5% of girls from all racial groups had precocious puberty. Although figures for boys are unknown, they are likely to be much lower.[21]
>
> Adolescent girls reach puberty today at earlier ages than were ever recorded previously. . . . For example, the average age of the onset of menstrual periods in girls was 15 in 1900. By the 1990s, this average had dropped to 12 and a half years of age.[22]
>
> Around the world, the age of puberty has reduced over recent generations and it is recognised that puberty is earlier in certain ethnic groups such as Afro-Caribbean and South Asian adolescents.[23]

In clear contrast with the 'problem' of late blooming, thus, early puberty is perceived as an issue increasingly affecting entire populations globally.

Earlier development: clinical implications and contentions

> There are a lot of terms that relate to puberty, and you may know many of them. One of the terms many parents don't know is Secular Trend. What is the secular trend and why are there concerns about changes in this phenomenon as it relates to puberty in recent years?[24]

In the 1960s, on examining a statistical collection with respect to several European countries and the US, Tanner (1965: 49) pointed to a 'trend towards earlier maturing during the last hundred years'. Within the next three decades, several researchers offered new evidence of this secular trend[25] (e.g. Brundtland, Liestøl and Walløe 1980; Wyshak and Frisch 1982), even when contending that the decrease in the average age of puberty onset in 19th-century Europe had not been as linear and steep as Tanner argued (Brundtland and Walløe 1976; Brudevoll, Liestøl and Walløe 1979; Rosenberg 1991). The late 1990s witnessed a forceful comeback in researching and debating this phenomenon. A number of studies have since then suggested that the average ages of girls' pubertal onset have continued to decline in recent years, namely in China (Ma et al. 2009;

Meng et al. 2017), Denmark (Aksglaede et al. 2009), the UK (Morris et al. 2011), and the US (Biro et al. 2013). The trend has also been recently found among boys in the US and elsewhere (see Herman-Giddens et al. 2012).

The rebirth of this trend as a matter of medical and social concern owes much to a controversial article by US paediatrician Marcia Herman-Giddens and associates, from the Pediatric Research in Office Settings (PROS) network. In 1997, they published their cross-sectional analysis of clinical data on 17,077 female patients aged between 3 and 12. Their findings suggested that US girls were starting puberty significantly earlier than had been reported in previous surveys. On average, the onset of breast and pubic hair growth occurred one year earlier in white girls, by age 10, and two years earlier in African-American girls, between 8 and 9 years of age. 'At age 7', more particularly, '27.2% of African-American girls and 6.7% of white girls had evidence of breast and/or pubic hair development with the proportions increasing to 48.3% and 14.7% respectively, by age 8' (Herman-Giddens et al. 1997: 507). Yet, the average ages at menarche in white and African-American girls were nearly the same as before – about 12.8 and 12.1, respectively – the implication being that US girls, especially the African-American, were starting to mature at younger ages but also taking longer to finalise sexual development. In that same year, a research team based in Hong Kong reported a similar lengthening in the pubertal timing of Southern Chinese girls (Huen et al. 1997).

The Herman-Giddens findings prompted a group of paediatric endocrinologists to write a letter to *The Lancet* arguing that the age guidelines for clinical assessments should be revised accordingly (Elders et al. 1997). On behalf of the Lawson Wilkins Pediatric Endocrine Society (LWPES) network, Paul Kaplowitz and Sharon Oberfield (1999) took up the call, proposing the lowering of the age limits of 'normal' puberty onset to 6 years for African-American girls and 7 years for white girls. 'In most cases', they asserted, 'evaluation of girls with early breast and/or pubic hair development to look for a pathologic etiology of precocious puberty need not be performed for white girls older than 7 years of age or for African-American girls older than 6 years of age' (Kaplowitz and Oberfield 1999: 940).

The statement provoked a critical chorus in the field. Robert Rosenfield and colleagues wrote a letter to the journal *Pediatrics* (Rosenfield et al. 2000: 622) warning that 'liberalizing the definition of normal carries the risk of overlooking pathology'. Furthermore, they disputed the empirical support of the initiative:

> We are of the opinion that the study [by Herman-Giddens and colleagues] has a fundamental flaw: the prevalence of the early signs of puberty was not ascertained in a sample of children drawn at random from the general population. . . . [I]n support of the possibility that the study may be flawed was the notable finding . . . that puberty is beginning earlier, but that its tempo is slower, for which there is no explanation.

In their response, Herman-Giddens, Eric Slora, and Richard Wasserman (2000: 622–3) maintained that 'the large numbers of girls studied would make it unlikely that they were different from the population as a whole'. As to the lengthening of puberty, they noted that it had also been reported in Hong Kong (as referred above), suggesting it was not particular to the US data. Despite the study's limitations, which they fully acknowledged, they stressed that, in any case, their findings would be more accurate for the US population than the data underpinning current standards, collected in the 1960s under Tanner's direction at the Harpenden Children's Home. 'Thus, we feel that our data provide a far better estimate of the age distribution of the onset of puberty in US girls than the Marshall and Tanner study of 192 institutionalized white British girls published in 1969 upon which the 8-year cutoff has been based'. They conceded that some early pubescent girls might be at risk of pathology, and that the general trend 'may not be "normal"'. Yet, they still disputed the standardised 'recommendation that all girls with the sole factor of breast development or pubic hair growth before 8 and 9 years of age, respectively, have a diagnostic evaluation'.

However, others remained reluctant about the perceived trend and its alleged implications: 'It is inappropriate to dramatically lower the "normal" ages of puberty as might be suggested by some of these reports; parents must still be educated to carefully observe and report signs of development to their primary care providers' (Reiter and Lee 2001: 989).

A little later, in France, Martin Chalumeau et al. (2002) retrospectively examined a cohort of 197 girls under age 8 with central precocious puberty, seen between 1982 and 2000 in a Paris paediatric hospital. They found that of the 11 girls in whom the condition was not idiopathic but due to cerebral disorders, two would not have been referred for brain imaging examination if the 1999 recommendations were followed. Citing a study conducted in Italy (Cisternino et al. 2000), they noted that among a total sample of 167 true precocious pubescent girls, three were diagnosed with brain abnormalities at age 7 and would not have been seen until age 8 according to the LWPES guidelines.

Nonetheless, Chalumeau et al. (2002: 66) ultimately agreed that the established age limits for the 'normal' onset of puberty signs in girls (i.e. thelarche onset) needed revision, 'as clearly demonstrated in the United States by Herman-Giddens et al (1997) and in China by Huen et al. (1997). It is probably true in many other countries. We also agree that a systematic approach using invasive dynamic biological tests and brain imaging in all cases of breast development before 8 years of age is not cost-effective' – the implication being that an exponential increase in the number of clinical referrals would become unaffordable for the health system. However, given their and others' findings, Chalumeau et al. called for further population-based research so as to enhance the screening of precocious puberty. They also noted that the 1999 proposition was anchored in the Herman-Giddens study, 'in which the cause of precocious puberty was not assessed. . . . The real impact of the LWPES's recommendations should now be tested on American girls' (p. 66).

Actually, by then, such research had already been conducted in the US by L. Kurt Midyett and colleagues. They asked 'Are Pubertal Changes in Girls Before Age 8 Benign?', assuming potential criticism at the outset: 'The hypothesis of the current study is that the new guidelines, if followed, will lead to significant under-diagnosis of endocrine conditions' (Midyett, Moore and Jacobson 2003: 47). Accordingly, they drew on a convenience sample of 223 patients referred for precocious puberty within a five-year period, specifically composed of white girls aged 7 to 8 and African-American girls aged 6 to 8 – for these would dispense with endocrine assessment under the new guidelines. They found that 47.1% had true precocious puberty, and that 12.3% of these girls had been diagnosed with more or less serious endocrine conditions – which would have passed unnoticed at those ages under the new norms.

> On the basis of the results of our study, we will continue to recommend referral of any girl who is younger than 8 years and has 2 signs of puberty. We will also continue to recommend (at a minimum) a bone age evaluation on all girls who are younger than 8 years and have even 1 sign of sexual development.
>
> (Midyett, Moore and Jacobson 2003: 51)

Furthermore, they claimed, there had been no decrease in the number of patients sent to their clinic following the 1999 recommendations, suggesting that these were not being recognised by practitioners.

In addition, they conducted their own statistical examination of the data supporting Herman-Giddens et al.'s (1997) findings. Contrary to what the Herman-Giddens study and subsequent papers suggested, Midyett and colleagues (p. 51) concluded:

> Only 22 girls out of the entire population of 17 077 girls (0.1%) of the ages and races in question would have met the definition of true precocious puberty under the definitions of precocity at the time. Subspecialty referral of 100% of girls with 2 signs of puberty would hardly overwhelm the current health care system, even with the current shortage of pediatric endocrinologists.

Finally, they refuted the statistical significance of the racial differences inferred from the PROS data, arguing that these 'do not provide a scientific basis for using separate guidelines for black and white girls between the ages of 6 and 7 years' (p. 51).

In the following year, Herman-Giddens, Kaplowitz, and Wasserman (2004) elaborated a critical review of, and responses to, articles hitherto published by one of the main hosts of the debate, the journal *Pediatrics*. In the end, they spoke of three fundamental problems in Midyett et al.'s arguments.

First, these authors made the 'erroneous assumption' that central precocious puberty in girls implies the presence of both breast and pubic hair growth;

rather, Herman-Giddens et al. explained, the latter 'is related to adrenal androgen production, the regulation of which is independent of the hypothalamic-pituitary-gonadal axis' (p. 914). This is to say, the pubertal activation of this endocrinal axis is best indicated by breast development and acceleration in linear growth, even if thelarche and adrenarche usually occur at about the same time. Consequently, they argued, Midyett and colleagues' reinterpretations of the PROS data 'are flawed', both in terms of the likely incidence of true precocious puberty and its perceived racial differences (p. 914).

Second, Herman-Giddens et al. noted that their critics 'used the wrong denominator in their calculations' – i.e. the whole 17,077 patients of the PROS sample, instead of the total of 1390 girls comprising the two racial/age groups addressed in the analysis – 'a common error that occurs when cross-sectional data are treated as longitudinal data' (p. 915). If done correctly, they added, the number of girls with one pubertal sign amounted to '9.4% of the population of 7-year-old white girls and 6- to 8-year-old black girls, not 0.8% as stated by the authors' (p. 915).

Finally, they insisted on the burdening costs of not adopting revised guidelines. After estimating that there were about 195 400 US girls below 8 years old with pubescent pubic hair, and about 650 paediatric endocrinologists in the country, they gave Midyett et al. a *priceless* response: 'If all these girls truly need an evaluation, then each endocrinologist would have to see, on average, 300 of these girls. If we estimate the cost for a basic evaluation as proposed by the authors of an examination and bone age films (including radiologist interpretation) at $250, the cost to evaluate these girls would be $48 850 000' (p. 915). While readmitting that the 1999 guidelines entailed the risk of tardy diagnoses – 'No system of screening is perfect' – they stressed that clinicians should in any case resort to age norms 'in conjunction with' the careful assessment of various non-chronological, maturational signs (p. 916). A short exchange between the two groups followed, each of them reasserting their statistical readings as well as their physiological definitions of, and clinical approaches to, precocious puberty (Jacobson, Midyett and Moore 2004; Kaplowitz, Herman-Giddens and Wasserman 2004).

Nevertheless, despite all the antagonistic views and tensions in the field, there is generalised agreement that, whatever statistical proportions the condition is said to assume, the majority of girls aged 6–8 referred for assessment for precocious puberty turn out to be true, idiopathic cases. Once the child is proven to be healthy, the parent might think, there's nothing else to do at the clinic: "not so quickly", many specialists will reply.

Possible consequences and their clinical prevention

> Sometimes, treatment of a related health problem can stop the precocious puberty. But in most cases, no other disease is triggering the condition, so treatment usually involves hormone therapy to stop sexual development. . . .

> Dramatic results are usually seen within a year of starting treatment . . . which is generally safe and usually causes no side effects in kids.[26]

Arguably, if 'normal' puberty can already be challenging – as stated by online medical sites – precocity might cause the child to experience behavioural troubles and psychosocial difficulties in more dramatic ways. In addition, it has been known since the 1940s that earlier hypothalamic activation leads to the premature closure of the epiphyses, which might reduce the child's final height. Strictly speaking, none of these possible outcomes constitutes pathology. Yet, there is a pharmaceutical treatment for them: doctors may prescribe gonadotropin-releasing-hormones (GnRH) agonists in order to halt pubescence and postpone its completion. Furthermore, parents might be warned that there's a chance that early maturing children will engage in conduct risky to health, such as early sexual activity or alcohol drinking (let alone being victims of sexual abuse), or that girls will have a higher risk of breast cancer in adult life.

Recently, Celia Roberts (e.g. 2015) and Peter Hayes (e.g. 2016) have critically delved into the logic, conundrums, and methodological support of the ensemble of dangers constructed around early pubescent bodies. As these science studies scholars show, a polyphonic corpus of research has reasserted those problematisations over the last two decades, ultimately facilitating or even promoting a normalising, treatment-based approach, rather than supporting children through celebrating diversity and focusing on their rights. Drawing from a feminist stance, in particular, Roberts highlights the ways in which health concerns about early development entwine with gendered expectations and moral panic about girls' sexualisation and the loss of childhood (see also Roberts 2013a). As these authors contend, where efforts have been made to correlate earlier puberty onset with the incidence of clinical and social problems, the same energy has not been spent on consistently testing its said implications. Instead, 'evidence is fitted to confirm that there are medical (or medical-sounding) threats to [girls'] health, rather than genuinely testing whether these threats are real and significant, or questioning whether they are truly medical' (Hayes 2016: 10).

To be fair, several of the above arguments were not alien to various of the doctors publicly engaged in the debate around pubertal timing and the 1999 guidelines. Already then, Kaplowitz and Oberfield (1999: 938), in framing their rationale, suggested that pathology was not the only or even the principle reason for girls between ages 6 and 8 being systematically sent for clinical work-up:

> Puberty in most such cases is idiopathic and central. . . . What then are the arguments that support aggressively evaluating and subsequently suppressing puberty in these girls? Behavioral problems have been noted in girls with precocious puberty, although there are few well-designed studies of this issue.

Speaking to one such study, which reported psychosocial issues in non-treated patients (e.g. aggression and depression), Kaplowitz and Oberflied argued that 'it is not clear which, if any, of these behavioral problems would have responded to hormonal therapy' (p. 938). In addition, they suggested that there were more sensible ways for parents and clinicians to engage with, and give psychological support to, early developing girls:

> A related concern is that early-maturing girls will have difficulty coping with early menarche if no treatment is offered. The 7-year-old who has Tanner 2 breasts [i.e. in the earliest pubescent stage] will in most cases not have menarche for another 2 to 3 years, allowing the paediatrician and parents ample time to prepare the child for this event.
>
> (Kaplowitz and Oberfield 1999: 938)

In their literature review, they found that, actually, the most frequent justification for hormonal therapy was the risk of height loss. They contended that before the treatment's introduction (in 1981), 'many girls with precocious puberty achieved adult height well within the normal range' (p. 938). This, as they showed, was evinced by subsequent studies aimed at testing the therapy's results (see also Hayes 2016). Regarding those attempting to demonstrate otherwise, they left an important reminder:

> Many studies have shown increased predicted adult height (based on bone age) after 1 to 3 years of therapy, and a smaller number have shown increased adult height over that predicted before the onset of therapy. It is not possible, however, to conclude from these studies that GnRH analogs are beneficial in *all* early-maturing girls.
>
> (Kaplowitz and Oberfield 1999: 939, our emphasis)

Regardless of whatever successes were announced in randomised studies, in other words, no doctor can assure parents that the drug will be effective – or that girls won't grow to their estimated final stature or overcome psychosocial issues without treatment, for that matter. In view of the data published by then, they concluded 'that in the girls with pubertal onset at 6 to 8 years, little if any beneficial effect on adult height is obtained [with treatment] in the majority of cases' (p. 939).

A few other paediatricians also stressed that treatments are usually not needed in such cases – namely some of the earliest critics of the 1999 norms, Rosenfield et al. (2000). Many other experts, however, would continue to suggest lessened height potential as a self-evident problem requiring medical intervention. In France, for example, Chalumeau et al. (2002: 66) insisted, 'Predictors for short final height . . . identified by rigorous statistical analysis, need to be established'. Discussing their US clinical data, Midyett, Moore, and Jacobson (2003: 50) maintained, 'Perhaps of greater concern than the pathologic diagnoses was the additional finding of advanced bone ages, indicating diminished growth potential in a larger subset of girls'.

By the 1990s, as seen above, doubts about height treatments for girls older than 6 years had been planted in paediatric literature, both in terms of their advisability and supposed success. Hayes (2016) relates that, in 1999, two randomised control trials suggested as much. While, to a great extent, recommendations for hormonal therapy as prevention against (slight) height loss have prevailed until the present, he notes a most interesting discursive transformation. After the 1999 reports had demystified the drug's height-enhancing powers, the rationale for its prescription as offered in medical literature started focusing much more on behavioural issues than previously. Since then, besides suggesting it as a solution for height 'problems', reports have consistently referred to the treatment as a means to 'help [girls and parents] cope with the emotional and social implications of early development' (Hayes 2016: 13).

By 2006, Herman-Giddens spoke to the challenges of earlier pubertal maturation in a piece on the secular trend in the US. Regarding adverse clinical consequences, she made a point that is still valid in today's scientific knowledge: 'The question of whether there is an optimal age for puberty and the negative effects of too early an age of sexual development (such as psychological stress or an increased risk of breast cancer in girls) needs to be answered' (Herman-Giddens 2006: 945). Meanwhile, ethical questions about treating young bodies on the basis of poor findings, and on behalf of uncertain and non-pathological outcomes, remained the elephant in the paediatric room.

Possible causes, alarming implications

> Puberty research, like so much scientific research, is a mirror onto our fears.
>
> Lisa Belkin (2000)[27]

Journalist Lisa Belkin noted the above in an interesting article on early puberty published by *The New York Times Magazine* in 2000. After Herman-Giddens et al.'s (1997) findings, the announced maturational trend and the subsequent scientific debate quickly caught the US news media's attention (Roberts 2010). Navigating theories, contentions, and calls of alarm, Belkin reported the views of several experts on the matter, starting with her encounter with Herman-Giddens at her research office. With the help of a slideshow, the paediatrician took Belkin through the main hypotheses on what might be causing the trend: 'Obesity', 'Cow's milk', 'Estrogen simulators in the environment, chemicals and plastics', and 'households without biological fathers'. Besides these, Herman-Giddens spoke of another possible cause which she clearly found very distressing:

> Considering the various theories has led her to develop a hypothesis of her own. "If you watch somebody cut a grapefruit from across the room,

> you're going to salivate," she says, "which is just one example of how what you see can have a biological effect on your body. We worry about what all the violence is doing to children. Well, what about all the sex? While we're doing all this research, we ought to be researching that".

In the background of this call for research, a range of anxieties may be discerned. These anxieties resonate strongly with academic and policy-driven claims about today's premature and undue 'sexualisation' of youth, as famously advocated since 2007 by The American Psychological Association (APA) Taskforce on the Sexualisation of Girls (see Roberts 2013a). From this standpoint, it is argued that both mainstream media and consumer culture are increasingly exposing children to age-inappropriate forms of sexual representation, from popular music and advertising to clothing and toys. The sexualising effects of these representations on youngsters' perceptions of the world and themselves, the APA reports suggest, potentially forces them into states of psychological vulnerability, such as unhealthy expectations about their bodies and problematic (early, risky, permissive) sexual conduct.

A body of feminist research has complicated such views, generally arguing that the 'sexualisation' framework narrows the debate by positioning girls as passive recipients of cultural messages (e.g. Egan and Hawkes 2008; Hawkes and Egan 2008; Jackson 2015). Feminist scholarship has vigorously illuminated young people's complex engagements with sexualised materials and their agency in negotiating meanings, hence offering alternative ways of thinking about and researching youth, sexuality, and cultural change (e.g. Attwood and Smith 2011; Renold and Ringrose 2011; Vares, Jackson and Gill 2011; Renold, Ringrose and Egan 2015). In the meantime, nonetheless, concerns about the effects of popular media on young girls' sexual behaviour have unsurprisingly been revived in psychosocial research on early puberty, as the study by Brown, Halpern, and L'Engle (2005) about 'Mass Media as a Sexual Super Peer for Early Maturing Girls' illustrates.

Reflecting this widespread fear of 'sexualisation' in her interview with Belkin, Herman-Giddens took a step further: she hypothesised that the sexualising effects of culture are not only behavioural but also physical. Belkin correctly suggested that this was (and still is) a marginal hypothesis in the scientific field. However, unlike Belkin asserted, Herman-Gidden's 'theory' is certainly not 'of her own'; it is actually quite an old one, systematically yielded by a long tradition of scientific sexism, as we shall show in our book. In any case, as her slideshow illustrated, there were other worrying hypotheses.

In 2001, after re-examining the PROS data, Kaplowitz and colleagues (Herman-Giddens included) hypothesised a causal link between increasing obesity and earlier puberty among US girls (Kaplowitz et al. 2001). Likewise, subsequent studies correlated being overweight and earlier sexual development in girls (Wang 2002; Anderson, Dallal and Must 2003), drawing on other US data sets, namely the National Health and Nutrition Examination Surveys (NHANES).

Meanwhile, based on their analysis of the NHANES data, Herman-Giddens, Wang, and Koch (2001) suggested that African-American, Mexican-American, and white boys were also starting genital and pubic hair growth earlier than before. Within the next two years, based on analyses of the NHANES data (Wu, Mendola and Buck 2002; Chumlea et al. 2003) or alternative official sources (Freedman et al. 2002), researchers continued reporting racial differences in US girls' pubertal timing. 'The Wu et al analysis', Herman-Giddens, Kaplowitz, and Wasserman stressed, 'provides the important additional information that racial and ethnic differences among the NHANES populations are independent of select social and economic factors' (2004: 911).

Considering the above set of biomedical findings and correlations, questions as to how they speak to issues of class and racial inequality can be posed. Are those racial differences in girls' ages of sexual development an indicator of the structural inequalities that have affected specific populations, namely the African-American communities? As Roberts (2013a: 144) writes, the perceived trend 'raises complex questions about the biological and developmental effects of racism', especially in view of the inevitable tangling of racial difference with poverty and lack of social support.

While researchers have often remained silent about such issues in discussing their findings (Roberts 2015), they have consistently hypothesised earlier puberty as the result of a complex entanglement of biological and social actors. In their inaugural article, Herman-Giddens et al. (1997: 511) noted that, according to a 1994 study, 'hair products containing estrogen and placenta may be related to some increased prevalence of early puberty in African-American girls', and recommended inquiry on possible 'estrogen-related physiological effects' of other chemical agents. In their later review, Herman-Giddens, Kaplowitz, and Wasserman (2004: 915) insisted that, 'given the remarkable changes over the last few decades in the environment with regard to factors suspected of affecting puberty such as endocrine disrupters and the epidemic of overweight and obesity, pubertal events may be a sensitive indicator of conditions that are not healthful'. Research work on these topics 'should continue' (p. 916).

By 2006, Herman-Giddens listed the scientific 'theories and speculations' about the trend's incidence, pointing to a number of possible endogenous (congenital and psychosomatic) and exogenous (social and environmental) triggers:[28]

- Genetic differences among racial/ethnic groups
- Overweight and obesity, decreased physical activity
- Pre and postnatal exposure to endocrine disrupter chemicals
- Infant soy-based formulas
- Girls born small for gestational age
- Stress, absent fathers, unrelated males in the household
- Effects of different types of diet
- Exogenous hormones
- Hypersexualization of culture.

(Herman-Giddens 2006: 245)

Making yet another call for further inquiries on the causes of earlier puberty, Herman-Giddens stressed that 'the cumulative effects of multiple factors must be included' in such investigations (p. 245). She thus proposed research that reflected a biosocial, multi-factorial understanding of the trend. Such an approach enabled not only addressing clinical and ecological concerns but also the requirement for educational interventions, starting with sex pedagogy: 'The timing and content of sexual education in schools may need revision' (Herman-Giddens et al. 1997: 511).

Despite the careful and multifaceted approaches to early puberty voiced by leading health experts – most of them pointing to non-clinical, social-familial ways of engaging with cases – the general response of the paediatric field has not been that nuanced. In her readings of epidemiological, social scientific, and mainstream media discourses on early development, Roberts (2013b: 301) sees 'a widespread mode of thought that . . . creates a sense of ecological, medical and moral crisis demanding pharmaceutical intervention'. Cozzi and Vinel (2015) offer a similar critique. After reviewing expert literature and interviewing health professionals working in Italy and France, they painted the landscape of anxieties around early (and 'normal') maturing bodies as follows:

> Notwithstanding the lack of evidence in the studies and the controversies over puberty timing, a social alarm is spreading by, disseminated by press screamers. Not only are preadolescents precociously sexually active: they are prone to consumerism and substance abuse, as an imitation of adult's misconducts. Childhood is shorter and shorter, and physical signs demonstrate it.
>
> (Cozzi and Vinel 2015: 294)

As a result, their findings strongly suggest, medical engagements with early maturing children have remained heavily oriented towards the clinical preventive management – i.e. hormonal treatment – of the behavioural risks associated with the condition, as Hayes' (2016) analysis also indicates.

Puberty in crisis, knowledge in crisis

> "The 'why' is the important part," Herman-Giddens says as she sets up a slide projector and dims the lights. "We don't know anything if we don't know why." She takes the remote control in hand and runs through the prevailing theories. . . . "Is it going to keep getting lower? Are kids going to get to be 5 and 4 and 3? And is this supposed to be happening? I don't think so. I don't think that's what nature intended".
>
> Belkin (2000)[29]

At present, as Roberts (2015) illuminates, puberty is construed across a range of scientific and popular arenas as being itself in a state of crisis. In the dominant narratives on earlier puberty, 'the bodies and lives of girls, childhood more broadly and even humanity's reproductive futures are said to be at stake' (Roberts 2013a: 143). Ultimately, the puberty-in-crisis discourse evokes a crisis of the culturally established limits and meanings of 'nature', as crystallised in Herman-Giddens' musings reported by Belkin: this is not what nature intended.

Looking into today's 'puberty', as shown throughout our brief overview, the perceived crisis of pubertal timing – which announces an unnatural event with social consequences – may be said to entangle three major levels of concern: moral, biopolitical, and epistemological.

First, the idea of children going through puberty earlier and earlier, in a world perceived as extremely sexualised and increasingly 'risky', troubles established values of sexual morality and child development itself. Not only is early puberty systematically depicted as a predictably disquieting situation for parents, the reported trend raises questions around appropriate and inappropriate sexual conduct, age-opportune sexual education, and proper parenting. Likewise, the condition provokes new dilemmas about children's 'moral development', as 19th-century doctors often termed it.

In expert and mainstream health discourses, moreover, the onset of puberty – both precocious and 'normal' – is conflated with dangers associated with 'the end of childhood', or 'the loss of innocence',[30] most notably expressed in relation to girls. As Roberts (2013a: 148) contends, 'scientific, news media, environmentalist and public policy debates around early development and sexualisation tend to represent all young girls as sexually innocent and thus requiring protection from (their own and others') desires'. Where early pubescent girls are concerned, suggestions of possible psychological harm and inadequate sexual behaviour parallel the eminent fear of sexual predation.

Second, while requiring clinical, parental, and pedagogical interventions targeted at early developers, earlier puberty also constitutes a challenge to the government of the population. The fact that an increasing number of young people may be engaging in behaviour considered risky to their and others' health – from having 'premature' sex to taking drugs – sets off alarms about a dysfunctional and unmanageable social body. Likewise, the trend in pubertal timing amplifies reproductive and epidemic-related anxieties within public health which are entangled with questions of gender, class, poverty, and racism (Roberts 2013a). Ultimately, thus, early development brings the biopolitical surveillance and protection of the species into play.

Finally, the puberty-in-crisis discourse encapsulates a crisis of paediatric medicine, and of puberty science in particular. Earlier pubescent patients who are otherwise healthy trouble the ethics, theories, and standardised practices of a whole medical profession concerned with child and adolescent development. In unsettling established norms and provoking calls for their revision, earlier puberty renders current clinical distinctions between normality and abnormality uncertain. As a result, it produces powerful tensions in the paediatric management of pubescent bodies: some advocate new guidelines (for both health-related and economic reasons), others caution against possible under-diagnoses; some suggest possible over-prescription of hormonal treatments, others depict them as crucial and successful. In the end, however, the success of these treatments cannot be guaranteed, and their iatrogenic effects are still waiting for further testing (Hayes 2016).

Furthermore, not only are the reported health risks of early development controversial, no scientist can say what triggers puberty's endocrinal mechanisms, be their timing 'normal' or 'abnormal'. Today, in short, alongside the prevailing ignorance about the natural *causes* of sexual maturation, there is a very clear understanding of *how* pubescent bodies work. The puberty-in-crisis discourse inescapably talks to the ethical and disciplinary discomfort of not knowing enough to explain the 'abnormal' while knowing enough to intervene on the child's body.

With this in mind, in our genealogical research we have departed from a twofold question. On the one hand, how did puberty become such a self-evident and yet controversial biomedical object? On the other hand, how and when did pubertal medicine attain its modern scientific status, henceforth allowing for systematic forms of scrutiny and intervention in the lives of children and those around them?

As we show in this book, the perceived crisis of puberty is not exactly new. Concerns with moral and biological decay and the current tensions within pubertal knowledge-practice, whilst seemingly provoked by new configurations in child development, have actually been at the heart of puberty science's emergence and expansion. The current crisis of puberty is rooted in the confusion of immaturity and maturity within the very young body, as construed in early 19th-century clinical discourse. That crisis replicates racial, gendered, and class-based anxieties about sexual morality and reproductive futures voiced in the statistical studies of pubertal timing from the 1830s–40s. Within its own technical and disciplinary dilemmas, the ongoing crisis of pubertal knowledge recapitulates medicine's early embarrassment with the fact that the monstrous and abnormal child could be controlled and corrected, but not cured.

Throughout our introduction, we have navigated a swirl of powers, discursive manoeuvres, and injunctions around sexual development. On behalf of a healthy and timely puberty, parents are medically advised about how to deal with their children, and children are encouraged to monitor themselves; doctors call for tighter surveillance over maturing subjects, inciting governmental authorities to act upon environmental and social issues endangering public health; preventive treatments for healthy developing bodies are often deemed advisable by the clinical profession and justified in reference to parental concern. This state of affairs is not at all recent, as we demonstrate in the chapters to come.

Following Michel Foucault (1988: 101), our interest in investigating the past is to 'make the present situation comprehensible and, possibly, lead to action'. Our contribution to the ongoing study and discussion about pubertal timing is one that brings the historical conditions of today's puberty science into the centre of the debate. Therefore, rather than a history of medical conceptions of puberty, we propose a critical inquiry into the problematisations by which certain practices and relations of power took shape around sexually maturing children. Accordingly, our main aim is to trace the epistemological and political roots of today's pubertal apparatus – i.e. the ensemble of norms, anxieties, and modalities of intervention within which pubescent subjects are medically figured and managed worldwide.

On doing the genealogy of puberty science

Our project in this book is heavily inspired by Foucault's academic work and activism. In our research, we have extensively used (several of) the analytical notions, standpoints, and methods of what he called 'the archaeology of knowledge', and later, in complement, 'genealogy'. The epistemological and philosophical implications of Foucault's analytics for critical scholarships have been extensively discussed (e.g. Dreyfus and Rabinow 1983; Diamond and Quinby 1988; Mahon 1992; McNay 1992; Huffer 2009). Here, we restrict ourselves to briefly clarifying the general points of our archival-genealogical framework in terms of its key historiographical approaches and conceptual tools.

Subjects, events, and discourses

A few years before his death, Foucault (1982: 77) famously wrote that his principle endeavour over two decades 'has been to create a history of the different modes by which, in our culture, human beings are made subjects'. He argued that the constitution of subjects as cultural realities – namely the sexually precocious child – is embedded in interdependent relations of knowledge *and* power. He insisted that 'there is no power relation without the correlative constitution of a field of knowledge, nor any knowledge that does not presuppose and constitute at the same time power relations' (Foucault 1995: 27). In our research, we assume this power-knowledge nexus as the general system allowing for medical subjects to emerge and transform over time, but also as a most effective 'instrument' to render 'the relationship between subjects and truth' comprehensible (Foucault 2000: 290).

In historicising puberty science, thus, we have investigated the different modes in which, on the basis of knowledge deemed true, medicine and psychiatry have idealised, construed, and positioned pubescent subjects until the present. In tracing those 'modes of subjectivation', we have also traced their adjoining 'modes of objectification': once human beings are figured and categorised through any institutionalised form of knowledge – by others but also by themselves – they necessarily become the object of some truth, thereby *subjected* to its explicit and implicit effects upon their lives (Foucault 1982, 2001a). While analysing subjects' construction and positioning in scientific discourse, in short, we have also looked into the ways and reasonings by which young people, or features within them, have qualified as necessary *objects* of study and control.

Foucault termed this twofold line of inquiry 'archaeology', or the study of an 'archive' – i.e. 'the ensemble of the discourses effectively pronounced . . . which continues to function, to transform throughout history, allowing for other discourses to appear' (Foucault 2001b: 800).[31] Archaeology's final aim is to illuminate the practices and events underpinning the reconfiguration or replacement of what Foucault called an *episteme*: bluntly put, the discursive game of rules – the regime – governing scientific statements and techniques within a certain period. Accordingly, researchers conducting archival work are not interested in the *meaning* of something stated at a given time and place but rather in its strategic function in a field of power-knowledge relations. 'The history which bears and determines us', as Foucault (1980a: 114) later said, 'has the form of a war rather than that of a language: relations of power, not relations of meaning. History has no "meaning", though this is not to say that it is absurd or incoherent'. In reading scientific literatures, likewise, we treated statements as *events*, as discursive *facts*, which necessarily correlate with other events recorded in the same or other disciplinary or institutional domains.

The correlation between events, as Foucault clarified towards the end of the 1960s, is embedded in a 'game of dependencies', which are to be decomposed by the discourse analyst according to three fundamental levels: (i) *intradiscursive dependencies* – i.e. 'between the objects, the operations, the concepts of the same formation'; (ii) *interdiscursive dependencies* – i.e. 'between different discursive formations'; and (iii) *extradiscursive dependencies* – i.e. 'between discursive transformations and [transformations] that are produced outside discourse' (Foucault 2001c: 708). This method led us to organise the materials around major discursive themes (described below), allowing us to highlight patterns across the data irrespective of the texts' provenance or specific fields.

Struggles and 'subjugated knowledges'

By the late 1960s, Foucault argued for 'a work of excavation' of knowledge as a way to critically inquire: 'what are we today? What is that "today" in which we live?' (Foucault 2001d: 641). This question led him to progressively reshape the rational of his work according to what he later termed genealogy, or 'the history of the present' (Foucault 1995: 31). In the spring of 1983, he explained as follows:

> What I mean by archaeology is a methodological framework for my analysis. What I mean by genealogy is both the reason and the target of analysing those discourses and events, and what I am trying to show is how those events have determined in a certain way what constitutes our present and what constitutes ourselves – either our knowledge, our practices, our type of rationality, our relationship to ourselves and to others.
>
> (Foucault cit. Mahon 1992: 105)

In terms of 'both the reason and the target' of our research, we have oriented towards what Foucault called (2003a: 7) 'the insurrection of subjugated knowledges': our analysis resurrects 'confrontations and struggles' concerning puberty that run deep in medical history, but which 'have been buried or masked in [the] functional coherences and formal systematizations' inherent in scientific disciplines. For us, rediscovering those struggles in the multidisciplinary science of puberty has been a useful way to contextualise important shifts in medical discourse and practice. In particular, by unpacking doctor's standpoints, contentions, and respective discursive strategies, we have been able to show the ways in which their biopolitical concerns shaped, and were shaped by, their studying of pubertal development and timing. Finally, in paying attention to struggles – this is to say, in theorising networks of disputes, validations, and resistances as a ground on which to historicise medical sciences – we have not looked for an analytical field wherein the 'hidden' contradictions could finally be exposed. Instead, we have framed those struggles as coherent historical mechanisms allowing for new knowledges and respective power relations to emerge.

Puberty science: clinical and social

In historicising the scientific study and management of puberty, we have assumed that there is no real divide between clinical and epidemiological or 'social' medicine. The emergence of new techniques of examination, diagnosis and therapy, and the expansion of a clinical market stimulated by private demand – 'the great medical edifice of the nineteenth century' – is inseparable from the establishment of a health politic concerned with the community: 'both derive from a common global strategy' (Foucault 1980b: 166–7). As our genealogy shows, the modern clinical medicine of pubescence was the same medicine that concerned itself with the quality of housing in working-class districts, the health of the nation's 'racial' make-up, the gendered organisation of schooling, or the social issues posed by juvenile delinquency.

Looking into the 'socialisation' of pubertal knowledge, in particular, we have kept in mind that this socialisation historically intertwines with the modern construction of society as an organic reality, an amenable *body* (Rose 1994). As Foucault (1980b) argues, one of the main strategies through which medicine spread its power across the social body was the medicalisation of the family and the home. During the 18th century, the so-called cell-family rose as an extension of the hospital and the clinic. The domestic space was now to function as 'a dense, saturated, permanent, continuous physical environment which envelops, maintains and develops the child's body'; henceforth, parents were required 'to produce – under the best possible conditions – a human being that will live until the state of adulthood' (Foucault 1980b: 172–3). As our study highlights, pubertal development has been a key technology for the establishment of those power relations between parents and doctors around the child.

The normal and the pathological

During the analyses of medical and psychiatric texts, we often encountered the conflation of abnormality and pathology in the doctors' accounts. As Foucault (2003b) shows in his lectures on the *Abnormal*, the early 1800s saw the rise of a normalising power which *does not* operate in the same manner as medicine's traditional power which permits the doctor to assign disease and cure. From a medical perspective, the world is not simply populated by the ill and the non-ill, but also by those who either do or do not conform to certain norms. People's medicalised existence is foremost bent on 'the permanent distinction between normal and abnormal, the perpetual enterprise of restoring the system to normality' (Foucault 2001e: 50).

As current medical views of puberty attest, there is a universe of clinical subjects who escape the possibility of healing because, quite simply, they embody no illness to defeat. Their 'problems', or the dangers they represent, do not take the forms of physiological degeneration or sickness that translate into pain, agony, disability, or even death. While being subjected to treatments, the vast majority of early developers are not to be cured but rather corrected, transformed, enhanced. This is to say, the power of pubertal knowledge, the effects of its 'truths', are not only pathological but also, and perhaps more importantly, normalising. Following Foucault's genealogical work, thus, we have kept the important theoretical distinction between the abnormal and the pathological, while attending to their intricate interplay. From around the mid-19th century, as we show in Chapter 7, pubertal abnormalities (bodily and behavioural) have figured in health sciences as a principle – a risk factor, as we say today – for disease.

Pubertal knowledge as scientific

In talking of the birth of puberty *science*, of puberty as a *scientific* subject matter, we refer to a process that was part of a relatively long episode in the history of science: a broader transformation concerning the production of truth in medicine and other scientific fields. We particularly mean that, by the mid-19th century, pubertal medicine had fully embraced an epistemic modality wherein the assertion of true knowledge requires its *demonstration* through replicable, positive methods, 'a technology of demonstrative truth':

> [F]or scientific practice in general, there is always the truth, the truth is always present. . . . The truth in itself permeates the entire world, without break. . . . This means that for a scientific type of knowledge nothing is too small, trivial, ephemeral, or occasional for the question of truth, nothing to distant or close to hand for us to put the question: what are you in truth?
>
> (Foucault 2006: 235–6)

Unlike the old Hippocratic management of sickness, as later addressed in this book, modern medicine no longer concerns itself with 'a truth which will only speak or appear from time to time, where it wishes to', and only via the ritualised activities of 'privileged agents and bearers' (p. 237). For the earliest scientists of puberty, likewise, its truth could and should be discovered everywhere across the planet, provided that proper scientific techniques were wisely employed. While drawing on 'scientific' knowledge and its presumed universality, therefore, we have drawn on the premise 'that scientific demonstration is basically only a ritual . . . and that the discovery of truth is really a certain production of truth' (p. 238).

Speaking of change

To sum up, with the above standpoints in mind, the goal of our archival research was to frame the epistemic regimes sustaining the production of pubertal knowledge, and to trace the discursive practices and events by which those regimes gave way to different ones. When looking at these transformative events closely, such fractures or breakups of epistemic regimes can be described in terms of radical and abrupt changes – as they sometimes are in our historical narrative. Yet, putting them in genealogical perspective, one can also see that they entail 'a slow preceding evolution of practices which, at a certain moment, passes a threshold and takes on the character of a mutation' (Castel 1991: 281).

While pointing to 'births' as well as discursive discontinuities, thus, we have attempted to locate them within broader networks of historical processes and agents of transformation operating inside and outside scientific worlds. It is precisely in this sense that we use the term 'apparatus', which is the usual English translation for Foucault's analytical notion of *dispositif*. Whenever we talk of an apparatus during the study, we mean an ensemble that 'consists of: strategies of relations of forces supporting, and supported by, types of knowledge' (Foucault 1980c: 196). In theorising the historical apparatus allowing for an event or regime to rise in puberty science, we speak to this heterogeneous formation of strategies of power, technical-material arrangements, and modes of knowledge construction: in this sense, we articulate 'the said as much as the unsaid' (p. 194).

Setting-up, constructing, and reading the archive

Our first research step was to conduct a systematic literature search for medical, paediatric, and psychiatric journal articles concerning puberty. We chose the five oldest periodicals (published in English) indexed in the Web of Science database under the categories 'medical' (established in the early 1800s), 'psychiatric' (appearing in the second half of the 19th century), and 'paediatric' (only founded in the first decades of the 20th century). All the 15 journals have been active from their inception to the time of writing this book (although intermittently and under different titles, in several cases). The medical journals are:

Journal of the Royal Society of Medicine, *The New England Journal of Medicine*, *The American Journal of the Medical Sciences*, *The Lancet*, and *British Medical Journal*. The psychiatric journals are: *British Journal of Psychiatry*, *American Journal of Psychiatry*, *Addiction*, *The Journal of Nervous and Mental Disease*, and *American Journal of Orthopsychiatry*. The paediatric journals are: *JAMA Pediatrics*, *Acta Paediatrica*, *Archives of Disease in Childhood*, *The Journal of Pediatrics*, and *Pediatrics*. Most of these publications are associated with the establishment of important royal societies and national associations of medicine and allied sciences.

Our systematic literature search followed very simple criteria: we looked for all articles with 'puberty' (or any derivative term) in the title, published since the founding year of each journal until 1950.[32] Here, our strategy was basically to generate a sample of a manageable size, but also to ensure that the articles' main focus was on pubertal development. This initial data corpus consisted of clinical reports, empirical studies, essays, literature reviews, and doctors' letters, comprising 123 pieces. As to our periodisation, the decision was also based on historical reasons. By 1950, puberty's endocrinal and metabolic mechanisms were fairly well-known and the medical-psychiatric foundations of today's paediatric science had been laid. Also, by then, a clinical apparatus concerning sexual difference, particularly the treatment of what 1940s doctors still called 'hermaphroditism', was set in place. In that decade, finally, the non-pathological, 'constitutional' type of precocious puberty was described and asserted as the most common type of the condition.

Our second step was to explore and organise the initial body of materials into major themes. Those discursive themes were constructed such that they could be read independently of each other as coherent systems of discourses, but also reflect links and discontinuities between them. The overarching themes produced in our research are: *monsters*, *abnormals*, and *the surveillance of all*.

These first materials guided us into a wealth of other texts, from journal articles to medical monographs, written in English or French. This second body of data (totalling over 100 documents) allowed us to explore important knowledge formations and academic debates further, and to dig more deeply into the work of specific authors such as the first instigators of a 'true' science of puberty (e.g. Roberton in England or Boismont in France, amongst others).

During the research, we became aware that our periodisation missed out a seminal episode in the formation of today's pubertal apparatus: Tanner's statistical capturing of the secular trend towards earlier maturing. Our concern around Tanner's work was not that the genealogy would not cover the Harpenden Growth Study and the subsequent construction of the Tanner Scale. Not only has the Harpenden project been extensively reviewed and critiqued by Roberts (2015: 61–90, 2016), pubertal standards for clinical assessment were (tentatively) established and strongly advocated in the 1940s, namely by Richard Ellis in the UK. Nevertheless, whilst our archival work allowed us to address the conditions of possibility for the problematising of earlier puberty, we simply could not historicise the emergence of the trend through steps 1 and 2 described above.

The third step of our archival study, therefore, consisted in tracing the knowledge generated on the trend from its earliest assertions and re-elaborations to the present. Here, our gathering of data was neither exhaustive nor systematic. At the outset, we wanted to see how the discursive rationality supporting the postulated biosocial causes and implications of the trend has changed over the decades. Our final aim was to theorise the links of that rationality to a general apparatus of prevention against the unnatural as part of a modern politic of life. Starting off with Tanners' earliest texts on growth and the trend, we tracked publications referencing and/or critiquing his arguments until the 1990s. For the period from the late 1990s to the 2010s, we compiled a body of journal articles and important reviews/discussions from the paediatric-epidemiological field (e.g. Parent et al. 2003; Euling et al. 2008; Walvoord 2010) via searching reference lists and a number of databases (Cumulative Index to Nursing and Allied Health Literature [CINAHL], Directory of Open Access Journals [DOAJ], eMedicine, Global Health, Google Scholar, MedicLatina, Medline, Scopus, and Web of Science). Then we organised this last set of materials – from the mid-20th century onwards – around two main themes: the puberty-in-crisis discourse, on the one hand, and risk-treatment practices, on the other. Our history of today's 'puberty' ends with a genealogy of the bio-historical discourse of pubertal crisis, and of the peculiar subject position of the child patient who is to be treated for uncertain health dangers.

At the start of our research, we became acquainted with Tanner's superbly detailed volume, *A History of the Study of Human Growth*, published in 1981. This text, in our view, is not a critical history. In fact, at some points, we would say it is quite aseptically written. For one, while he describes his own momentous contributions to the field (in the third person), he chose to leave out the 'discovery' of the trend and the explicitly eugenic mood in which it was introduced. Nonetheless, regardless of the criticisms one may make concerning Tanner as a growth scientist, as we do later in the book, his historiographical devotion and the unique wealth of information he provides should be acknowledged. For us, Tanner's *History* was extremely useful in checking the historical relevance and making sense of our own data in relation to pubertal growth. It ultimately supported us in theorising the complicated affair between growth phenomena and sexual maturation in the genealogical developments of puberty science.

Finally, our research is bound up with a polymorphous body of writings, most notably by feminist and queer theorists, historians of childhood, biopolitics scholars, historians of science and technology, and scholars whose inquiries move across those fields. We are especially indebted to the critiques, histories, and counter-stories by Anne Fausto-Sterling, Celia Roberts, Erica Burman, Ian Hacking, Londa Schiebinger, Lorna Weir, Nancy Stepan, Maria Tamboukou, Nikolas Rose, Paul Rabinow, Rex and Wendy Stainton-Rogers, and Roy Porter. In some, we found important support to our analyses; in others, we found thrilling theoretical complicities: in one way or another, they all have been close 'companions' in our venture.

The book: parts and their chapters

> The historical record is like the night sky: we see a few stars and group them into mythic constellations. But what is chiefly visible is the darkness.
>
> Roy Porter (1998: 13)

Roy Porter wrote these beautiful words in the introduction to his colossal history of medical sciences. Like him, we kept grouping and regrouping multiple constellations of events, always encountering the 'darkness' of our own theorisations, our incapacity to link as many dots as we would have liked. Besides, unlike the sky, our space here is very limited: we chose to follow some of the paths instead of others. There remains an endless universe of stories to be told about puberty science, children, and the regulation of young people's lives. This book, therefore, is also an invitation for others to continue the paths we take, challenge them, or take alternative ones.

Drawing from the overarching themes produced in our archival work, our genealogy unfolds in three main parts:

I Precocious little monsters

We begin Chapter 2 by introducing the figure of the child monster, as produced in medicine's first encounters with 'precocious' or 'premature puberty'. In the early 1800s, the characteristic discursive regime governing doctors' problematisation and objectification of the condition was that of human monstrosity. Precocious pubescent children personified the undue yet fascinating mixture of maturity and immaturity, thereby upsetting both natural and social laws. Following Foucault's (2003b: 56) definition of the monster, we argue that these children were the great representors of 'the spontaneous, brutal, but consequently natural form of the unnatural' in 19th-century medical discourse.

Confronted with their dilemmatic condition, clinicians suggested concerns about whether such children were to develop towards an able, reproductive, and intellectually sound adult state. As shown in Chapter 2, this threefold preoccupation took on a highly gendered shape, distribution, and emphasis, reflecting patriarchal expectations regarding those children's future roles in society. Pubertal precocity immediately posed the problems of survival and education; but it also anticipated a set of medical and social dangers: most notably, the distressing eventuality of a child delivering another child – the monstrosity of the monstrosity, the extreme biological and social unnaturalness.

A simultaneous line of enquiry was established in early case reports: whether the child's behaviour also revealed precocious sexual manifestations. Two gendered figures emerged: the masturbating young boy and the 'modest' young girl. Rather than conveying the unnatural, these figures embodied an 'innocent' mind abnormally driven by the instinctual force of sexual pleasures and desires. In short, they posed the problem of a behavioural rather than a biological monstrosity. From this standpoint, the problem of pubertal precocity was increasingly invested with the technologies and normalising power of a nascent sexual psychiatry. In Chapter 3, after tracing this shift of the child monster into a moral monster, we describe the technical-discursive apparatus supporting the management of precocious pubescent children deployed throughout the 19th century: an intimate and extremely detailed clinical gaze combined with a meticulous vigilance at home.

Finally, in Chapter 4, we elaborate on speculations of the causes of precocious puberty circulating in 19th-century clinical reports. In looking into doctors' 'family portraits' of young patients, in particular, we find the interweaving of hereditary-racial and socioeconomic-environmental features, all of which suggest a possible causal background in the cases under discussion. In clinical discourse, in short, the 'premature body' emerged as a biosocial phenomenon. From the earliest clinical studies of the child monster, there emerged a biosocial thinking about early pubescence, and so about puberty itself, which undermined the discourse of the pubertal monstrous body from the outset.

2 From biological to cultural monstrosities

The 1830s–40s saw the birth of modern research on pubertal timing. As we show in second part of the book, this event took place on the basis of two interlinked surfaces of emergence. On the disciplinary plain, there was a conversion of pubertal medicine to a statistical technology of truth-demonstration which defied previously adopted views of pubertal timing. Within the first statistical debates on the causal triggers of menarche, puberty figured as a multifactorial, biosocial phenomenon, rendered sensible by the promising powers of 'the numerical method'. On the biopolitical plane, those studies and debates were bound to angsts about the 'uncivilised' in a changing colonial world, on the one hand, and increasing worries about child factory labour and the precarious living conditions of the working classes, on the other. More particularly, while some talked of 'monstrous' social settings forcing girls into earlier puberties outside the 'civilised' West, others descried the 'evil' effects of 'civilisation' upon girls' maturation into a 'proper womanhood'. Reading novels, watching a theatre play, or listening to music were activities the developing girl should avoid – seemingly more so, according to several doctors, than working in a textile factory.

Across Chapters 5 and 6, we draw on the historical apparatus underpinning the inception of age norms of puberty onset in different 'races' and socio-professional classes. We argue that this apparatus encompasses three strategic forces: the scientific demands of medical jurisprudence, the intertwined debates of scientific racism and scientific sexism, and movements of colonial and metropolitan reform. In Chapter 5, we conclude with John Roberton's evolutionary causal theorisation of early puberty among the Hindu, and its reflection of a discursive shift from an excluding and de-humanising racism to an inclusive and normalising one. In Chapter 6, moving across the findings and contentions of the first statisticians of puberty, we conclude with James Whitehead's inquiries on menarcheal ages among labouring populations and 'educated ladies', showing the rise of an epidemiological notion of pubertal risk in his discourse.

3 The surveillance of all

From the 1940s onwards, puberty science enormously expanded the scope and the reach of its intervention: from the management and correction of the few to the surveillance of all. In the final part of the book, we elaborate on three major discursive events/regimes by which pubertal medicine's normalising power was generalised to all maturing individuals: the construction of pubescence as dangerous; the production of the Normal pubertal body; and the assimilation of an epidemiological reasoning around risk into a clinical rationale for pubertal corrections.

Puberty as dangerous

Starting with Raciborski's re-elaboration of puberty as a time of 'crisis', as discussed in Chapter 7, the discourse of 'puberty as dangerous' was actualised again and again in countless attempts to explain, prevent, and find remedy for a range of conditions affecting youth. During the 1870s–90s, the correlation of pubertal 'growth acceleration' and the onset of sickness was widely espoused, both statistically and in clinical etiological hypotheses. Henceforth, from a physiological angle, puberty-as-crisis foremost referred to the temporality and intensity of pubertal changes; the rapid and energy-demanding evolution seen to characterise that period became problematic in and of itself. Here, again, girls' puberty looked particularly vulnerable, with many doctors protesting against the damaging effects of school 'overpressure' during such a 'critical' period of girls' maturation into proper and serviceable womanhood.

By the late 1800s, from the viewpoint of modern psychiatry, every pubescent subject could well become a mental case. After 1900, the whole problematic of the instincts was re-codified by endocrinal knowledge and recycled evolutionary truths. This approach proved resilient. In the mental medicine of the 1920s–40s, puberty-as-crisis fundamentally implied a war between natural drives and the moral self. In light of with this 'pubertal struggle against the instincts', as Joseph Lander put it in 1942, parents, doctors, and pedagogues were all enrolled in helping children in managing their conduct across the 'storm' of life. If they failed, it was maintained, criminal behaviour was a likely consequence, especially for the 'mental defectives' and 'maladjusted' who quickly became school-dropouts. 'Petty and serious crimes committed by this large army of juvenile delinquents are a matter of common knowledge', asserted US doctor Alfred Gordon in 1921.

The Normal *pubertal body*

In Chapter 8, we draw on the anthropometric and physiological apparatus allowing for the birth of the 'normal' body of pubescence and its modern surveillance during the first half of the 1900s. From the early forging of growth standards, and the subsequent discovery – or invention – of a 'physiological age', to the first efforts to standardise pubertal growth and metabolism on the basis of that notion, we delve into a new network of normalising views of the pubescent body. In the end, as several specialists suggested, those views complicated the very notion of pubertal normalcy and the attempts to capture it. Simultaneously, the production of this 'normal' body foregrounded a new system for the correction of sexual abnormality in the young, provoking dilemmas as to the advisability of procedures and treatments. Focusing on the surgical and pharmaceutical technologies employed in puberty science in the 1920s–40s, we explore the contentious politics and ethical views on which such interventions were voiced in paediatric discourse.

Within that period, owing to quick advances in endocrinal knowledge and surgical practice, the theoretical separation between pathology and abnormality became well-pronounced: a long biological dynasty of sexual monsters reached its end. By 1944, Novak called attention to the 'constitutional' type of pubertal precocity in girls, showing it to be the most common. This event completed a 100-year transformation in medical discourse: as J. Flamand Christensen pointed out in 1947, the 'gigantic' child of early medical memoires dissolved into a little abnormal; rather than unnatural, precocious puberty was, in most cases, a natural 'anomaly'. However, he also suggested, early pubescent girls were at risk, not only of sexual abuse, but also of not being able to 'to lead a normal life' as adults. The only remedy available to prevent such dangers was, in a word, pedagogy.

Pubertal risk

In a few decades, clinicians would actually be able to directly intervene upon early maturing bodies, not to treat sickness or any health complication, but on behalf of risk and risk alone. In the concluding chapter, we historicise the technical-discursive apparatus sustaining today's paediatric management of early development. We start by briefly redrawing the main lines along which puberty progressively moved from being a state of health into being a source of danger, reviewing both statistical and clinical modalities in which pubescent subjects were construed as 'at risk' and 'to-be-corrected' from the early 1800s to the 1940s.

Then, resuming the genealogy where we have left it (i.e. 1950), we engage with Tanner's contributions to the field. After briefly elaborating on the Harpenden Study as to its theoretical, clinical, and disciplinary implications, we critically explore what Tanner saw as a decline in pubertal ages across the industrialised world since the 19th century. Drawing on the trend's bio-historical discourse, we argue that its construction was a key event in the transposition of epidemiological risks associated with early puberty into clinical (and parental) anxieties about pubescent bodies. At the same time, this event allowed for a multidisciplinary scholarship to develop around the problematic of earlier development, and for a new discourse to emerge with it: puberty itself is going through a crisis. While tracking important changes in the discursive regime supporting the biosocial knowledge of the 'trend' from its inception to the present, we theorise its continual articulation with old ideas of collective degeneracy and monstrous sociocultural settings.

In the chapter's final part, we go back to Novak's 'constitutional' precocity and trace the emergence of today's corrective technology of early developers. According to its current politics, healthy children should be submitted to treatments as a form of risk prevention. After discussing the ethical and epistemic complications fuelling the ongoing crisis of puberty science, we conclude with a reflection on our 'today and tomorrow' as construed in paediatric and epidemiologic discourses on pubertal timing.

Notes

1 The NHS website, 'Stages of puberty: what happens to boys and girls'. Available at: https://www.nhs.uk/live-well/sexual-health/stages-of-puberty-what-happens-to-boys-and-girls/
2 MedlinePlus, The US National Library of Medicine, 'Puberty'. Available at: https://medlineplus.gov/puberty.html
3 KidsHealth, The Nemours Foundation, 'All about puberty/Time to change'. Available at: https://kidshealth.org/en/kids/puberty.html#kha_11
4 KidsHealth, The Nemours Foundation, 'All about puberty/Change can feel kind of trange'. Available at: https://kidshealth.org/en/kids/puberty.html#kha_51
5 KidsHealth, The Nemours Foundation, 'I'm growing up – but am I normal?'. Available at: https://kidshealth.org/en/kids/growing-up-normal.html
6 KidsHealth, The Nemours Foundation, 'All about puberty/Developing differently'. Available at: https://kidshealth.org/en/kids/puberty.html#kha_52
7 Verywell Family, 'Tips for talking to your tweens about puberty'. Available at: https://www.verywellfamily.com/talking-about-puberty-to-your-tweens-3288357
8 MedicineNet, WebMD Network, 'Puberty / What are the medical concerns associated with normal puberty?'. Available at: https://www.medicinenet.com/puberty/article.htm#what_are_the_medical_concerns_associated_with_normal_puberty
9 KidsHealth, The Nemours Foundation, 'Delayed puberty / What is delayed puberty?'. Available at: https://kidshealth.org/en/teens/delayed-puberty.html#kha_11
10 KidsHealth, The Nemours Foundation, 'All about puberty/Time to change'. Available at: https://kidshealth.org/en/kids/puberty.html#kha_11
11 You and Your Hormones, Society for Endocrinology, 'Precocious puberty/What is precocious puberty?' Available at: www.yourhormones.info/endocrine-conditions/precocious-puberty
12 KidsHealth, The Nemours Foundation, 'All about puberty / Developing differently'. Available at: https://kidshealth.org/en/kids/puberty.html#kha_52

13 You and Your Hormones, Society for Endocrinology, 'Precocious puberty'. Available at: www.yourhormones.info/endocrine-conditions/precocious-puberty
14 You and Your Hormones, Society for Endocrinology, 'Delayed puberty'. Available at: www.yourhormones.info/endocrine-conditions/delayed-puberty
15 KidsHealth, The Nemours Foundation, 'Delayed puberty/What causes delayed puberty?'. Available at: https://kidshealth.org/en/teens/delayed-puberty.html#kha_21
16 You and Your Hormones, Society for Endocrinology, 'Delayed puberty/What causes delayed puberty?'. Available at: www.yourhormones.info/endocrine-conditions/delayed-puberty
17 KidsHealth, The Nemours Foundation, 'Precocious puberty/Causes of precocious puberty'. Available at: https://kidshealth.org/en/parents/precocious.html#kha_22
18 You and Your Hormones, Society for Endocrinology, 'Precocious puberty/What causes precocious puberty?'. Available at: www.yourhormones.info/endocrine-conditions/precocious-puberty
19 KidsHealth, The Nemours Foundation, 'Precocious puberty / Causes of precocious puberty'. Available at: https://kidshealth.org/en/parents/precocious.html#kha_22
20 You and Your Hormones, Society for Endocrinology, 'Delayed puberty/How common is delayed puberty?' Available at: www.yourhormones.info/endocrine-conditions/delayed-puberty
21 You and Your Hormones, Society for Endocrinology, 'Precocious puberty/How common is precocious puberty?' Available at: www.yourhormones.info/endocrine-conditions/precocious-puberty
22 MedicineNet, WebMD Network, 'Puberty/When does puberty occur?' Available at: https://www.medicinenet.com/puberty/article.htm#when_does_puberty_occur
23 You and Your Hormones, Society for Endocrinology, 'Precocious puberty/How common is precocious puberty?' Available at: www.yourhormones.info/endocrine-conditions/precocious-puberty
24 Verywell Family, 'The secular trend, menarche, and puberty'. Available at: https://www.verywellfamily.com/definition-of-secular-trend-3288342
25 The term 'secular trend', traditionally used in econometric as well as anthropometric work, refers to a phenomenon lasting over a century (*secular*) or a relatively long period.
26 KidsHealth, The Nemours Foundation, 'Precocious puberty/Treatment for precocious puberty'. Available at: https://kidshealth.org/en/parents/precocious.html#kha_32
27 Belkin, L., *The New York Times Magazine* website, 'The making of an 8-year-old woman'. Available at: https://www.nytimes.com/2000/12/24/magazine/the-making-of-an-8-year-old-woman.html
28 To these, we shall add that it has also been suggested that internationally adopted children can experience early development (see Hayes 2013; Roberts 2013b, 2015: 147–8).
29 Belkin, L., *The New York Times Magazine* website, 'The making of an 8-year-old woman'. Available at: https://www.nytimes.com/2000/12/24/magazine/the-making-of-an-8-year-old-woman.html
30 In their beautiful *Stories of Childhood*, amongst their deconstructions and reconstructions of childhood narratives that prevail in popular and scientific discourse, critical psychologists Rex Stainton-Rogers and Wendy Stainton-Rogers (1992: 141–61) offer a fundamental critique of the 'childhood's end' theme.
31 Foucault's 'archaeology' laid the basis of many critical discourse analytic methods used nowadays in research (see, for example, Arribas-Ayllon and Walkerdine 2008; Parker 2002).
32 Within this time frame, we found no articles in the psychiatric journal *Addiction* with 'puberty' or derivative terms in the titles, or, alternatively, in the body of the text.

Part I

Precocious little monsters

Chapter 2

Child monstrosity and the dilemma of nature

Until well into the 1800s, what mostly concerned and fascinated the clinical profession about puberty was the monstrous manifestation of its 'signs' on the body of the infant and the young child. In this chapter, we show that doctors' earliest reports addressed the overarching question of whether these children were to grow into an able, reproductive, and disciplined adulthood. Pubertal precocity immediately raised issues around developmental health and education. But it also anticipated a specific set of medical and social dangers: most notably, child pregnancy and young girls being subjected to sexual predation. From the start, the modern problematisation of early sexual developers assumed markedly gendered narratives, in which the reproductive girl child was a main focus of regulation.

Faced with the child monster, clinicians were required to determine the multiple features of the condition and, however precariously, articulate them within a coherent symptomatology, according to the scientific rules of the time. As the first part of this book suggests, the rise in the early 1800s of a new scientific study of pubescence – combining anatomical observations with analyses of physiological and intellectual functions – is tightly bound to the problem of 'precocious' or 'premature puberty'. Doctors' first attempts to establish *pubertas praecox* as a clinical entity were a crucial historical element in the epistemic conversion of the techniques and discursive rationalities of pubertal knowledge production during that century. Indeed, it should not be presumed that modern pubertal medicine turned its attention to the episodic cases of precocity as a smaller or secondary level of concern, only after having undertaken the grand investigation of puberty as a natural phenomenon and having revealed its scientific laws. On the contrary, rather, the modern science of puberty, on both the individual and the population levels, is rooted in the body of the monstrous pubescent child.

'Remarkable children': blending maturity and immaturity

In March 1809, a paper by British physician Anthony White was read in a meeting of the Royal Medical Society. It offered the 'Historical Account of Philip Howorth, a Boy, in whom Signs of Puberty Commenced at an Early

Age'. In introducing the case, White began by situating it in a long lineage of stories about 'remarkable children':

> The histories of remarkable children have been transmitted to us from the days of Pliny the elder, who lived in the reign of Vespasian. Philemon Holland, his translator, in book vii chap. 16, has the following observation: – "It is well known that there be some that naturally are never but a foot and a half high; others again somewhat longer, and to this height they come in three years, which is the full course of their age and then they die. We read, moreover, in the chronicles, that in Salamis one Euthimenes had a son who in three years grew to be three cubits, or four feet and half high, but he was in his gait slow and heavy, and in his wit as dull and blockish, howbeit in this time overgrown he was, and his voice changed to be great, and at three years' end died suddenly of a general cramp".
>
> An account is also given by Craterus, the brother of king Antigonus: the subject of which story was an infant, a young man, a mature man, and an old man, was married and begat children, and all in the space of seven years!
>
> (White 1809: 278–9)

At the outset, White allocated those 'remarkable children' to the realm of monstrosity. As occurred in clinical examinations of such children until well into the 1800s, he construed them via the discursive regime of the 'human monster', which Foucault (2003b: 55–75) historicises as the background-figure of the modern abnormal. As shown in Foucault's genealogical study, monstrosity was perceived in any subject who embodied the transgression of both natural and social laws: 'The monster combines the impossible and the forbidden' (p. 56). Overall, it is precisely within this double transgression that White's and other's case subjects were framed and positioned through the 1800s, as we elaborate in this chapter.

On the one hand, as outlined by Foucault, the monster violates the sovereign order of Nature's distinctions and classifications – it is the confusion or mixture of kingdoms, of species, of sexes, of individuals in the same body. For example, monstrosity appears in the half-human beasts of the Middle Ages, in infant bodies born only to live a few hours or days (the mixture of life and death), in Siamese twins (the mixture of two persons in one body), or in hermaphrodites (the mixture of the two sexes). As soon as a transgression of limits is found within the body, there is the monster. And yet, monstrosity is 'the spontaneous, brutal, but consequently natural form of the unnatural' (p. 56): it asserts nature's imperious force while standing outside its boundaries. Monstrosity is simultaneously the expression and the negation of nature. It reifies both the order and irrationality of nature by somehow escaping its laws.

White's 'remarkable children' also challenge natural order because – and here we find their monstrous specificity – they represent the mixture of maturity and immaturity in a very young subject. The ruthless manifestation of this ambiguity is found in their anatomical features and, even more dramatically, their capacity to reproduce. In addition, paradoxically, in White's quotes their bodies are seen as already anticipating a very short life, possibly ending in collapse.[1] From his account onwards, as we shall see in this chapter, this problem of the child monster's untimely death, and so the question of survival, is quickly dismissed and replaced by a totally different kind of problematic: that of a premature sexual-reproductive *life*.

On the other hand, as Foucault shows, monstrosity takes shape 'only when the confusion comes up against, overturns, or disrupts civil, canon, or religious law' (p. 63), and in such a way that 'Law must either question its own foundations, or its practice, or fall silent, or abdicate, or appeal to another reference system, or again invent a casuistry' (p. 64). Monstrosity, therefore, is not to be confused with disability. Whereas disability is given provision and protection by the law, 'the monster's power and its capacity to create anxiety are due to the fact that it violates the law while leaving it with nothing to say' (p. 56).

Likewise, White's 'remarkable children' had reached some degree of reproductive maturity before the laws of nature should permit it and the laws of society could provide for them. They, thus, provoked a set of scientific-social-legal puzzles. Are they children or adults? How should they be regarded legally? What about their civil and religious status: if indeed they are children, should they get married? And if they happen to reproduce, should they be legally recognised as parents? If they are to be seen as mature individuals due to the development of their sexual apparatus, should they be punished as adults? What is the place of these immature-mature subjects in a lawful society? Although White's and other early clinicians' reports did not address these questions, such issues were carefully considered in British medical jurisprudence a little later in that century, as shown in Chapter 5.

Nevertheless, White provided a discursive framework wherein those children loomed as sexual-reproductive little monsters. As such, as we shall see next, they constituted a type of monstrosity of a very unique medical-juridical substance. This uniqueness set them apart from the hermaphrodite, the great representor of sexual monstrosity from the Classical Age to the 19th century (cf. Foucault 2003b: 66–7).

Speaking to a few legal cases, Foucault shows that the figure of the hermaphrodite underwent a crucial mutation in medical-juridical discourse over two centuries: from being sentenced to die up until the late 1500s to being released in 1601 yet prohibited from having any kind of sexual relations, to finally being forced, in 1765, to behave according to their 'predominant' sex and live in 'heterosexual' conjugality. By the 18th century, this is to say, rather than being killed or banned from sexuality, hermaphrodites were punished as soon as their ambiguous bodies caused them to manifest monstrous *behaviour*. 'Monstrosity, therefore, is no longer the undue mixture of what should be separated by nature. It is simply an irregularity, a slight deviation, but one that makes possible something that really will be a monstrosity, that is to say, the monstrosity of character' (p. 73). Where pubertal precocity is concerned, this shift from biological to moral monstrosity started to take form some decades later, as we shall show in this and the following chapters. In any case, as Foucault's genealogy suggests, hermaphroditism remained an object of legal and social condemnation, whereas the 'remarkable children' described by White and others following him were, bluntly put, the good sexual monsters.

The benign monster: an 'extraordinary' excess of nature

Before introducing his own memoir, White jumped from old narratives of remarkable children to the early modern era, referring to the first clinical account of pubertal precocity ever documented in English medical literature:

> In January, 1747, Dr. Mead presented to the Royal Society the history of an extraordinary child, born at Willingham, near Cambridge, which is to be found in the Philosophical Transactions for the year 1745, vol. 43. This child, according to the relation of his historian, Thomas Dawkes, surgeon, at St. Ives, near Huntingdon, was not only remarkable on account of his bulk and height, but also for the external marks of puberty which were first observed at the age of twelve months.
>
> (White 1809: 279–80)

In 1858, another fellow of the Royal Society, Robert Smart, reported 'On a Case of Premature Puberty', also citing Dr Mead's seminal accounts in his introduction:

> The earliest instance of premature puberty which I have been able to find in an English volume is in the 'Philosophical Transactions' for 1745, where there are two letters, entitled "Some Account of the Gigantic Boy as Willingham, near Cambridge." This child, named Thomas Hale, was born Oct. 31, 1741; he was a lusty boy at birth, and the parts of generation were remarkably large. . . . The change of diet, consequent on his mother's death, has no retarding influence on his growth, as he continued to flourish amazingly, and, when he was two years and ten months old, Mr. Dawkes, surgeon, at Huntingdon, communicated the particulars of his case to Dr. Mead. At this time, he was three feet eight inches and a half high, and weighed, in his clothes, four stone two pounds. He possessed extraordinary strength, and could easily lift and throw from him a blacksmith's hammer, which weighed seventeen pounds. When provoked by other children, he did not fight with his fists and legs, but laid his opponent prostrate by sheer strength, treating thus even boys of eight or ten years of age. His voice was "like a man's very groom." The genital organs were of large size, and the pubes covered with long crisp and thick hair.
>
> (Smart 1858: 455–6)

Clearly, these subjects (from White's old child monsters to Thomas Hale) constitute quite the opposite of the mixture of sexes associated with the hermaphrodite: their bodies attest to the forceful order of sexual difference, even though anticipating it in a grotesque manner, that is, in a form that immediately disqualifies nature's power in sustaining orderly physical development. Their defective morphology offends natural laws because of an excess, instead of a lack of potency. In this sense, they are the natural antithesis of hermaphrodites. In stark contrast with them, these young sexual monsters are 'remarkable' and 'flourish amazingly'. They are the erratic brutality and limits of nature but, nonetheless, the cause of 'admiration'.

This is the overarching theme of Dr Mead's 1740s case report, but also of reports such as those on Philip Howorth (White 1809), Charlotte Mawer (Cooper 1813), James Savin (Breschet 1821), John Sparrow (South 1823), and Mary Dean (Smart 1858):

> On viewing the body naked from the pelvis upwards, he is nearly the exact representation of the Farnese Hercules reduced. The pectoral and serrati muscles, the abdominal, and those of the neck are eminently conspicuous; the muscles of the back, and around the scapulae, are also remarkable; the arm is truly herculean; the deltoid, when in powerful action, swells to an astonishing thickness, and its insertion is well marked; the fore-arm is muscular, the hand large, with the common integuments remarkably hard; the contour of the neck is beautiful, marking, from its formation where it joins the dorsal vertebrae, excessive strength; the chest is broad and fleshy.
>
> (White 1809: 283)

> The breasts are very full, and as large as most young women's of twenty years of age. She is very broad over her chest and loins. Her pelvis seems much larger than is ever observed at her age. The pubes is covered with a white-coloured hair, which began to shew itself when she had the first appearance of the catamenia. She is quite a little woman in her appearance, except as to her countenance, which is childish.
>
> (Cooper 1813: 208)

> His gait is free from the vacillation which characterizes that of children of his age, and his muscles are more developed, and more vigorous. . . . His voice is sonorous and corresponding in its tone to that of a youth of 16 or 18 years of age, and, in a word, has the character of puberty.
>
> (Breschet 1821: 446)

> When his clothes are stripped off, the trunk presents the appearance of that of an adult, except that he is not so large across the shoulders as he is round the pelvis, the clavicles being, comparatively with the rest of his body, short. . . . But it is the posterior view of the trunk which presents, next to the parts of generation, the most remarkable appearance.
>
> (South 1823: 80, 81)

> It will be seen, from the accompanying photographs, that her general appearance is wonderfully like that of an adult female, of short stature, and the resemblance is maintained in her functional economy, the menses recurring every month, as regularly as in their normal manifestation.
>
> (Smart 1858: 457)

If these children incite more than simple curiosity or pity, they provoke fascination with their spectacular bodily features and, in boys' case, their physical power. Unlike the hermaphrodite, their monstrosity is not to be punished by criminal law; their existence alone is not subjected to violence or condemnation. These clinical accounts are exemplary of a kind of medical narrative particular to the 18th and 19th centuries, which tells the story of little prototypes of men and women, ultimately asserting that, however unnatural, these precocious little monsters are neither unlawful nor biologically dysfunctional subjects. Thus, while disrupting the laws of nature and the norms of society, they are a very particular kind of monster: a benign monster.

Yet, in early 19th-century clinical discourse, premature pubescent children blended maturity and immaturity in biologically *as well as* socially deviant ways. The extraordinary appearance of pubertal signs in such patients cleaved apart the natural-unnatural divisions sustaining the biological-juridical order of child development, thereby up-ending both medical and societal principles of sexuality and reproduction. After all, as discussed later in this chapter, pubertal precocity was the aberrant manifestation of sexual maturity in those whose minds were still 'innocent', which raised behavioural concerns of significance to social life.

Assessing the child monster: able, reproductive, and disciplined?

Confronted with the child monster's natural-unnatural condition, doctors in the 1800s expressed concerns which, while in line with the general alarm regarding child mortality of the previous centuries (see Foucault 1980a), were also distinct from the traditional medical preoccupation about infants' survival and safeguarding childhood. In 19th-century reports on the condition, the management of childhood as a delicate and irregular path towards adulthood takes very specific gendered forms and focuses. At the outset, doctors suggested doubts as to whether such children would not merely to survive, but also reach a capable and sexually reproductive maturity.

This medical problem necessitated a certain kind of clinical scrutiny which, White regretfully remarked in his case introduction, had been neglected by the doctor who had examined Thomas Hale in the 1740s:

> This child, according to the relation of his historian, Thomas Dawkes, surgeon, at St. Ives, near Huntingdon, was not only remarkable on account

> of his bulk and height, but also for the external marks of puberty which were first observed at the age of twelve months. No evidence however has been given of the perfect development of the genital organs; their external appearance has alone been described, without any regard to the state of their functions.
>
> (White 1809: 279)

White's text illuminates a medical discourse in the making. It reflects the scientific call for a medical understanding of sexual bodies that objectifies their features as well as their workings. His report voices an expert clinical opinion that no longer contents itself with just looking at the sexual body: the clinician also ought to analyse its performance, the 'state' of its 'functions'. In short, it reflects a move from an external to an internal gaze of the pubertal body; or better, from a pseudo-scientific sexual anatomy of the surface to a corporeal knowledge that is not just visual but also functional. Accordingly, as we discuss in Chapter 3, White and others offered excruciatingly detailed corporeal and functional descriptions, revealing the enormous intimacy of their clinical approach to their young patients' precocious bodies.

Based on this type of examination, White (1809: 287) was able to conclude that in Philip Howorth's corporeality, 'nothing of monstrosity is to be found'. He was obviously not referring to the sexual monstrosity that nonetheless constitutes the central theme of this account, that is, the mixture of maturity and immaturity in a single subject. White uses the old medical term of 'monstrosity' to designate what later in the century would be seen as a bodily defect, a somatic abnormality (Foucault 2003b). His conclusive statement simply attests that Philip, despite his monstrous sexual features, is a healthy boy with a perfectly working sexual body.

In this respect, boys seldom raised any other concern besides the reproductive validity of their eventual sexual performance. In their case, the question of reproductive maturity was basically considered with regard to the normal size, shape, and functioning of their sexual apparatus – for example, if they had erections and if they produced semen:

> The penis and testes are as large as I have seen in some adults. The corpus spongiosum urethrae has outgrown the corpora cavernosa, which gives the penis a considerable curve, when in a state of erection. The testes are firm and perfect in their formation, and the chord may be distinctly felt; the prepuce is easily drawn back over the glans, and the secretion of the glandulae odoriferae is apparent.
>
> (White 1809: 284)

> The penis measured in length from the pubis to the extremity of the glans nearly four inches when in a flaccid [state], and five inches and a quarter when in a state of erection. The circumference of the glans in the former

> condition was three inches and a half; in the latter, three inches and three quarters. All the functions appear to be in a healthy and vigorous state. A spermatic odor exhales from his body.
>
> (Breschet 1821: 446)

Besides their sexual vigour, moreover, as early illustrated in doctors' portrayals of young boys, these immature-mature male patients were promptly positioned as rather powerful little men by their medical biographers:

> He possesses very considerable strength, being able to lift a weight of forty pounds without much exertion.
>
> (White 1809: 286)

> He does not fail to be master when he plays with other children, and uses his fist with good effect, to obtain from them any object which may particularly strike his fancy. . . . The spine is very erect; and from the nape of the neck to the pelvis, he is completely covered with hair, like a strong muscular man: in short, the back gives the idea of very great strength which he possesses, as he can lift a half-hundred weight with one hand, with great ease, and will drag an adult about on his rocking-horse, without much exertion.
>
> (South 1823: 79, 81–2)

Strength, tenacity, and even willingness and capacity to fight: all these figured as 'admirable' features, proper to the manly adulthood so precociously erupting in these children's physical existence. Their remarkableness reflected not only doctors' fascination with – or medical ignorance of, if you will – the condition, but also a certain anticipation of an adult citizenship in which those qualities would be desirable and useful in young men. In short, clinicians' notable interest in those features ultimately attested to these young boys' healthy conformity to a bodily able, and therefore productive, manhood.

The reproductive girl child: healthy but at risk

When it came to girls, while their constitution or 'frame' was often said to be strong and healthy, no comments were made about their physical power. Furthermore, the same central question of reproduction was put in far more complicated terms: female pubertal precocity posed the problem of child pregnancy. From the clinical standpoint of child monstrosity, this figured as the most fascinating as well as the most upsetting natural-unnatural outcome of the condition. The following is an early account of such a case:

> Matilda H. was born in New Orleans, Sept. 31, 1827, with her mammae perfectly formed, and the mons veneris covered with hair. At three years of

> age the menses appeared, and have continued every month, until the present time (May 1832), as copious as in any woman, each period lasting four days. She is now 42½ inches high (French measure), of handsome feature, her frame very strong; and the pelvis such as, in Dr. Le Beau's opinion, will allow her to bear children when she is eight years of age or sooner.
>
> (Le Beau cit. *The Lancet* 1833: 709)[2]

In early reports about girls, emphasis was given to their biological potential to procreate (eventually attested to by the clinically recorded occurrence of child pregnancies and subsequent births, as shown below). This anxiety comprised both a 'positive' and a 'negative' biopolitical discourse: positive, because the medicalisation of these subjects' fertility spoke to the reproduction and maintenance of the social body and the vitality of the nation; but negative as well, because their fertility meant, to put it in dramatic (monstrous) terms, a child giving birth to another child. Given that pregnancy was in this case to occur in what nonetheless was a still-developing body, the reproductive girl child appeared inescapably endangered by her physiological maturity. While seen as 'remarkable' or 'astonishing', such girls' premature sexual biology automatically situated them as subjects-at-risk due to, above all, the clinically alarming prospect of very early pregnancies.

Indeed, the doctors who were engaged with such cases showed no explicit interest in child sexual abuse in their reports. They addressed the problem of child pregnancy strictly from the ethos of a medical humanism that called for the protection and saving of life itself above anything else. Accordingly, their perplexities mostly drew on the physiological likelihood of a child delivering, and becoming the parent of, another child – the monstrosity of the monstrosity, the extreme biological and social unnatural.

Nevertheless, physiological anxieties around these girls' reproductive power also incited concerns as to the prevention of such situations, as illustrated in another short report, this time on a 'Case of Puberty and Pregnancy in a Girl of Ten Years of Age':

> Sally Deweese, daughter of John Deweese, was born in Butler county, Kentucky, on the 7th of April, 1824. She was of the ordinary size, but her hips and breasts began to grow rapidly in a few weeks after she was born, and at twelve months of age she began to menstruate, and her hips and breasts had become so large as to be the objects of common remark; and as she took no pain to conceal her condition, her menstruating so young, became a fact of public notoriety, which continued regularly till some time in the year of 1833, when she became pregnant, and on the 20th day of April, 1834, she was delivered of a healthy female child, weighing seven and three-fourth pounds. Thus, at the age of ten years and thirteen days, she became a mother of a child of ordinary size; which, however, refused to suck her, and has been so far raised by the bottle. It is as healthy as usual

> for children to be when raised from the bottle, and at the time of taking these notes it weighed eight and three-fourth pounds, and its mother weighed one hundred pounds.[3]
>
> (Rowlett cit. *American Journal of the Medical Sciences* 1834: 266)

Like the previous example, this account evokes the physiological anxieties referred to above, ultimately reassuring – this time with a matter of fact – that the girl child is indeed reproductive and can survive childbirth. However, as Rowlett's remarks also suggest, her immature maturity entailed an implausible motherhood. Upfront, alongside the concerns about her new-born's size and weight, Sally's fertility raised questions about her ability to nourish, or better, to breastfeed her child.

Simultaneously, a discourse around social risks and their prevention unfolds throughout the extract. The reproductive girl child is exposed to peril as soon as she becomes an object of 'public notoriety' and 'common remark'. Not only does she cause curiosity in others, she eventually provokes the sexual desire of older boys and men. The reader does not know the context in which this child conceived, nor if it happened with a peer or if she was victim of abuse (that is clearly not the question of 19th-century puberty science, or at least it remains silent within this type of medical literature). In the face of a possible premature sexual initiation, what nevertheless seems to emerge is a certain need 'to conceal her condition', the implication being that proper, restrictive measures directed at girls themselves should have been taken to avoid the pregnancy. While boys' spectacular features were accorded an environment of great social visibility in early 19th-century medical accounts, the same is not true with regard to precocious pubescent girls. Their space of developmental existence – girlhood, if you will – appears promptly constrained by the ubiquitous danger of premature sex, their bodies being positioned as its very trigger and consequently requiring a thorough and restrictive regime of vigilance.

The monster's challenge to morality and education

Alongside anxieties about reproductive futures, *pubertas praecox* raised the associated problem of how to educate and morally guide the child monster towards adulthood. These psychosocial questions were central to the formation of modern puberty science, as they provided the point of contact between monstrosity and abnormality in 19th-century clinical views of the condition. Returning to White's 1809 report, we can see the question of 'intellect' already at work:

> In the history of the boy related by Pliny, he describes him as stupid and dull of intellect; the reverse of this, however, is found in this boy. His understanding seems equal to that of a child of six years old, and many

> of his observations and inquiries appear to have been the result of mature reflection. It must however, be observed, that his general character is marked with a considerable mixture of childish playfulness. How far he is capable of receiving scholastic instruction has not yet been ascertained.
>
> (White 1809: 286)

As White's account illustrates, child monstrosity is not constituted through the premature body alone. In being the confusion of immaturity and maturity within the same individual, such monstrosity puts the child's 'intellect' into question as well. As earlier argued, pubertal precocity manifests in those whose 'understanding', as White wrote, is 'that of a child'. The 'considerable mixture' of these two elements is where child monstrosity truly resides and takes shape. It is precisely around this body-mind interface that the dilemma of maturity-immaturity is formulated in its complete scientific form. The first great scientific endeavour around pubertal precocity was not simply to know how sexually mature the young body was, but also the extent to which the child's mental development corresponded with that of her/his sexual apparatus.

This task obviously implied a kind of clinical approach that sought for signs of maturity in children's behaviour. To do so, doctors had to attend to the qualities of their 'character' overall, but also to their aptitude to learn and be disciplined. Hence, in pondering on whether and how the condition could influence or determine personality and conduct, clinicians automatically engaged with the question: are these children 'dull' or, rather, 'capable of receiving scholastic instruction'? In answering it, doctors necessarily drew on psychological comparisons between their patients and other, 'normal', children.

In child monstrosity discourse, this analytical framework served either to normalise and even praise (as in White's case) or disqualify (as in the following extract) the child's intellectual faculties. Either way, such assessments ultimately led doctors to the same conclusion: although sexually remarkable, the monstrous child was indeed just a child.

> His style of expression is laconic, abrupt, and often imperative. His intellect, however, does not appear to have a progress corresponding to that of the genital system; for though his memory is good, his judgment is not at all superior to what might be expected from his age and the education he has received, and his imagination is not peculiarly vivid.
>
> (Breschet 1821: 446)

Alongside their 'imagination', 'memory', and their cognitive potential overall, these children's attentiveness or ability to concentrate and stay quiet also became important objects in clinical analyses of immaturity-maturity. In assessing the extent to which the child monster's mind was morally mouldable and capable, this is to say, to use Foucauldian language, doctors inevitably pointed to their patients' *docility*, whether they were subjectable to authority or not.

> As to his disposition, from what I have observed, I have no doubt that his mother's statement is correct. When a stranger visits him, he is at first shy; but, by the kind manner which children expect and so well know how to appreciate, any thing may be done with him, which I have myself witnessed when I measured him, and at the time when Mr. Silvester, one of our students, was so kind as to make a sketch of him for me; which last took up full two hours at his first sitting, during which time he allowed himself to be put in any position we thought proper without the least opposition.
>
> (South 1823: 82)

In addition, the idea of a possibly monstrous 'intellect' called for observations focused on the normality – that is, the immaturity – of the child's habits, play, and forms of entertainment. In the end, physicians happily suggested that, however prematurely, the child monster walked the proper paths towards manhood and womanhood.

> He is of an intrepid disposition, conscious of his power, disdaining to engage with children of his own years; and placing his chief delight in contests of strength with those with whom he is a more equal match.
>
> (Breschet 1821: 446)

> Her mother describes her as being "old-fashioned in her ways," as being fond of babies and household employments, and as liking dress and display, loving to strut in some tawdry drapery hung fantastically from her shoulders.
>
> (Smart 1858: 459)

Thus, while addressing their intellectual capacities, doctors first and foremost scrutinised these children's thoughts, tempers, natural aptitudes, self-control, awareness about themselves and the consequences of their actions. Their intellectual analysis was primarily to understand if both patients' motivations and their personalities reflected the natural traits of childhood so that the stage of their moral development could be assessed. In short, insofar as child sexual monstrosity upset the very nature of childhood, doctors ought to analyse how childish these children were.

> He is remarkably inquisitive, asking the name of everything which is new to him, which he does not forget as children generally do. But still his faculties are only those of a child, though his body is so completely evolved: he still acts from the impulse of the moment, without reflection on the consequences of his wishes. He is satisfied with the common amusements of childhood, and can be amused for hours with a humming-top, or scribbling on a piece of

paper; whilst, on the other hand, if he be opposed in the most trivial thing, he will throw himself into a violent passion, chastise the offender, if it be in his power, or, if not, vent his indignation in a flood of tears.

(South 1823: 82)

In this detailed analysis of the child monster's 'faculties', 'amusements', and 'wishes', childhood itself is rediscovered within the non-pathological axis of normal-abnormal sexual development. This type of clinical gaze paved the way for the codification of puberty according to a sexed-gendered logic endemic to notions of developmental health circulating in 1800s medical-psychiatric knowledge (see Chapter 3). As precocious children were sexually monstrous and yet just children, a clinical approach to their psychology was enabled wherein the immaturity-maturity nexus is configured around children's natural lack of 'reflection'. After all, provided that patients were deemed healthy in most cases, it is due to this mental trait (lack of reflection) that the premature sexual body potentially constituted a real problem. Just as with South's patient, who seemed unable to reflect on 'the consequences of his wishes', the premature sexual body was often confirmed as being governed by a childish, impulsive mind. An unnerving problem rose: that of a possibly dangerous mind that may eventually result in unacceptable conduct.[4]

At all events, in this early clinical framework where the child is psychologically measured against his/her own sexual apparatus, the problematisation of the child's 'impulse' found fertile terrain on which to flourish. The questions of instruction and scholastic discipline were secondary to a more fundamental anxiety, which concerns the sexually premature child's character, and more particularly that child's impulsive behaviour. This notion of the impulse, of an instinctual conduct or 'propensity', as it is called in the next example, is the principal point of contact between the corporeal and possible monstrous behaviour. As such, it is also the theoretical passage through which the natural-unnatural dilemma of child monstrosity quickly gave way to the problem of the little moral monster in pubertal medicine's clinical discourse.

The intellectual and moral faculties of this child do not exhibit any signs of precocity at all commensurate with the forward development of the body. Her disposition is lively, but her mother says she has "her little tempers", in which she shows an obstinate resistance to authority, and she is less manageable than her sisters. She is certainly less intelligent than her elder sister; her education, however, has been neglected entirely, her mother being unwilling to send the child to school, lest tricks might be played with her. There are no positive indications of sexual propensities; she is coarse in her manners; but, perhaps, no more than other children of her class and age; there is the absence of all that grace and gentleness which accompany natural puberty in the female sex.

(Smart 1858: 458)

Throughout Smart's text, which corresponds to a more 'psychiatrised' stage of 19th-century pubertal medicine, the psychosocial question of child monstrosity is completely formulated. First, there is the problem of 'resistance to authority', and so the anxiety about how manageable the premature child is. At the same time, there is also the question about the child's 'intellectual faculties' and more particularly her intelligence: given that her sexual precocity is asymmetrical with her mental development, she needs to be protected within the school environment 'lest tricks might be played with her'. Second, there is the question of the child's 'moral faculties': given her 'obstinate' character, her sexual monstrosity becomes an object of greater preoccupation and tighter surveillance. We can see how, on the basis of the child's moral conduct, her intellect and discipline acquire a truly threatening status and are dramatised in the text.

Finally, the problem of morality, or rather the risk from whence all other anxieties radiate, is synthesised in the question of whether the child has 'sexual propensities'. Where was medicine to look for 'positive indications' of this moral monstrosity? In the child's general conduct, in her 'manners', but even more particularly in her level of 'grace and gentleness'. In other words, doctors needed to observe how feminine the child was as an indicator of the status of her sexual desire. To do so, doctors had to compare these qualities with those of 'other children of her class and age', but also with those of adolescent pubescent girls.

A double entanglement can be read in this clinical framework of sexual precocity, which would become fundamental, not only for puberty science, but also for medicine's entire power-knowledge apparatus. First, there is an association between the embodiment of femininity and the development of 'sexual propensities' – since the child is not yet feminine, she does not reveal a precocious female sexual drive, meaning she might not entail a moral monstrosity. Second, there is an association between the development of feminine traits and the 'natural' onset of puberty – the child reveals no femininity, and hence her sexual maturity is unnatural in a double sense. Once revealing no 'sexual propensities', the girls' pubescence is, in short, incomplete. In Smart's discourse, thus, although still unnatural, the condition appears less a monstrosity than a complicated natural mistake, a biological *error*. However, like hermaphroditism, it now comes to constitute a real peril to the child and the community: 'a monstrosity of *conduct* rather than the monstrosity of nature' (Foucault 2003b: 73; our emphasis).

The child monster as the precocious bearer of gender roles

Overall, what we see in Smart's and previous memoirs is the clinical elaboration of a gendered theory of pubertal sexual conduct that developed throughout the 1800s (see the following chapter). For the modern physicians of pubescence, the question of sexual-reproductive maturation was not merely about sexual difference understood biologically and juridically; in other words, it was not simply concerned with the natural order of the flesh and of the division of roles in society. Rather, it was principally about how sexual difference infuses conduct in the form of an instinct, an impulse, a propensity, an inclination, as well as the ways in which the development of an instinctual sexual self may be moulded through a healthy regime and proper education. Puberty science of the 1800s was interested in taking hold of the sexual system that belongs both to nature and culture, the individual and the society, instinct and discipline, flesh and morality – it was already interested in gender roles.

As shown in this chapter, while the child monster troubled biological and moral precepts of sexual development and reproduction, the orderly workings of sexual difference within the individual and the social body were taken up and reinforced in the reports. There is one issue, thus, in which no confusion or trouble was created: that of the sexual-gendered destiny of these young subjects in society. This can be seen in the developmental concerns assigned to the male and female young patients: whether boys are strong and can take on manly characteristics, and whether girls can procreate and manifest feminine traits in their attitudes and play.

The striking polarity of these questions does not suggest sex roles simply in the form of a sexual-social contract to which youngsters must conform while growing up. Rather, doctors' demonstration of their patients' early engagement with these roles had a naturalising function on two levels. First, it worked to validate the non-pathological character of the child monster: however unnatural, they healthily comply with the sex-gender order. Second, and consequently, the embodiment of such roles is rendered as a stamp of normalcy for every individual's evolution as a man or a woman, that is to say, as an intrinsic part of a healthy development overall.

This type of enquiry into pubertal precocity highlights how 19th-century medicine expected puberty to work: as a great natural machine of sexual polarisation. Parading the child monster in medical articles was never about displaying the grotesque, and even less a demonstration of the doctor's clinical expertise: after all, he had so much to show and yet so little to say in strictly diagnostic terms. On the level of power-knowledge relations, showing off pubertal monstrosity meant an opportunity to assert the enormous power that puberty offered to the modern science of sex differences, that is to say, to scientific sexism.

In 1800s case histories of early sexual developers, gender roles permeated not only these children's carnality and bodily potential, but also their aptitudes and motivations, their desires and pleasures, their voluntary and involuntary sexual manifestations. Those doctors' intimate, authoritarian methods of scrutiny provided the first sketches of a medical-psychiatric regime around pubertal maturation that we discuss further in the next chapter. At the core of that regime, there is the sexual instinct.

In the following, then, we trace how this notion of the instinct was appropriated and put to work in clinical examinations of premature pubescent children during the 1800s. In particular, we explore the ways in which 'signs' of a precocious sexual drive were deemed natural as well as unhealthy or deviant, quickly becoming the main dilemma from whence clinicians approached the whole problematic of early sexual development during that century. In doing so, we show how the gendering of souls started to take form in the modern clinical study of the immature-mature child.

Notes

1 We take up this theme in a different analytical context, which comprises the medical debates around early puberty taking place between the 1830s–40s (see Chapter 5).

2 This is basically the transcript of Dr Le Beau's original and similarly short report, published in *The American Journal of the Medical Sciences* (Le Beau 1832: 42–3): 'I take the liberty to acquaint you with an extraordinary case of prematurity in a child'. So 'extraordinary' it was, Le Beau made sure to call some fellow doctors, not to explain the 'prematurity', but quite simply to validate it: 'We, the undersigned, physicians practising in the city of New Orleans, State of Louisiana, do certify that at the request of our brother, Dr. Le Beau, we called at the dwelling of the parents of Matilda H., where, after having attentively and minutely examined the said Matilda H., confirm all that is above expressed. In truth whereof, we have signed the present certificate'.

3 Within our entire 1800s data set, this is the only clinical account that vaguely echoes the possibility of child sexual molestation and rape in connection to a case of female precocious puberty.

4 As previously noted, the problem of criminality in relation to pubertal development was not posed in clinical reports on precocious puberty at this stage. However, as we show throughout the book, it increasingly became a momentous preoccupation within the vast realm of puberty science.

Chapter 3

The monster, the modest girl, and the masturbating boy

As previously shown, the pubertal monster raised an overall anxiety amongst physicians about her or his capacity to attain an able, reproductive, and disciplined maturity. As soon as premature sexual characteristics and excitement were scrutinised, the problem of moral monstrosity also appeared. In 19th-century clinical reports on 'precocious' or 'premature' puberty, biological monstrosity (the dilemma of nature) entangled with, and was eventually subsumed in, the problem of sexual morality.

In those reports, as we continue exploring in this chapter, the dilemmatic *natural-unnatural* pubescent body often appeared as inhabited by a *naturally abnormal* sexual self. During the 1800s, doctors were notably concerned about whether their mature-immature patients showed any signs of an erotic or sexual conduct associated with 'natural' pubescence. Two distinctively gendered subjects emerged from this enquiry: the 'modest' girl and the masturbating boy.

In this chapter, we draw on the discursive and technical apparatus underpinning the clinical production and subjectivation of these two personas. Then, we show how the disparate regimes of behavioural abnormality and biological monstrosity co-constructed pubertal precocity as a clinical condition furnished with the positivity of measurements. Finally, we discuss how the assessments of the reproductive child, the little masturbator, and the 'modest' young girl may be seen as an anticipatory or primordial event in the emergence of a clinical practice concerned with standards of pubertal maturation.

Boys: aroused, 'seminal', and masturbatory?

Intertwined with the questions around reproduction and discipline, another line of enquiry arose in 1800s clinical encounters with precocious developers, which may be summarised as follows: do these children reveal sexual conduct as premature as their bodies? From the early years of the century, doctors' examinations endeavoured to assess the extent to which the child's physical make-up equated with precocious manifestations of a sexual impulse or drive – in short, instinctual sexual behaviour.

Where did physicians look for such behaviour? In boys, they focussed on forms of bodily behaviour perceived as both involuntary and sexual: namely, erections and the famous 'night emissions' (involuntary ejaculation). Unsurprisingly, they also focused on what was portrayed as a ubiquitous and alarming menace to health, which White, obviously embarrassed with the topic, addressed in Latin – in a footnote – in his 1809 report:

> Minimè praetereundum est, quod hic puer virilis, manstupratione interdum utitur. Semen tali modo paratum ipse ego bis vidi; et, me judice, perfectum et bene elaboratum evadit [It must not be overlooked that this young man sometimes masturbates. The seed (*semen*) is so readily produced that I myself have seen it twice; and, in my opinion, it is perfect and well-formed.] This has taken place, the mother informs me, from the completion of the second year.
>
> (White 1809: 286)

While White suggests vigilance, as the issue, at the outset, 'must not be overlooked', he does not problematise the little masturbator. White is far more interested in proving the great and remarkable vigour of this precociously sexual subject whom, when the clinical observation gets to his genitals, he prefers to treat, not as a child, but rather as 'young man' (or manly boy, literally translated). In other words, the physiological manifestation of a pubescent sexuality demonstrates that this 'young man' – a 3-year-old child, to be sure – indeed is biologically a sexual monster, but one of a remarkably benign character. After all, White's footnote adds to a statement with a similar discursive function in the text:

> We naturally suppose that a just union of health and excessive growth are incompatible. The continuance, however, of perfect health, during this rapid increase of height and bulk, has been in this subject very remarkable.
>
> (White 1809: 286)

Furthermore, White simply states 'the young man sometimes masturbates'. This is to say, the practice is suggested as a purely automatic consequence of a monstrous pubertal make-up and nothing more than that: the child's masturbatory conduct appears as an automatism in itself, with no relation to adult sexual desire or pleasure (however problematic its consequences were considered for one's health at the time).

In practically no time, in great contrast with White's ascetic footnote, 'seminal emissions' and 'onanism' took up much space in clinical reports on precocious pubescent boys:

> A spermatic odor exhales from his body, and the stains occasionally observed on his linen would lead to the belief that semen is secreted, although there is no other proof of this secretion taking place. . . . The sexual instinct has manifested itself by the frequent erection of this organ,

> on occasions calculated to excite it: it has not, however, led to the practice of onanism.
>
> (Breschet 1821: 446, 47)

> He does not seem at all aware of his situation; and, from what I can ascertain from his mother, has not the least inclination to play any tricks with himself. But it is remarkable, that whenever he has an emission in the night (now about once a week), and he is always waked by it, he calls out, 'Leave me alone; do not pull me about;' and will not go to sleep till his father goes to sit by him, when he immediately drops off.
>
> (South 1823: 83)

> His penis was as large as a man's, and was noticed to be erect every morning, though the testicles were rather smaller than those of an adult. . . . It is interesting to note that, in spite of the great development of his sexual organs, he has never given any evidence of sexual desire, and that no seminal emissions are known to have occurred.
>
> (Clarke cit. *The British Medical Journal* 1886: 263)

In reading these extracts, it must be borne in mind that until late in the 19th century, masturbation (or 'onanism', as coined in the early 1700s) was widely portrayed by the medical profession 'as the cause of every possible kind of illness' (Foucault 2003b: 238–9; see also Laqueur 2003). Doctors believed that the so-called 'solitary vice', and more particularly the spermatic waste of vital energy, crippled the body in a whole lot of ways and, of course, provoked madness (Harre 1962; Neuman 1975). It goes without saying, 19th-century puberty science had a lot to say about this 'fact', for masturbation was seen to naturally affect many pubescent children and adolescents who could hardly resist its forceful impulses.[1]

Hence, the possibility or site of a masturbating child indeed represented a 'real' danger of pathology, which was necessarily at stake in White's as well as the above quoted accounts. In the latter, however, the discursive rationality in which masturbation and involuntary emissions are conveyed is far more complex and problematising than in White's report.

Rather than being treated as a mere pubescent automatism, masturbation, or the question of a precocious or even aberrant infantile sexuality, is now linked to 'an inclination', to use South's term. Within this game of truth, night 'emissions' immediately suggest masturbatory conduct but also explicit concerns as to whether the child is prone 'to play any tricks with himself'. Moreover, besides 'seminal emissions' (involuntary or not), even the 'the great development of his sexual organs' is automatically articulated with the precocious installation of a 'sexual desire' in the child, as in Clarke's case. Likewise, to the doctor's great surprise, such a desire was not found in his precocious patient. In all the reports following White's, masturbation and seminal emissions are linked and seen as subjected to an impulsive, innate mechanism governing the whole of sexual conduct and desire, or what French doctor Gilbert Breschet already called 'the sexual instinct' in his 1821 report (read in the previous year to the British Royal Society).

This notion would later be importantly theorised by Heinrich Kaan in his seminal treatise on sexual perversions, *Psychopathia Sexualis*, published in 1844.[2] For Kaan, as Foucault (2003b: 278) illuminates, the sexual instinct – or *nisus sexualis* as he termed in Latin – is 'a dynamic manifestation of the functioning of the sexual organs', analogous to 'a dynamic of hunger that corresponds to the apparatus of nutrition'. As such, it is always natural and never pathological since it plays an essential part in reproduction. Yet, this instinct's power is inherently excessive and unruly, not only conducting sexual 'appetite' beyond its procreative end, but also emerging in people as early as the first years of childhood, that is to say, much before sexual-reproductive functions are expected to develop. As an evidence of this, Kaan pointed to the polarised roles that children so frequently took up in their play:

> Girls' games and boy's games are not the same, which proves [in Kaan's view] that the entire behavior of children, including their games, is supported and underpinned by a sexual *nisus*, a sexual instinct, which is already specified even though the apparatus it must drive and through which it must pass in order to lead to copulation is far from ready.
>
> (Foucault 2003b: 279)

As Foucault indicated, Kaan framed the sexual instinct as 'much too lively, precocious, and wide . . . [and hence] susceptible to a series of abnormalities; it is always in danger of deviating from the norm' (p. 279). From this perspective, infantile pleasure-seeking conduct was but the natural outcome of a sexual instinct that was already present in the child; but, given the sexual instinct's excessiveness and precocious calls for satisfaction, masturbation indeed became problematic as it could stimulate all sorts of sickness from very early on.

On the one hand, it may be argued that this conceptualisation of a natural infantile sexual behaviour does not correspond with the problematic of the instincts as posed in reports on precocious developers. In their case, to be sure, doctors searched for instinctual manifestations due to their patients' pubertal bodies, that is to say, because those young girls and boys were *not* exactly children.

On the other hand, however, the fundamental game of truth of Kaan's '*nisus sexualis*' – 'it is natural for the instinct to be abnormal', as Foucault puts it (p. 280) – is the same principle embedding the clinical analysis and problematisation of sexual conduct in premature pubescent subjects, as the previously quoted accounts about boys illustrate.

Overall, doctors connected the precocious pubescent body with sexual excitement, thus demonstrating or anticipating the child masturbator. This child is the main constitutive figure of the early maturing boy understood, not as unnatural, but as abnormal. Henceforth, he is no longer exclusively monstrous, the 1745 'gigantic' subject existing outside nature that White (1809) revisited in his clinical report. Rather, while this masturbating boy is still the figure of a little monster – he still blends maturity and immaturity – he now also embodies an instinctual apparatus. As such, his natural 'inclination' (South 1823: 83), his pleasure-seeking drives, may lead to behavioural disorders of medical and moral consequence.

In other words, this is a sexually precocious and possibly masturbating child: a child who may 'not seem at all aware of his situation' (South 1823: 83) but in whom the sexual instinct may have 'manifested itself' (Breschet 1821: 447). His monstrous pubertal development, therefore, in entailing instinctual sexual behaviour, invites what will soon become the real monstrosity of puberty, whether premature or not: a deviant pleasurable conduct, a morally degenerative and therefore dangerous sexual self.

What about girls' sexual drives? 'Modesty'

We started this chapter by reproducing one of the central questions of 1800s clinical reports on precocious puberty, which, as we have argued, opened up the very large field of abnormality to the scientific study of pubertal development. That question, to put it very shortly, concerned manifestations of an instinctual behaviour in precocious pubescent children. We have shown that, in the case of boys, doctors focused on masturbatory conduct. Now, when girls' sexual precocity was at stake, the question of 'solitary pleasures' was fairly mute.

Overall, boys' genital arousal and ejaculatory reactions were presented as the 'monstrous' physical stigmata of their reproductive capacity, as much as a regular menstrual cycle and a large pelvic diameter were in the case of girls. However, while menstruation was basically taken up as a premonitory sign of girls' procreative maturity with barely no articulation with sickness or problematic behaviour, boys' erections and 'involuntary seminal losses' – to which Lallemand famously dedicated three volumes (1836–42)[3] – suggested a morbid waste of vital energy, of their stamina, or even possible 'self-abuse'. As such, these bodily manifestations were something to be constantly watched over by parents. Where 'seminal emissions' were at stake, moreover, they were to be *treated* through clinical guidance and techniques. Herewith part of the 'History of a Case of Premature Puberty' documented by South, who, we irresistibly note, was clearly more worried about his 4-year-old patient's 'emissions' than with 'his usual allowance' of alcohol drinking:

> [The mother] noticed that his linen was stained two or three times in the week, when she had to dress him in the morning, and was then unconscious of the cause from whence it proceeded; but from his crying out whenever it occurred, as if hurt, and the circumstance of his being faint and pallid on the next morning, she was induced to watch him, and then

> ascertained the real cause, which, alarming her very much, she applied to her medical attendant, who recommended cold bathing of the whole body, three times a day. . . . The child's health became better . . . the emissions were less frequent, rarely more than once a week; but she noticed that if he took more porter or beer than his usual allowance, he generally had an emission the same night; she also states that since the time he has been in town (six weeks) the emissions have been more frequent than for some time previously.
>
> (South 1823: 78)

Like South's patient, boys' precocious carnality was expected to be excitable, and even ruled by a natural impulse to erotic pleasures, whereas early manifestations of a pubertal sexual drive in girls were, from the beginning, linked up with something quite different. In scrutinising girls' instinctual behaviour, rather than premature desires and self-indulgence, clinicians looked for a certain gracefulness or docility in mannerisms, a certain shyness or seclusion about the body, a manifest avoidance of boys and sexual affairs: in a word, they searched for signs of 'modesty'.

By the dawn of the 20th century, Havelock Ellis would eloquently elaborate on this notion, dedicating the first part of his famous volumes on sexual psychology to it. For him, 'modesty' is the most distinctive manifestation of the sexual instinct in the pubescent female. It plays a primordial role in the evolution of both 'men [sic] and animals' as a defence mechanism against the 'naturally aggressive attitude of the male in sexual relationships' (Ellis 1905: 29). As such, 'it may almost be regarded as the chief secondary sexual character of women on the psychical side. The woman who is lacking this kind of fear is lacking, also, in sexual attractiveness to the normal and average man' (p. 1). Thus, in the usual sexist and eugenic-driven tone of his writings, he worried that 'civilization tends to subordinate, if not minimize, modesty, to refer it a grace of life rather than a fundamental social law of life. But an essential grace of life it still remains, and whatever delicate variations it may assume we can scarcely conceive of its disappearance' (p. 48). For Ellis, most essentially, 'modesty' consists of an 'instinctive fear [of sexual exposure or intimacy] prompting to concealment' (p. 1), as well as an 'aptitude for disgust' regarding sexual acts and the genitalia (p. 30). In other words, 'this essential grace of life' (p. 48) implies an inherently defensive, conflicting, and even repulsive relation to sexual pleasure and desire of any kind in the 'normal' pubescent female.[4]

The prospect of a 'self-abusive' young girl, who gives herself up to 'solitary vice', would necessarily trouble this game of truth, in which can be found the archetype of a pervasive and widely familiar double standard. If we look back at the first English medical memoir on female premature puberty, we find that 'modesty' is already the standpoint of Cooper's analysis of the young girl's sexual instinct:

> She plays with children of her own age [four years old], and does not seem to have any sexual feelings, or an uncommon degree of modesty . . . [Two years later] she has a degree of modesty not formerly noticed, and does not now like to walk in the streets, because some boys have teazed her about her appearance.
>
> (Cooper 1813: 208)

In trying to understand this gendered disparity in behavioural examinations of pubertal precocity, it is important to avoid the argument that young maturing girls were medically portrayed as sexless and seen to somehow escape the ubiquitous 'evils' of masturbation. By the early 1800s, as our genealogy clearly shows, the problematic existence of a female infantile sexuality was already planted in both medical discourse and family life.

The anti-masturbation crusade appeared to target boys more directly than girls. Its somatic imageries were infused with sexist and heteronormative anxieties about the spermatic loss of stamina, without which individuals – men – but also civilisation as a whole could not evolve. Indeed, this is a central theme in the crusade's discourse. We find it in Tissot's 1758 medical treatise on onanism (Foucault 2003b), obviously in Lallemand's monumental work on 'seminal losses' referred to above, or even later, in Hall's (1904) famous text, *Adolescence*. However, at least from the early 1800s onwards, young girls became increasingly at stake in medical problematisations of pubertal masturbation.

True, celebrated physicians such as Adam Raciborski (1844), in line with the dominant expert opinion of his time, maintained that onanism was more a male than a female issue. Yet, as we shall see in Chapter 6, his lancet was ready to 'treat' masturbation in girls once and for all. As Foucault (2003b: 252) writes, while Lallemand 'proposed inserting a permanent probe in the urethra' of masturbating boys, or 'the insertion of needles in [their] genital area', the 'cauterization and removal of the clitoris' was also suggested and practiced by a number of doctors. In 1835, for example, Deslande, 'the great theorist of masturbation' according to Foucault, saw no big a problem in what he described as a 'sacrifice [of] the secondary for the principle, the part for the whole':

> "The greatest disadvantage" is to place this woman in the "already very large category" of women who are "insensitive" to the pleasures of love, "which does not prevent them from being good mothers and devoted wives".
>
> (Deslande cit. Foucault 2003b: 253)

From our perspective, there are interlinked epistemic-political reasons why, in early medical encounters with early developing girls, masturbation was ostensibly absent from their doctors' inquiries. First, the notion or at least the discourse of 'modesty' was a key element in the 19th-century clinical construction of female hysteric behaviour – a significant object in the history of sexual psychopathology (Foucault 2006). 'Modesty', we would argue, is the discursive root or principle of a vast range of behavioural disorders consistently associated with female sexual development and reproductive functions until well into the 1900s – e.g. fainting fits, emotional outbursts, sexual 'frigidity' – all of which were brought together under the rather malleable rubric of 'hysteria'.

In other words, 'modesty' may be seen as the regime sustaining the medical-psychiatric fiction widely known since the 1800s as the hysterical woman: bluntly put, a persona whose neurotic ailments, in one way or another, are the result of women's 'endemic' complications, reservations, and complexes regarding sex. 'Modest' pubescent behaviour, in particular, precedes and overlaps with the hysterical woman's famous lack of interest in 'the pleasures of love', to use Deslande's words (above). Being the condition of possibility for this type of discourse, second, 'modesty' reinforced a patriarchal heteronormative style of parental authority, particularly widespread in 19th-century bourgeois ideology and medical thought, the ideal of which was sexual abstinence until marriage (Neuman 1975).

In short, while fuelling the development of a new sexual psychopathology rising in the 19th century, 'modesty' gave scientific support to the social regulation of women's sexuality, which in turn incited the medical profession to objectivise the 'modest' maturing girl.[5] From this angle, it is unsurprising that, instead of auto-eroticism, forms of 'modest' behaviour (e.g. gracefulness, sexual shyness, avoiding boys' company) constituted the main object in doctors' examinations of precocious pubescent girls' sexual instinct:

> There are no positive indications of sexual propensities; she is coarse in her manners; but, perhaps, no more than other children of her class and age; there is the absence of all that grace and gentleness which accompany natural puberty in the female sex. She is not at all shame-faced; she does not shrink from being examined, nor does she blush when stripped; she has manifested no preference for the society of the opposite sex, indeed, she is reported to avoid the company of boys.
>
> (Smart 1858: 459)

In bluntly neglecting the possibility of masturbation and seeking instead for signs of 'modesty' and similar traits, Smart's type of analysis actually fed scientific constructions of female sexual development as inherently complicated, conflicted within itself, and eventually producing typical neurotic states in both young and adult women. Not only did he remark that his patient did not present the modest character of 'natural puberty in the female sex' – meaning she wasn't truly pubescent – he made sure to add that this 5-year-old girl, despite her premature reproductive biology, 'has never been given to fainting fits, or any other forms of hysteria' (p. 460).

From the beginning, this is to say, the clinical questions around boys' and girls' precocious sexual drives reinforced and refined the modern dimorphic language of sex and reproduction, providing the patriarchal regulation of female sexuality with ever-more sophisticated rhetoric. Order, rather than transgression, was the substantial theme underpinning the analysis of unnatural-natural pubescence. In looking for a gentle, somewhat secluded, possibly disordered behaviour in precocious pubescent girls, on the one hand, and for a sexually excited and possibly auto-erotic behaviour in precocious pubescent boys, on the other, doctors were after all asking – and attempting to confirm – how orderly the gendering of these little monsters was.

In our view, as suggested above, a misogynist scientific culture of notable repressive effects cannot entirely explain the gendered disparity in clinical approaches to pubertal precocity. The historical analysis of 'modesty', as well as that of anti-masturbation discourse, should not be reduced to the function of repression. As Foucault (1978, 2003b) illuminates, the repressive effects of medical-psychiatric discourses on sexual abnormality are both the means to, and the by-product of, a markedly productive, inventive, and transforming system of power, the strategic rationality of which has been the establishment and constant reinforcement of particular forms of knowledge and control over bodies, thoughts, and actions. Rather than merely denying girls sexual pleasures until the 'right' time, the discourse of modesty – just like the prohibition of masturbation – strengthened the interplay of familial and medical relations around childhood and sexual development.

Intimate bodies, intimate knowledges

> At the crossroads of the body and the soul, of health and morality, of education and training, children's sex became both a target and an instrument of power.
>
> (Foucault 2001f: 259)

As we have seen throughout this chapter, the monitoring of precocious pubescent children's sexual behaviour during the 1800s was importantly performed by parents – especially the mothers.[6] Every little trace of sexual excitement or dangerous pleasure was tracked, for example, in children's games around the house, in their play with each other and with themselves, in how they dressed, their actions in their rooms, inside their beds, under the sheets, in their expressions and odours after waking up. This kind of policing activity was inextricably bound to doctors' expertise and, of course, to their power to instruct mothers regarding how to watch over and manage their children.

As earlier suggested, the medicalisation of pubertal precocity from the early 19th century onwards provided a historical stage for the establishment of tight parent-doctor bonds on behalf of the child's sexual-reproductive health. While mothers served as key agents of medicalisation and main medical informants, doctors became the closest witnesses, the expert guardians of children's 'natural history' and 'remarkable' development:

> From my repeated visits, a perfect acquaintance and familiarity with the boy has been established; and he has been induced to visit me frequently at my own house, where, as he acts without restraint, I had most favourable opportunities of becoming acquainted with whatever is remarkable in his formation, or interesting in his natural history.
>
> (White 1809: 282)

> Thus far his mother. The rest of the narrative has come under my own observation: I have had frequent opportunities of seeing him, both at the place where he resides, and at my own house, to which he has been several times; the result of which I shall now endeavour to lay before the Society, whose indulgence I must crave, should I not do that justice to him which his remarkable figure requires.
>
> (South 1823: 79)

From the moment that the parents called the family doctor, he was given a particular power of examination over the young patient that shaped the medical construction of the child monster, that is to say, the predecessor of the early developing child of our present. This power is not the usual medical power of examination of the ill individual, nor does it concern traditional diagnostic assessment of someone's health. Rather, it is the specific clinical power producing, and produced by, pubertal monstrosity.

This power has two main features. The first is that it allows for an extremely intimate relationship between the doctor and the child's bodily condition. More precisely, it allows for the child's 'monstrous' mixture of immaturity and maturity to be submitted to a very detailed and extensive observation wherein all the clinician's senses are at work. By means of thorough observations, manipulations, palpations, and smells, the doctor discovers that mixture or confusion across almost every limb, every surface, every secluded spot, every 'sexual' function of the child's body:

> The nipple is prominent, and the areola well marked, and incircled with a small quantity of hair. The axilla is without hair, but the secretion has the peculiar characteristic odour of the adult. . . . The testes are firm and perfect in their formation, and the chord may be distinctly felt.
>
> (White 1809: 284)

> The [menstrual] discharge is as copious as in most women, and it generally continues about four days; it is the colour of venous blood, and does not coagulate. . . . [T]he hair has begun to grow in the axillae; her countenance has not near so much the childish appearance; her voice is much rougher.
>
> (Cooper 1813: 208)

> The penis, scrotum, and testicles are as large as those of an adult: the prepuce being always drawn back, or perhaps, it may be said, not existing at all; the glans penis is constantly uncovered. The pubes and scrotum are covered with thick dark curling hair. . . . His voice is very deep and hoarse, and he laughs loud and heartily; but the larynx is not so much developed as might be expected, the thyroid cartilage being by no means prominent; which, however, may perhaps be less noticed from the great size of his neck, which is very fat.
>
> (South 1823: 81, 82)

> The voice is strong, without any other peculiarity. The bust is full and womanly, as is well seen in the photographs. The breasts are larger and more protuberant than those of most girls who have recently attained puberty, and the characteristic lobular structure of the [mammary] gland is easily perceived on manipulation. . . . The labia externa and nymphae are large, the latter included within the fissure of the vulva. The vagina is capacious, and has a fringe-shaped hymen.
>
> (Smart 1858: 458)

All these detailed and intimate observations, together with parental accounts, compose what could be called an anatomical symptomatology of the child monster. This symptomatology has a rather peculiar quality: at the outset, none of those bodily elements in which doctors find the 'remarkable' traces of sexual maturity are suggested as indictors of pathology. Those bodily features appeared at the 'wrong' time, but they did not represent illness. As we argued in Chapter 2, all these elements discursively serve to show that the child is healthy, the little monster is sexually benign. Thus, the doctor, whose medical expertise is requested by the family in first place, is able to intervene – and in an exhaustive fashion – directly on the precocious pubescent body despite the fact that the young patient, to be sure, cannot be cured. This is the second main quality of the medical power of examining the child monster.

Precisely because these subjects are not to be cured, they nonetheless are to be measured. Alongside the profuse inspection of the child's flesh, measurements form another fundamental technique in the clinical construction of the little sexual monster's symptomatology.

> I have subjoined a table of admeasurement of the principal parts of the body. His height and weight I ascertained in August 1808. The dimensions, however, of the other parts were taken, with great accuracy, in January 1809.
>
> (White 1809: 284)

> She is four feet and an inch high, is broader across the pelvis than the shoulders, measuring only fourteen inches and three quarters from one acromion scapulae to the other, but seventeen inches from the anterior superior spinous process of one ilium to that of the other.
>
> (Cooper 1813: 208–9)

> I have, at a further part of this paper, given an exact measurement of almost the whole body.
>
> (South 1823: 79)

These measurements play an important part in the twinned history of abnormality and child development. First, they produce a more or less regular field of physical marks of 'monstrosity' on the basis of which precocious puberty, while not being construed as an illness, can be related to a pathological realm, according to the discursive rules of medical science. This is, in a phrase, the formal discursive function of measurements in reports on early development.

Second, they serve to confirm the clinician's power of examination over the young body, not simply in terms of his authority and the reciprocal docility of the child (and the rest of the family), but in terms of the real power endowed by the parents to the doctor to thoroughly inspect, connect with, and profusely know his patient, to the extent that such an intimate knowledge can be translated into metrics. This is, if you will, the power or disciplinary function of measuring precocious pubescent children.

Moreover, doctors' assessment has the power to set a scene – a both playful and authoritarian environment – where children's more or less docile subjection to such a detailed examination becomes in itself an indicator or 'symptom' of their (sexual) character. For example, in stating that the young girl of his case 'does not shrink from being examined, nor does she blush when stripped', Smart (1858: 459) is asserting that, despite her physical sexual precocity, she presents no manifestations of modesty ('there is an absence of all that grace and gentleness which accompany natural puberty in the female sex'). South's remarks on the docility of his patient quoted in Chapter 2 and repeated below are also exemplary of this discursive effect produced on the child's behaviour by the clinician's scrutinising power:

> As to his disposition, from what I have observed, I have no doubt that his mother's statement is correct. When a stranger visits him, he is at first shy; but, by the kind manner which children expect and so well know how to appreciate, any thing may be done with him, which I have myself witnessed when I measured him, and at the time when Mr. Silvester, one of our students, was so kind as to make a sketch of him for me; which last took up full two hours at his first sitting, during which time he allowed himself to be put in any position we thought proper without the least opposition.
>
> (South 1823: 82)

South's discussion of the case is analogous to Smart's (1858), in which the young girl's lack of shyness during her examination indicated that she was not yet 'modest', meaning that her behaviour was not pubescent. Likewise, South's assertion of this boy's absolute controllability serves to stress that, despite his 'night emissions' and precociously developed sexual organs, he nonetheless shows no signs of a pubescent, hence naturally less docile, behaviour that would be considered 'monstrous' at his age. Most importantly, South's report is also a fine reflection of that simultaneously playful and orthopaedic technique of power that consists of measuring, drawing (in South's earliest case), and photographing (in Smart's later account): in a word, *figuring* the mature-immature child.

Ultimately, this rudimentary anthropometric activity enveloping the precocious pubescent body throughout the 1800s, and partly constituting it, was also an important historical surface for the rise of knowledge about maturational standards in pubertal medicine. In doctors' attempts to codify the child's 'monstrous' development into quantifiable bodily stigmata, measurements were made that necessarily called for comparisons against standardised figures, against bodies deemed 'average', hence enabling the production of norms. Pubertal norms did not arise, thus, from the sheer curiosity of a few illuminated medical minds who, at some point during the 1800s, wished to determine the 'right' size and shape of a boy or a girl at the time of puberty, and when that vital change is expected to happen. As shown in the second part of this book, those norms – or the earliest attempts to elucidate them – took shape as the necessary data against which pubertal abnormal phenomena, and early development in particular, could be scientifically monitored on both the individual and the collective levels, and for both medical and political reasons. In challenging the rules of biological and social life, the child monster's most original and extraordinary power was that of compelling a flourishing medical biology into the formulation of newer and more thoroughly quantifiable understandings of puberty.

Indeed, for the most part of the 1800s, measurements of premature pubescent bodies were never compared to maturational norms for the simple reason that either such figures did not yet exist or, from the 1840s to the late 19th century, were hardly agreed upon by the medical world. Until at least around the middle of that century, what existed was an imprecise, loose, disconnected pubertal knowledge, basically composed of the bits and pieces of data gathered in clinicians' hospital and private practices, and sparsely laid down in medical dictionaries and treatises (see Chapter 5). Overall, such knowledge based itself upon a regime of medical *opinions* attested to by the expertise of the doctor's gaze alone, rather than a regime of demonstrable and generalisable truth.

By the early 1820s, for instance, South spoke to the growth of facial hair in his patient as follows: 'There is no beard on the chin; but the upper lip is darkened with hair, such as is *generally noticed* in young persons of fifteen or sixteen, accompanied also with inspissation of the sebaceous matter about the alae of the nose, *usually observed* at the same period' (1823: 80, our emphasis). While mentioning 'generally noticed' or 'usually observed' phenomena, thus evoking the authority of a traditional understanding of pubertal development commonly shared by the profession, such statements did not actually refer to systematic studies of pubertal characteristics and the timing of maturation. By the late 1850s, Smart still objectified the maturity-immaturity of his patient's body against what he bluntly calls 'the type of childhood' – i.e. a measurable entity according to his own discourse, but whose 'relative proportions' are not stated in the article, nor are these 'proportions' validated by reference to anything other than his own expertise:

> The configuration and relative proportions of the torso differ widely from the type of childhood. The subcutaneous cellular tissue is abundantly supplied with fat, by which the unseemly angularities of unripe years are cushioned over and lost in the rounded contour of maturity.
>
> (Smart 1858: 457)

Alongside this traditional, non-systematic ideal of 'normal' pubescence, the other typical standards used for comparison by the clinicians were the measurements made on occasion of the patients' brothers or sisters, whose bodies were basically assumed to be 'normal' for their ages by the doctor's experienced eye:

> Her eldest sister, aged about seventeen years, has never menstruated, and there is very little fullness in her breasts [unlike observed in the precocious pubescent girl], though she is in good health. One of her sisters, aged ten years and five months, is four feet and two inches high, and is not so broad across her pelvis as her shoulders; she measures fourteen inches and a half from one acromion scapulae to the other, and thirteen inches from the anterior superior spinous process of one ilium to that of the other.
>
> (Cooper 1813: 209)

> In the preceding measurements the elder sister has served as a convenient standard of comparison. The differences observable between the two children are most emphatic, where the data relate to girth, and are chiefly due to the greater volume of the soft parts in the younger girl, and less to the expansion of the osseous framework. The most practical importance is attached to the determination of the pelvic diameters, which do not, however, seem to be notably increased.
>
> (Smart 1858: 462)

In being part of the same progeny of the patient, 'normal' young siblings were the most exact and readily available control group for the clinician's analysis of pubertal monstrosity. Yet, their random measurements paradoxically functioned as the 'norm' itself, without any reference to the general population. Therefore, they merely worked to show the absolute exceptionality of the young patient by suggesting the lack of any hereditary sort of pathology in the family.

Nevertheless, all these bodily measurements constituted the rudimentary form, or at least the embryonic rationality, of the statistical normalisation of pubertal development as we know it today. From the early 1900s onwards, as we show in Chapter 8, clinicians' intimate assessment of precocious pubescent bodies was replaced by a new and rather 'colder' style and technology of examination in which both anthropometric and molecular quantifications play a major role. Nonetheless, the essential features and power relations particular to the clinical assessment of the child monster prevailed in 20th-century puberty science, namely full-body measurements, pictorial (i.e. photographic) records, and close inspection of genitalia and other secondary sex characters.

Early puberty scientists' observations of the child monster unveiled a very powerful object or field of phenomena: 'normal' development. Consequently, those doctors engaged in a non-pathological clinical practice, the power of which was not so much to cure as it was to monitor, manage, and even correct those who are biologically 'monstrous' and yet not ill. Ultimately, while dealing with pubertal precocity as a natural-unnatural 'condition' (although the term is not yet employed in most of their reports), the early scientists of pubertal precocity also discovered that child development can be entirely analysed from the both diffuse and rather comprehensive notion of abnormality, rather than the stricter and episodic problem of illness. And thus, they found themselves in the powerful position of being able to medicalise the child's body and behaviour, and to do so in the name of a real medical authority, without having to refer to a pathological episode or process.

Monstrous bodies with abnormal drives: two powers, one subject

To sum up, the problematic of sexual drives in early cases of precocious puberty produced two distinctive figures: briefly, the masturbating young boy and the 'modest' young girl. Although they necessarily take part in the construction of pubertal monstrosity, their framework is quite different from that of the child monster. Above all, in terms of their discursive constitution, these figures were not excluded from the realm of nature. Unlike the child monster's general morphology, their sexual drives were suggested to be completely natural in themselves – i.e. chronologically congruent with the premature onset of puberty. Rather than the exceptional, these drives or impulses represented everyday phenomena and were commonly associated with the coming of age.

While construed as a natural manifestation of puberty's sexual-reproductive impulses, however, masturbatory behaviour and 'modesty' (not to mention the expectation of hysterical episodes) also pointed to excessiveness, irregularity, deviancy, especially given the young age of the children at stake. The sexual instinct was the discursive technology of the masturbating young boy and the 'modest' young girl. The completely different games of truth sustaining these figures, and their specific articulations with the problematic of sexual precocity, were organised around the power-knowledge rationality of an *instinctual* pubertal subject.

Within the 1800s clinical apparatus of pubertal precocity, thus, medical and parental practices concerning the reproductive child monster intertwined and overlapped with those concerning the 'modest' and the auto-erotic child. The former dealt most prominently with the measurement, surveillance, and management of monstrosity, without any truly corrective end. The latter, on the other hand, effectively put a normalising power to work; they ultimately aimed at reshaping children's behavioural eccentricities according to established precepts of what sexual maturation and adult life should look like. Obviously, controlling the 'modest' or the little 'onanist' also called for practices of surveillance and assessment distributed between the clinic and the family home. But these practices were not concerned with the sizes, shapes, and functions of the sexual-reproductive body, or even with the learning capacities of the child monster. Their scrutiny was far more specific: it focused on the movements within the bed, the stains on the bedsheets, children's roles in games, their feelings and imaginations – all sites and circumstances where sensuousness and sexual excitement were to reveal themselves.

Unlike the supervision of the child monster, in short, this kind of behavioural inspection pre-supposed corrective investments. Doctors prescribed hygienic regimes to stop young boys' 'night emissions' and endorsed domestic strategies to avoid early sexual excitement in young girls (namely by sleeping in their parents' bedroom, as we shall note in the next chapter). In the 1800s, unlike biological monstrosity, the 'tendencies', 'inclinations', or 'propensities' of precocious pubescent children already formed a medical object upon which family doctors (via the parents) intervened as medical healers, not merely by monitoring the child's sexual behaviour, but also by moulding, reforming, 'treating' – normalising it.

In early puberty science, the child monster's biology could not be fixed for the very simple reason that clinicians did not yet have the corrective hormonal-surgical technologies to enable such treatment (they were only put in place in the 20th century, as later shown in the book). Hence, the discursive technology proper to the analysis of biological monstrosity was monstrosity itself, that is, the simultaneous transgression and reaffirmation of the absolute demarcations between the natural and the unnatural. Yet, the clinical enquiry into the sexual behaviour of precocious children afforded a more complex and nuanced approach. Here, the clinical dilemma was not the (impossible) reconciliation of the natural with the unnatural, but rather the tricky distinction between the voluntary and the involuntary, and between the normal and the abnormal, in the sexual conduct of early maturing children. Was auto-eroticism or 'modesty' mere automatisms or determined by a precocious pubertal drive? Was the child's sexual instinct to be considered normal given her/his sexual-reproductive prematurity, or should it be deemed abnormal due to the child's chronological age?

Stemming from 1800s reports, these dilemmas formed a productive source of behavioural discourses around pubertal precocity. On the one hand, they constituted the dead-end intrinsic to doctors' questioning; meaning that, along with the problem of monstrosity – is the precocious children natural or unnatural? – they were solvable from neither scientific nor philosophical methods. In other words, doctors could not capture the condition in terms of a regular system of bodily standards that did not yet exist, nor could they separate the normal from the abnormal in the child's conduct, thus leaving the confusion of immaturity and maturity unsolved. Precisely due to these two inextricably unsolvable paradoxes, both biological and behavioural monstrosities enabled a number of dangers to surface in social imaginaries and a number of measures to be taken accordingly – not only medical but also juridical, as we discuss in Chapter 5.

On the other hand, whereas the dilemma of nature appealed to the language of pathology (i.e. monstrosity as illness), the dilemmas of child sexual conduct, in being based on the discourse of the instinct (i.e. sexual abnormality as natural), completely dispensed with medicine's pathological power. Quite simply, therefore, the premature sexual conduct did not demand a cure. Rather, premature sexual drives were meant to be either kept in or brought back into a state of 'health' that implied a regime for the shaping of souls. In contrast with the benign medical figure of the child monster, the main discursive positioning of the 'modest' or the masturbating young child was being destined to correction from the start.

In short, within the foundational apparatus of pubertal precocity, two different frameworks coexisted, with complementary knowledges and techniques, but with completely disparate technologies of power. The first, the framework of monstrosity, functioned through the old medical power of pathology and dealt with the insurmountable impossibility of curing the unnatural. The second, the framework of behavioural abnormality, conveyed the newer rationality of the sexual instinct, putting the normalisation of precocious pubescent children's attitudes and imaginations into practice.

The discourse of the instinct – i.e. the confrontation of naturalness and abnormality within one's behaviour – allowed for early puberty science to open up to a vast field of *naturally* abnormal phenomena particular to pubescent subjects' conduct. Within the last third of the 1800s, while physiological medicine still struggled to consolidate the principles and norms of puberty, the new psychiatry of sexual-reproductive development consistently showed what normal and abnormal pubertal conduct meant. By the early 20th century, the sexual instinct had become the most important technology in the analysis of pubertal behaviour (see Chapter 8).

Until at least the 1850s, nevertheless, the main clinical framework of 'premature' puberty was that of child monstrosity. The first clinical narratives on the condition were chiefly about a little monster and her/his 'remarkable' sexual-reproductive maturity. Their crucial question was about the mature-immature child developing towards a medically sound and morally proper adulthood. However, in some of these accounts, the enquiry into the young patients' sexual traits flourished alongside the general issue of biological monstrosity, bringing the analytical nexus of normality-abnormality into the nascent puberty science.

This shift would not be completed without a third line of inquiry in early reports on precocious pubescent children, which revolves around the enigmatic question that haunted puberty science since its inception: "why?" In the following chapter, we engage with the tentative explanations and implicit speculations about the causes of the condition conveyed by these children's clinicians in their memoirs.

Notes

1 By 1883, British physician R. Clement Lucas introduced a distinctive type of rickets which he called 'rickets of adolescents' (later classified as 'renal rickets'). In the following year, he clarified his argument as follows: 'I have been accused of clouding the cause of this condition in language which so far obscured my meaning, as to leave the reader in doubt as to what I intended to convey. The unpleasant nature of the topic is sufficient excuse for the obscurity; but I do not wish again to be misunderstood, and I will distinctly state that the invariable cause of this form of rickets associated with albuminuria is masturbation. The absurdity of treating such cases merely by mechanical appliances, by division of tendons, by osteotomy or excision of bones, when there is an underlying habit causing a general constitutional disease, will be at once obvious' (Lucas 1884: 852).

2 According to Foucault, the earliest scientific theorisations of the instinct did not take place in the field of sexuality. Rather, they emerged in the context of criminality, and responded to a dilemma with which the judicial system was suddenly confronted in the first decades of the 1800s: murderers presenting with no apparent reason for committing their monstrous offences – the medically enigmatic and judicially embarrassing cases of motiveless crimes. Such cases posed a problem to a penal system based on the premise that all crime excludes madness, or conversely, the mad cannot be criminal. Medical-psychiatric elaboration on the 'instincts' served as an essential instrument for the judicial system to work, that is to say, for a conduct that was previously deemed motiveless, and thus inexplicable, to be made intelligible, and therefore punishable. 'We have gone from the motiveless act to the instinctive act' (Foucault 2003b: 131).

3 'In the course of 13 to 14 years', Lallemand asserted in the *Avant-Propos* to his oeuvre, 'I have collected over 150 observations of *involuntary seminal losses*, serious enough to alter health profoundly, and even to cause death' (1836: 1).

4 A few years later, a 1907 paper on 'The Psychology of Puberty' by psychiatrist and criminologist Antonio Marro was reviewed by Hamilton Marr, who paraphrased (and maintained): 'Two mental conditions are noticeable in the [pubescent] girl: first, amiability when this is exaggerated it is called "coquetry", and by it the girl attempts to make herself more pleasant in the eyes of men and her companions. The second condition arising in the girl is modesty or reserve, which is represented morally as bashfulness, physically as virginity' (Marr 1910: 143).

5 As Londa Schiebinger shows in her beautiful *Nature's Body*, the scientific constructions of female modesty can be traced back to the work of naturalists from the 17th and 18th centuries who 'saw' – and portrayed – the universality of that trait in the modest behaviour of female apes, or even in parts of plants (see Schiebinger 2004: 99–106).

6 From the 18th century onwards, as Rose (1994: 65) puts it, 'the mother is to be brought into a kind of alliance with the doctor that will secure her role against the patriarchal authority of the father, but at the price of transforming her into an agent of medical supervision of the domestic sphere'.

Chapter 4

Accounting for the mature-immature body

From the start of the medicalisation of 'premature puberty', i.e. the birth of a modern clinical medicine of puberty, the dilemma of immaturity-maturity made room for anxieties about monstrous behaviours and their dangerous consequences, as we initially outlined in Chapter 2. With the introduction of and increasing emphasis on an instinctual technology and problematic in clinical analyses of the condition, as seen in Chapters 3, child sexual monstrosity became foremost a behavioural issue – a shift that only reached its climax in the first few decades of the 20th century, as we illuminate in Chapter 8.

At the same time, the young child's pubertal biology itself began to change from being monstrous to being abnormal. Until at least the 1850s, to be sure, pubertal precocity figured in clinical discourse as the dilemmatic separation of, and encounter between, the natural and the unnatural in a single body. Yet, within that period, this framework started giving way to another, wherein the early maturing body was understood as natural, regardless of its abnormal constitution, and early puberty as provoked, possibly, by both biological and social forces. The rise of this discourse, as we show in this chapter, is tightly anchored in clinicians' musings, assertions, and implicit suggestions about the causes of the condition.

These causal hypotheses and assumptions, as articulated in the medical texts of that century, can be grouped into two general categories: endogenous – i.e. hereditary-racial and constitutional or inborn – and exogenous – i.e. socioeconomic and environmental. As argued in this chapter, although authors would at times emphasise one or the other, the history of their clinical uptake and discursive formulation in the puberty science of the 1800s is much more about theoretical complementarity than mutual exclusion and antagonistic debate (see also Chapter 6).

Starting with inborn and constitutional triggers, we trace the earliest explanatory models of pubertal precocity – one natural, the other pathological – via which medicine was afforded the first gaze beyond the monstrous anatomy of the mature-immature child into the domain of organic abnormality. Then, still in the endogenous plane, we explore the hereditary-racial nexus, which was the central trope of the little monster's 'family portrait', usually presented at the outset of the reports. Looking into these 'family portraits', we often find a tangle of clinical 'facts', either internal or external to the child, all of which are implicitly suggested as forming a possible causal background of the case.

We then move on to the exogenous triggers and shapers of pubescence as outlined in reports across the 1800s: namely, the quality of nutrition, the early and undue sexualisation of the child, and the natural properties of the environment. Overall, we locate this network of causes within the rise of a modern apparatus around the biological and the species wherein scientific sexism and racism played important roles. In the end, we sum up our main argument: the simultaneous rise of physiological abnormality and of the biosocial in tentative explanations of immature-mature bodies created a breach in child monstrosity discourse through which a modern rationality around physical maturational norms emerged.

Fantastical brains and actual tumours: discovering biological abnormality

In the beginning of 1809, surgeon Anthony White finalised his 'Historical Account on Philip Howorth', the first case of its kind presented to the British Royal Society of Medicine in that century. Philip, a 2-year-old at the time of White's clinical assessment, showed signs of 'premature puberty', which had taken shape soon after his birth in 1806. Since August 1808, White had thoroughly examined and measured this 'boy', and also collected a great deal of information from the mother. After about six months of observations, he reached a conclusion:

> From a review of this history, I think we may safely infer, that the changes which have taken place in this boy had their origin in utero. The development of the genital and other organs after birth has been extremely rapid, but remarkable for regularity.
>
> (White 1809: 287)

Thirteen years later, another fellow of the Royal Society, John South (1823), delivered his 'History of a Case of Premature Puberty', the subject of which, John Sparrow, was a boy born in 1818. His pubertal features and pace of development were similar to those reported in White's case. Like his predecessor, South had followed a clinical regime that combined very close observations, multiple measurements, and biographical data collection from the mother – 'both at the place where he resides, and at my own house' (South 1823: 79). At the end of his memoir, he contended:

> The case is rare and curious; one only of the male sex having previously appeared before the Society, and published in the first volume of their Transactions. I am not satisfied, as Mr. White seems to have been with his case, "that the changes which took place in this boy had their origin in utero".
>
> (South 1823: 85)

These two doctors' analytical approaches show a significant difference, which is reflected in South's final remarks. Rather than a disagreement, this difference is about the extent to which the hypothesis of an inborn or constitutional cause of premature puberty is advanced and addressed by both. South states being 'not satisfied' with the argument that 'the changes which took place in this boy had their origin in utero', as White suggested. To be sure, South did accept this conclusion as valid in both cases. For him, it was not enough to say that the phenomenon had inborn causes; one also had to look for – and demonstrate – the physiological system *responsible* for triggering such 'rare and curious' changes in these patients. In attending to this question, South focused his clinical gaze on the proportions of the boy's cranium, that is to say, on his brain.

In fact, both White and South resorted to recollections from the mothers about the development and shape of their patients' heads. The primary rationale behind that specific enquiry was merely to assert whether the closure of the cranium's junctions (or fontanelles) presented in these children signs that could, in one way or another, be theoretically correlated with the precocious development of their bodies:

> At the birth, the head of the child was covered with a profusion of hair of a considerable length; the sutures of the cranium were closed, not leaving the smallest vestige of a fontanelle; and he was at this period considered, in point of size and appearance, as a large and healthy child.
>
> (White 1809: 280–1)

> She says that [when her son was about sixteen months old] the fontanelles were very large, but soon closed; but that "down his forehead was so open that you might lay your finger in it," (to use her own expression) "and also the sides of his head behind his ears," putting her fingers in the direction of the lambdoidal suture, and that these were not closed for a very long while, but she does not recollect how long.
>
> (South 1823: 78–9)

Unlike White, South goes further in his analysis. As the below statements highlight, he examined the child's skull as an indicator of the size and shape of his brain. In doing so, South appealed to a knowledge system launched at the dawn of the 19th century, the 'science' of phrenology, which famously related cerebral constitution to the development of sex (and racial) differences in the human organism. When describing his first encounter with John Sparrow, South remarks:

> When I first entered the room where he was, I was much struck with the size and form of his head and neck. He has a fine high and spacious forehead; but the occiput is extremely prominent, from the enormous size

> of the cerebellum, which Drs. Gall and Spurzheim state is always the case when the genital organs are developed in a great degree.
>
> (South 1823: 79–80)

Whereas White had nothing to say about his patient's brain, South drew on the phrenological belief that the 'little brain' – the cerebellum – worked as primordial sexualising part of the cerebrum, directly connected to the shaping of male and female individuals' sexual characteristics. His analysis clearly suggests 'the enormous size of the cerebellum' as the causal principle of the child's premature 'genital organs', in reference to the work of two well-known phrenologists of his time: Austrian anatomist Johann Franz Gall, who founded phrenology in 1795; and German physician Johann Spurzheim, Gall's disciple, who was one of the greatest proponents of phrenology at the time of South's report (cf. Stepan 1982: 21).

In his 1825 'Lectures on Phrenology' (published by *The Lancet* in that same year), the German phrenologist defined his science as 'the doctrine of the manifestations of the mind, and the relations which these manifestations bear to certain bodily conditions' (Spurzheim 1825a: 41, our emphasis). For Spurzheim, the locus of this 'doctrine' was the brain, the biological lodge of the mind itself, where the causes of sex differences in behaviour, for example, were to be studied and eventually demonstrated. As he claimed (with no experimental proof) in his 1815 phrenological treatise, 'the manifestations of the faculties of the mind are modified in both sexes. Some faculties are more energetic in men, others in women' (Spurzheim quoted in Stepan 1982: 23–4).

Together with its measurements and analyses of cranial features, or what Spurzheim (1825b: 102) called 'protuberances', phrenology offered a psychosomatic narrative of human development in which brain differences were at the centre of the plot. This technical-discursive apparatus was highly appealing for the emerging science of puberty, that is to say, for a science that was striving for an explanatory model that could trace sexual-reproductive maturation within the physiologies of young children. In 1820, only two years before South's publication of his case, the superintendent of the Anatomical Department of the Faculty of Medicine in Paris, Dr Gilbert Breschet, presented his paper on a 3-year-old pubescent boy to the British Royal Society of Medicine. According to the abstract published in the following year, Breschet promptly resorted to phrenological expertise by calling Spurzheim himself to make an evaluation of the case:

> Dr. Spurzheim, who was desired by Dr. Breschet to examine the external form of the head of this boy, reported that the cerebellum appeared to have acquired a very considerable development; and he seemed to think even that very few adults have that organ of so great a size. Dr. Breschet,

> however, expressly states that he declines giving any opinion as to the truth of the peculiar physiological system which relates to the influence of the cerebellum on the genital system of organs.
>
> (Breschet 1821: 447)

In line with South's report, Breschet entertains the possible 'influence of the cerebellum on the genital system of organs'; he is significantly more careful about the argument, though. It is unsurprising that Breschet avoided 'giving any opinion as to the truth of the peculiar physiological system' proposed by Spurzheim. While phrenology had become popular, that does not mean that it was widely accepted or even well-regarded in most circles of 19th-century biomedical science – namely in France, where pathological anatomy and post-mortem tissue analysis were sovereign, or in England, where physiology was the dominant trend in clinical research (Porter 1998). Consequently, in the inaugural presentation of his 'Lectures' by *The Lancet*, the journal introduced Spurzheim in the following manner:

> We have this day the satisfaction of introducing to the attention of our readers the first of Dr. Spurzheim's excellent Lectures on the science of Phrenology, a science which by far the greater portion of the English public have never yet heard mentioned, unless accompanied by ridicule, abuse, or misrepresentation. . . . It will now be seen whether Phrenology is a 'fraud', a piece of 'specious quackery', a system of 'bumps and lumps', and its 'pretended discoverers philosophical impostors', or a system founded in nature, and having truth for its basis.
>
> (Spurzheim 1825a: 41)

The above statements give a good picture of the profusion of disqualifying terms used by many 'serious' scientists and clinicians in speaking to phrenology around that time. However, as Nancy Stepan (1982: 20) notes in her brilliant history of scientific racism, 'Phrenology . . . though discredited by many leading experimentalists, nevertheless shaped the views of a generation of scientists in Britain', ultimately occupying a 'fundamental place . . . in the scientific, social and intellectual history of Europe in the nineteenth century'.

In puberty science, in particular, the tacit assumption that cranial size and form were but the external manifestation of a cerebral structure underpinning sexual physiology proved resilient. Obviously, on the one hand, it did not take long for a new neurological science to demonstrate that the brain organisation predicted by the phrenologists was wrong. On the other hand, however, the endocrinal functions of certain cerebral organs in pubertal development (e.g. the pituitary glands) and respective assessment technologies would only be discovered in the next century (see Chapter 9). Thus, albeit based on a great deal of (unstated) speculation, the assessment of 'cerebellar enlargement' and cranial 'protuberances' as possible symptoms of accelerated sexual maturation can be found in clinical analyses from the second half of the 19th century:

> There is nothing unusual in the volume or shape of her head, neither inspection nor mensuration discloses any indication of cerebellar enlargement.
> (Smart 1858: 457)

> The girth of the head round the occipital and frontal protuberances was twenty-one inches, which is certainly not very small for his bulk.
> (Clarke quoted in *The British Medical Journal* 1886: 263)

Despite their very limited utility and consequence in terms of aetiological knowledge, these phrenological assessments performed important disciplinary functions in clinicians' discourse.

To start with, measuring cranial features was a fashionable activity in 19th-century biological research. Widely figured as determinant elements of the 'human races', cranial differences equated with 'natural' variations around, or gradations of, an evolutionary ideal that ultimately functioned as the 'normal', the standard of humanity – a racial norm understood as desirable rather than simply the average. For most, needless to say, that norm was the 'white' skull, that is, the 'white' mind (see Chapter 5). In examining their young patients' skulls, second, physicians were saying "we can indeed look into the child's body and attempt to know how it works". In 'entering' the precocious pubescent body through the skull, moreover, the first organ that they 'saw' was, of course, the brain. And in 'seeing' it, they also 'saw' a sexualising brain with a *natural yet abnormal constitution*. This view of the brain, as inherited from phrenology and conveyed in 19th-century reports on early development, is puberty science's first point of entry into the field of biological abnormality.

White, we said in Chapter 2, had moved from a quasi-scientific sexual anatomy of the body's surface to a corporeal knowledge connected to the body's 'inside'. Yet, his clinical gaze was mainly concerned with 'the state of [sexual-reproductive] functions' (White 1809: 279). White made no claims as to the physiological system responsible for maturation in the child. Ultimately, he could not see beyond monstrosity – he was first and foremost interested in demonstrating it, hence the importance of the functional analysis of sexual organs in his clinical discourse.

By the early 1820s, however, doctors dealing with similar cases suggested a physiological system in which the prematurity of sexual organs was influenced or even determined by brain size and shape. Within this game of truth, the apparent constitution of their patients' brains did not figure as monstrous in itself. For one, these children were clinically regarded as physically and mentally sound. Furthermore, as suggested above, the inspection of their heads revealed no pathology: while looking for an explanation in the brain, doctors explicated a condition that, within the discourses that they deployed, in no way resembled an illness. Rather, in seeking for skull 'protuberances' and speculating about brain 'enlargements', these doctors pondered whether the child's mature-immature body, despite its seeming unnaturalness, could after all be a natural condition caused by an abnormal physiological phenomenon.

A case of exception: the doctor gazes at the dead body

Within the whole of the 19th century, we found only one case in which pubertal precocity was linked with a pathological scenario from the outset. It is, therefore, in absolute contrast with *all* other reports published within that period in important Anglo-American medical literature. In those reports, as shown in this and the previous chapters, the question of pathology is either dismissed or not at all present. This 'Instance of Early Puberty', very briefly documented by *The Lancet* (1827: 468), constitutes a historically exceptional event for a second reason: it provided puberty science with one of the first – perhaps the earliest documented – post-mortem gaze of the immature-mature child. In this case, according to the autopsy, the young girl succumbed to 'an inflammation of the intestines'.

Dr Gedike, a Berlin physician, 'was called to attend on a child seven years old, of a most extraordinary figure. . . . The external parts of generation were very much developed, and covered *with hair*' (emphasis in original). At first sight, it appears that this doctor was still in the presence of a pubertal child monster. However, the seeming unnaturalness of the patient's 'extraordinary figure' fell apart as soon as Gedike palpated her body:

> On touching the abdomen, there could be easily felt in the neighbourhood of the pelvis a solid body, having an irregular form; moreover, a round and yielding tumour was also discovered. The child died of an inflammation of the intestines; and, on examination, there were discovered several steatomatous tumours situated in the cavity of the pelvis round the uterus, which they displaced from its natural situation. The right ovary and fallopian tube were distended, and contained three to four ounces of deep coloured liquid; the left was not so large, and was lost in the substance of the tumours.
>
> (*The Lancet* 1827: 468)

Following this post-mortem description, no further considerations are added. The autopsy had been conducted, the cadaver and her derangements described in detail, the cause of death found, all of which corroborating the doctors' initial exam – case closed. Had Gedike or any other doctor known about endocrinology, perhaps the journal would have had something to say about the relation of those 'steatomatous tumours' (i.e. sebaceous cysts) to the development of secondary sex-characteristics. All that knowledge was about a century away (see Chapters 7 and 8). Yet, the causal relation between the onset of such organic disorders and early pubertal development was suggested. In this way, a little after the emergence of a phrenological brain in tentative aetiologies of pubertal precocity, the death of this unnamed child was the second event allowing for puberty science to enter the domain of biological abnormality.

Family portraits: the hereditary-racial nexus

As indicated earlier, both White and South were inclined to believe that their young patients' pubertal changes were somehow integral to the child's gestation itself: they 'had their origin in utero'. In fact, whereas these clinicians *explicitly* attempted a conclusive explanation for what they saw as the onset of puberty in a very young child, most of the 19th-century doctors reporting on the condition did not venture into the etiological domain. However, in these texts, White's and South's included, there is often an implicit assumption of a number of concurrent possible underlying causes.

Those causal suggestions were most notably entertained in a certain portrait of the child's family, usually presented in the introduction of the case. These 'family pictures' of the case subject was a prevailing feature of clinical reports on early and very early developers until well into the 20th century.[1] White's, South's, and Smart's reports are exemplary of the manner in which different causalities – heredity, race, and class – circulate and interweave within the 'portrait', the so-called family history of the patient:

> Philip Howorth was born in Quebec Mews, Pott-man-square, on February 21, 1806. His parents are middle aged, and poor but industrious people. The father is a coachman in a gentleman's service, and the mother is constantly employed in nursing and rearing a family of ten children, of which Philip is the ninth. The father is a healthy and muscular man; the mother a middle sized woman and rather delicate; the rest of the children are of the ordinary stature and appearance.
>
> (White 1809: 280)

> The subject of the following memoir, John Sparrow, was born Sept. 6, 1818, at Long Melford, in Suffolk. His parents are laboring people, and at the time of his birth were about twenty-seven years of age. The father is a thin, but healthy rustic; the mother a dark little woman; has borne four children, a girl and three boys, of which this child is the youngest but one.
>
> (South 1823: 76)

> History of Family. – The mother of this child will be aged twenty-six next July. She is a small, spare brunette, and was formerly a factory-hand. She began to menstruate at the age of sixteen, and was married in two years after. She has had four children, all of whom are girls, and are still living. . . . There is nothing remarkable in the appearance of Mary's sisters. . . . The

> father, aet. 26, is of light complexion, and of medium height; he is a "maker-up" in a warehouse. It has not been ascertained at what age he acquired virility. No example of sexual precocity has been known to occur in the ancestry, or in any collateral branch of the family.
>
> (Smart 1858: 460, 461)

In the above statements, the clinicians make sure to indicate that their patients' parents and siblings are all in good health. The fathers are described as strong and productive man. The mothers figure as capable reproducers, having given birth to several 'ordinary' children. As Smart specifies in his more sophisticated analysis, no other episodes of 'sexual precocity' are to be found 'in the ancestry, or in any collateral branch of the family'.

In short, these 'family portraits' simultaneously refuted and entertained what may be called the hereditary hypothesis of pubertal precocity. Their authors showed concern as to whether the condition was caused by a line of descent producing biological 'degeneration', to use a popular notion of that century's scientific jargon and thought. At the same time, they promptly dismissed that possibility in their cases. 'It is worthy of remark', White (1809: 287) pointed out during his anatomical examination of his patient, 'that he retains a very close resemblance of countenance to the rest of his family' – a puzzling piece of evidence for him, since the premature pubescent child was nonetheless a monster in his discursive framework. That is to say, independently of the unnatural biological order of the child's pubescence, as White perceived it, the mechanisms of descent seemed to be working as naturally as expected.

From the early decades of the 1800s, even if very briefly stated, these hereditary 'pictures' constituted a dominant feature in clinical reports on pubertal prematurity:

> Charlotte Mawer [is] the daughter of a water man at Lincoln. . . . Her eldest sister, aged about seventeen years, has never menstruated, and there is very little fullness in her breasts, though she is in good health.
>
> (Cooper 1813: 207, 208)

> James A. Savin, the subject of this memoir, was born at Montmorillon, October 20th, 1817, of healthy and well-formed parents.
>
> (Breschet 1821: 446)

> Sally Deweese, daughter of John Deweese, was born in Butler county, Kentucky, on the 7th of April, 1824. . . . She was the fifteenth child her mother had given birth to, and was born when her mother was forty-five years of age. There had been no previous case of early puberty, or premature old age in either the family of the father or mother.
>
> (Rowlett cit. *American Journal of the Medical Sciences* 1834: 266)

Unlike the above examples, White's, South's, and Smart's 'family portraits' did not simply assert the non-pathological procreative 'quality' of descent within their patients' families. In speaking to the hereditary hypothesis, the three doctors also spoke to the racial 'quality' of their patients' parents. Philip's, John's, and Mary's fathers are respectively depicted as 'healthy and muscular', 'a thin, but healthy rustic', and 'of light complexion, and of medium height'. Their mothers are portrayed as, respectively, 'a middle sized woman [with] rather delicate [features]', 'a dark little woman', and 'a small, spare brunette'.

These doctors' intertwining of hereditary considerations and descriptions of skin colour and body types – features consistently racialised in 19th-century scientific discourse – is in harmony with the biological knowledge constructed throughout that period. At the time of their reports, heredity was widely accepted as a fundamental mechanism in the perpetuation of perceived racial marks in individuals and populations, such as different body shapes or colours of skin (Stepan 1982). Likewise, in White's, South's, and Smart's clinical discourse, the family's racial 'type' is confirmed by the suggestion of the child's acquisition of certain anatomical traits:

> [T]he head [is] small, but well formed; the eyes blue, the hair brown and coarse, the eye-brows large, and the complexion rather brown.
>
> (White 1809: 283)

> Soon after weaning, light curling hair began to appear very fast on the temples and sides of his head, which had been before bare, and the black hair on the occiput and vertex falling off, was replaced by light hair, but not for a considerable time.
>
> (South 1823: 78)

> She is of a robust habit; her complexion is clear, rosy, and slightly inclined to be fair; she has grey eyes, and rather dark brown hair.
>
> (Smart 1858: 457)

In an academic and political climate of heightened debates about the 'human races' and their differences, these doctors found it necessary to speak about their patients' hair, eyes, or skin colour (not to mention head shape). In his very short account, Dr Le Beau was direct and typological in his racial objectivising of the precocious pubescent girl brought to him:

> I take the liberty to acquaint you with an extraordinary case of prematurity in a child, which fell under my observation in this city [New Orleans]. Matilda H. was born of a white family in low circumstances, the 31st of September, 1827.
>
> (Le Beau 1832: 42)

The meanings and language of race, as outlined by Stepan (1982), have always been polymorphous and have changed across the history of scientific racism. In the new statistical science of puberty of the 1800s, as shall be seen in Chapters 5 and 6, race was a synonym for (and the confusing entanglement of) a variety of things such as anatomical characteristics, nationality, and religion.[2]

But, regardless of the repertoires used to racially portray premature pubescent subjects, this discursive event must not be reduced to a clinical style or an automatic expression of doctors' own racist views. The indication of their patients' race (via indications of hair colour or skin hue, for example) was a strategic way of asserting the scientific actuality and thoroughness of the analysis. Furthermore, the racial objectification of case subjects carried an important aetiological value in these reports. In medical texts whose implicit problem ultimately was that of causality (even if unstated or inexplicable), doctors selectively used a descriptive biological 'fact' that could be equated with structural differences between individuals, hence inevitably suggesting it as a factor to be considered in such extraordinary cases.

Ultimately, the clinical establishment of bodily phenomena such as premature puberty was moulded by the great scientific debates in which the medical profession was involved. Across the 1800s, clinicians addressed early puberty through a range of themes typically entertained at their time whenever human biology was at stake – race and heredity being prominent ones. As Stepan's work suggests, race differences and their hereditary transmission constituted a compelling nexus from whence 19th-century biomedicine drew ideas on human development, which the 1900s would not completely let go of:

> By the middle of the nineteenth century, everyone was agreed, it seemed, that in essential ways the white race was superior to the non-white races. . . . In 1850, the Scottish anatomist, Dr Robert Knox, exclaimed: 'With me, race or heredity descent is everything; it stamps the man.' While disagreeing with Knox's blatant racism, most British scientists shared by mid-century, almost unconsciously, Knox belief that fixed and distinct racial types provided the key to human history and destiny.
>
> (Stepan 1982: 4)

In specifying children's hereditary-racial 'types' in early accounts of premature development, implicitly or not, 1800s clinicians promoted a new space for scientific racial speculation: could race somehow influence or even determine the age of puberty? This question, as we know, haunts puberty science to the present day (see Chapter 1).

Exogenous triggers: the problem of living conditions

Alongside the hereditary and the racial hypotheses, an exogenous plane of causalities emerged in early reports on premature puberty. Looking back at White's, South's, and Smart's texts, one can see that, besides speaking to biological descent and race, their 'portraits' of their patients' families also position them within a socioeconomic status. Philips' parents are 'poor but industrious people. The father is a coachman in a gentleman's service, and the mother is constantly employed in nursing and rearing a family of ten children' (White 1809: 280). Mary's father 'is a "maker-up" in a warehouse'; her mother 'was formerly a factory-hand', meaning that she became, to use Smart's phrasing, 'constantly employed' in rearing her daughters (Smart 1858: 460, 461). Finally, for South (1823: 76), John's parents 'are laboring people'.

Such descriptions are also found in a couple of 'family portraits' quoted above. British doctor Astley Cooper (1813: 207) starts his brief report by indicating that 'Charlotte Mawer [is] the daughter of a water man at Lincoln' (with no further references about the parents). Doctor J. Le Beau (1832: 42), from the US, introduces his short account by stating that 'Matilda H. was born of a white family in low circumstances'.

In short, these families belonged to the lower classes of society. In indicating it, clinicians showed apprehension as to the situation in which the pubertal child had been born and raised, but also suggested a physiological relationship between material living conditions and their patients' development. Within their 'family portraits', this is to say, class emerged as an exogenous shaper of pubertal maturation and growth (the theoretical uses and implications of 'class' in the early history of puberty science are to be traced in Chapter 6).

The nutritional hypothesis

At the centre of medical anxieties around exogenous causes there was, of course, the issue of nourishment (which, in some cases, appeared alongside class-related concerns). In reflecting on White's conclusions, South (1823: 85) pondered whether his own patient's sudden 'loss of flesh', rather than a typical 'precursor' of pubescence as suggested in White's report, actually was 'the effect of the child having its customary and natural food withheld, which we know frequently produces the most fatal consequences to children'. As to White, he certainly did not disregard the implications of diet in his patient's development. During his account, he remarks: 'His food has been very simple, and chiefly of the farinaceous kind; his choice, however, appears to be animal food, of which he eats enormously, and, with great eagerness' (White 1809: 287). A similar statement about a voracious appetite is found in Clarke's later report on 'Early Puberty':

> The boy was the third child in a family of five, and he was bigger than the eldest child, who was over seven years old. He was suckled for nine months. At about one year of age he began to grow rapidly and to eat voraciously, so that nothing seemed to satisfy him.
>
> (Clarke cit. *The British Medical Journal* 1886: 263)

In the late 1850s, though, Smart carried the theoretical question of diet further. To start with, in citing 'the earliest instance of premature puberty' published in an English medical volume – the 1745 account of a 'gigantic boy' (see Chapter 2) – he drew special attention to the 'influence' of nutrition on this pubertal child monster:

> The minister of the parish writes: – "He grew to admiration three quarters of a year, having only the breast sustenance, when his mother died suddenly, and, as is supposed, he was accessory thereunto, by drawing away her vital nourishment." The change of diet, consequent on his mother death, had no retarding influence on his growth, as he continued to flourish amazingly.
> (Smart 1858: 455)

In Smart's view, however, the quantity and quality of what precocious pubescent children eat was to be considered not simply as a contributing factor in their growth but also a trigger of their maturation. When reporting on his own patient, he firmly situated diet as one of the main possible 'exciting causes' of the condition:

> An inquiry into her habits does not reveal an exposure to any of the assigned exciting causes of early puberty. She has occupied the same bedroom as her parents, and has never slept with any of the other sex; her sisters have been her usual associates. In diet she has fared like the rest of the family.[3]
> (Smart 1858: 459)

In stating that none of the 'assigned' triggers of the condition were met in his patient's case, Smart implies that diet and family environment were deemed 'exciting causes' by several other clinicians around that time, as we confirm in the second part of the book.

As to the nutritional hypothesis, its likelihood is reinforced in the footnote quoted below Smart's main statement, where he entertains an analogy between child development and animal biology. Drawing on the 'sexual development' of bees, he suggests that, just like 'the larva' that mutates into a 'queen', a girl's premature transformation into a true 'female' could be partly caused by her diet, if not by 'aliment [nourishment] alone'. Or better, he opens up the possibility in similar instances, even if it was not true in his case (for 'she fared like the rest of the family'). This analogy is perfectly aligned with the modern episteme established by then. Towards the end of the 18th century, the French founding father of comparative anatomy and functional analysis, George Cuvier, broke with the traditional external, formal gaze of the natural historians. Opening the door to modern biology, he launched the notion that every organism is governed *within* itself by a system of discrete processes that are constantly affected by the external world. In his *Archaeology of the Human Sciences*, Foucault argues:

> The living being [for Cuvier] . . . provides the outline of an organic structure, which maintains uninterrupted relations with exterior elements that

> it utilizes (by breathing and eating) in order to maintain or develop its own structure. . . . In order that the living being can live, there must exist several functional structures, all irreducible one to another, and also an uninterrupted movement between each one of those structures and the air it breathes, the water it drinks, the food it absorbs.
>
> (Foucault 2002: 298)

In Cuvier's account of the biological, in short, 'The living being, by the action and sovereignty of the same force that keeps it in discontinuity with itself' – as in the case of the mutating larva or the premature pubescent girl – 'finds itself subjected to a continuous relation with all that surrounds it' (p. 298). Unsurprisingly, based upon the principle that the structural evolution of human subjects is inherently bound, for example, to what they eat, the linkage between diet and pubertal maturation became an important vector in the scientific pursuit for the causes of puberty onset throughout the 1800s and the following century.[4]

It should also be noted that in Cuvier's type of analysis, the structures governing the organism – the functional structures of the brain, for example – are to be found in, and compared between, various living beings belonging to the same as well as different species.[5] As Stepan (1982) illuminates, the rise of a modern science concerned with human differences necessitated knowledge about animal biology on the basis of which such differences – racial and sexual – could be demonstrated as universal, constantly permeating and structuring the natural organisation of the entire animal, vegetable, and human realms (see also Schiebinger 2004).

By the 1830s, as will be seen in Chapter 5, the old naturalist comparisons between female pubescence and the blooming of flowers gave way to a new type and style of scientific sexism.[6] With this shift, as illustrated in Smart's theorising, analogical reasoning did not vanish from medical discourse, but was rather refashioned in line with new biosocial understandings and codifications of human development and life itself (see the second part of this book).

The other hypothesis contained in his causal statements also draws on a class-related issue but of a wholly different kind and origin. Smart confirms that, unlike what could be medically (theoretically) expected, the girl 'has occupied the same bedroom as her parents, and has never slept with any of the other sex; her sisters have been her usual associates'. In short, Smart's musings spoke to the problematic of promiscuity within the (poor) family home raised around that time. It basically presumes that early sexual contact or exposure may lead into sexual precocity and anticipate the arrival of puberty – a theorisation whose discursive technology is the psychosomatic dynamic of the sexual instinct, as discussed below.

The instinctual hypothesis

Towards the mid-19th century, governmental authorities in Europe initiated a campaign aimed at a new and rapidly agglomerating urban proletariat. The campaign was specifically preoccupied with the 'proper' partition of the family space, or better, with the sexually 'hygienic' division of the house and its rooms where that close-knit and affective body called the family cell was supposed to live. Foucault (2003b: 270) describes the advocates in this campaign speaking out 'against shared bedrooms, against parents and children, and children "of a different sex", sharing the same bed'. Essentially, they rallied against sexual (and possibly incestuous) promiscuity within the household. Besides getting married and legitimately procreating, working-class people were called to demarcate their homes and the relationships within them so that the interdependent proximity between relatives of different ages and sexes, and the necessary closeness of the family cell, could be, somewhat paradoxically, reduced to the minimum. 'The ideal in the workers' cities being planned at this time', as Foucault argues, 'is the well-known small house with three rooms: a living room for all, a room for the parents and a room for the children', or a specific room for boys and another for girls (p. 270).[7]

The idea of an adult sexuality as inherently dangerous *vis-à-vis* the child, highlighted by institutional propaganda of that period, was an important trope in the inception and expansion of pubertal power-knowledge. It is most notably seen in reports on female precocious puberty, particularly in the 'monstrous' cases of child pregnancy (see Chapter 2). In those accounts, however, concerns about sexual abuse are rather tangential, if not completely absent. Doctors were first and foremost worried about (and, we could say, marvelled at) the biological and social 'monstrosity' of a child giving birth to another child. Their medical interest was mainly focused on the physiological possibility of a safe pregnancy and healthy progeny in such a case.

Yet, as soon as the coupling of the question of behavioural abnormality and the sexual instinct is firmly established in clinical approaches to precocious puberty, the problem of a promiscuous family setting is discursively framed thus: on the one hand, as discussed in Chapter 3, a healthy development equates with the 'normal' evolution of the sexual instinct from infancy to puberty, for which parental supervision is expected. On the other hand, however, that instinct has the potential to fall off the 'right' track and manifest itself in the child's conduct in abnormal ways. Not only is it naturally excessive (i.e. non-procreative), it is also precociously excitable or 'awakened' (besides being markedly heterosexist). Therefore, the fact of a child living or sleeping too closely with older bodies, or with other children of a different sex, could now be linked to an abnormal process of maturation by force of the psychosomatic logic of the sexual instinct and its unpredictable power. Unsurprisingly, this discursive event took place at about the same time that the campaign for the 'proper' partition of the house gained ground.

Thus, while evoking class-related fears about adult sexuality, the problem of promiscuity around the child gained significant epistemic value in 1800s puberty science: it is the first truly medical-psychiatric explanatory model of early maturing understood as a natural yet abnormal condition, as clearly conveyed in Smart's scrutiny of his patient's 'habits': 'She has occupied the same bedroom as her parents, and has never slept with any of the other sex; her sisters have been her usual associates'. Once bodily promiscuity between children and older or sexually different relatives could be theoretically established as dangerous for the child's physical and behavioural development via an instinctual, mind-body mechanism, the possibility of pubertal precocity appears: this is the discursive rationality of Smart's statements. Accordingly, he was clear in indicating that the girl occupied the same *bedroom*, but not the same bed as her parents (nobody 'of the other sex'). Hence, these 'exciting causes' of early puberty were ruled out.

Ultimately, the technology of the sexual instinct, or what Smart (1858: 458) called 'sexual propensities', enabled him to interconnect (even though in a rather speculative manner) the morphological and behavioural abnormalities of pubertal precocity within a sort of bio-neuro-instinctual system. Consequently, those forms of promiscuity concerning the child were to be seen as 'exciting causes' of the condition simply because, in Smart's discursive framework, the bodily and the instinctual shape one another. As such, these 'exciting' promiscuities, bodily proximities, and all kinds of sexually suggestive settings or imageries, to be sure, historically form an early and rather productive element in the long and polymorphous domain of possible causes of early puberty (and, thus, of 'normal' puberty as well).

As will be seen in Chapters 5 and 6, some of the anxieties expressed by the first statisticians of pubertal timing were infused with this discourse of the sexual instinct, and more exactly with a notion of instinctual triggers of puberty – or female puberty, to be precise – prompted by the external world. Most notably, they saw those triggers in the hyper-sexualised cultural settings of the 'uncivilised', the 'improper' factory milieu surrounding the working-class girl, or the sassiness of new female education spreading among the cosmopolitan upper classes.

The environmental hypothesis

Another exogenous causal hypothesis was entertained in early clinical encounters with premature puberty: the environment. We find this in Dr Rowlett's 'Case of Puberty and Pregnancy in a Girl of Ten Years of Age':

> There had been no previous case of early puberty, or premature old age in either the family of the father or mother. . . . Her father lived in Butler county until she was two years old, and then removed to the place on which he now lives, in Hickman county, one mile south of Mayfield's Creek, and ten miles east of the Mississippi river, in latitude 36° 59' N; but I presume that latitude nor atmosphere has had any influence in this truly, (to me,) astonishing case. I think it is an over-match for the case of the Swiss girl spoken of by Haller.
>
> (Rowlett cit. *American Journal of the Medical Sciences* 1834: 266)

According to Rowlett's statements, as previously found in other 'family portraits', his hereditary inquiry produced negative results: neither cases of early puberty nor instances of what he and other 19th-century doctors saw as a relatable condition – 'premature old age'[8] – had occurred in the patient's family. Ultimately, Rowlett implicitly suggests an endogenous, inborn causal mechanism (given the absence of exogenous influences, in his opinion), and so the presence of a non-degenerative and actually reproductive biological process.[9]

Nevertheless, notwithstanding Rowlett's scepticism about environmental effects, heredity, and climate figure in his account as *concurrent* natural forces possibly producing the premature onset of puberty. Of course, his reasoning may be located within the new biological episteme of which Cuvier is an originator: from Rowlett's hypothetical standpoint, the structural and functional organisation of the living being is to be understood in 'an uninterrupted movement' with its own conditions of living, that is to say, 'the air it breathes, the water it drinks, the food it absorbs' (Foucault 2002: 298). Within our data corpus, to be sure, Rowlett's is the only case report on pubertal prematurity published in the 1800s where the environmental hypothesis is considered. Yet, as we discuss in Chapters 5 and 6, environmentalism represents a crucial trope in the scientific normalisation of pubertal timing, the emergence of which is inextricably bound to the scientific and political arguments about 'human races' and the geographical locations where they lived.

Abnormal and biosocial: connecting the monstrous body to a new power

Throughout the first part of this book, we have shown that, during the first decades of the 1800s, the pubertal monster mutated into an abnormal child via two interlinked clinical pathways: the child's premature sexual conduct, and the child's sexual-reproductive functions and carnality. Focusing on the latter in this chapter, we started with the rise of biological abnormality in reports on pubertal precocity, which links up with two distinctive lines of aetiological inquiry: natural, non-pathological triggers theoretically associated with the brain, on the one hand, and physiological anomalies of harmful consequence actually seen and located inside the body, on the other.

In the latter, exceptional case, reported on a post-mortem, the cause of the girls' death quite simply overrode the need for further inquiries on the possible relationship between the organic disorders found next to her uterus and her 'extraordinary figure'. At all events, this case did not provoke the same interest among the clinical profession as all other stories of premature pubescent boys and girls who seemed so remarkably healthy and destined to live, even reproduce.

In such cases, drawing on phrenological discourses, a few physicians 'discovered' a brain whose natural organisation was said to shape sexual physiology and its growth. While resorting to anatomical comparisons and examinations of sexual functions – i.e. the sovereign methods in early analyses of the confusion of maturity and immaturity – these doctors also appealed to knowledge and measuring practices by which the monstrous body was reconnected to natural phenomena. Reading cranial 'protuberances' as indicators of brain 'enlargements', they speculated about a physiological apparatus in which the child's 'irregular' skull was an anatomical anticipation of the precocious development of the sexual organs.

Although the phrenologists' prophecies about the human brain were eventually dismantled by neurophysiology, a new endocrinal science would offer the 'correct remake' of the principle that certain cerebral parts are implicated in the body's sexual maturation. Nevertheless, despite being construed on a fairly speculative basis, this idea rose within the problematic of premature puberty by the early 1820s (Breschet 1821; South 1823). At that moment, the child's corporeal monstrosity began to break down from within: the abnormal body emerged.

Alongside this explanatory body of pubertal precocity, another discursive event took place in clinicians' reports that undermined the old framework of biological monstrosity. Deeply bound to the emergence of a pubertal abnormal physiology, this event centred on a discursive formation concerning the causes of the condition that may be called, in a word, the biosocial.

Starting already with White (1809), an ensemble of concurrent endogenous and exogenous causalities – or 'latent' hypotheses, in many cases – circulated in doctors' reports. For example, in several of the 'family portraits', hereditary evaluations and/or racial descriptions interweave with socioeconomic considerations (White 1809; Cooper 1813; South 1823; Le Beau's 1832; Smart 1858). Rowlett (cit. *The American Journal of the Medical Sciences* 1834), who finally suggested the condition as constitutional, also contemplated a hereditary cause, at the same time pondering (even though distrustfully) the possible effects of the environment. Alongside the hereditary, racial, and class-related views composing their 'family pictures', a few of these clinicians inspected the issue of living conditions in their analyses. White (1809) and South (1823), who ultimately pointed to the possibility of an inborn causality, showed concerns as to what their patients ate. In his 1858 report, Smart explicitly advanced diet as a main causal hypothesis of premature puberty, as well as early bodily/sexual contact with others, especially with those of the 'opposite sex', facilitated by a promiscuous family space and environment.

In all these reports, this is to say, nature and nurture do not figure as mutually exclusive: their subjects' problem is suggested as the plausible result of a constant dynamic between the contingent settings of society and the laws of life itself. Simply put, the premature pubescent body emerged as a biosocial product. As soon as the question of causes was (implicitly or explicitly) posed in early reports on the condition, there appeared a network of hypotheses that, in responding to the problem of immaturity-maturity, paradoxically undermined the discursive exclusion of the premature pubescent body from the realm of nature. While that body was by and large construed as the natural outcome of the unnatural, it was already being inserted within a continuum between the subject's particular organic structures and all the exogenous conditions allowing it to live – as Cuvier proposed in the late 1700s. To sum up, from the very inception of puberty science, there was the emergence of a biosocial thinking around the causes of early pubescence, and so about pubertal development *tout court*, through which the seminal framework of biological monstrosity started to collapse.

This shift in medical history, it should be borne in mind, is inextricably bound to the historically subjugated knowledge of the child monster, that is, her/his unique capacity to inhabit the unnatural rather naturally. This discursive quality constituted the greatest dangerousness of this figure to the social body, its order, its system. From the genealogical perspective of struggles and resistances, pubertal monstrosity signified a real counter-knowledge with regard to established institutions, one able to defy the socio-political rules sustaining and sustained by the scientific meanings of 'nature'. Pubertal monstrosity, therefore, had to be filtered and codified according to those meanings in order to be eventually reintegrated in the very natural system that excluded it. During a brief stage in the history of modern puberty science, that is to say until the 1830s, the discourse of biological norms, the norms of nature, had not yet been formulated in statistical terms, as will be seen in the next chapter. Nonetheless, early reports already conveyed a clinical discourse by which the child's monstrous body could be excluded from, and at the same time reconnected to, the 'natural' imperatives of the family, the whole reproductive social fabric, the population.

Of course, the child monster represented the exceptional. However, monstrosity is not intelligible in itself (Foucault 2003b); that is to say, the child's exceptionality could only be demonstrated by contrast with her/his 'natural' counterparts, the siblings being the usual 'control group'. Furthermore, as also discussed in Chapter 3, clinicians were overall fascinated by the regularities of the little monsters' sexual bodies. These regularities, while constituting the very symptomatology of the condition, figured in their accounts as analogous, to a greater or a lesser extent, to the pubertal changes observed in 'natural' circumstances. Hence, their scrutiny entertained notions of puberty as a biologically ordained bodily process, while inviting a more refined formulation of its laws. In this sense, early medical encounters with immature-mature subjects gave rise to what can be seen as the earliest modern clinical analyses of pubertal development. In assessing and objectifying 'premature' bodies against healthy bodies developing in correct chronological order, those doctors consequently dealt with issues of natural *variation* and *limits*; that is to say, they already deployed a type of scientific thinking around pubertal norms.

Delving into the nascent statistical science of puberty, our task in the following chapter is twofold. On the one hand, we analyse the discourses and practices by which, within the 1830s–40s, variations in pubertal timing within and between different populations were hypothesised, constructed, and normalised as a biosocial phenomenon. One the other hand, we trace the historical conditions of possibility of this medical advent. From the 1830s onwards, the figure of the pubertal monster was continually filtered by a new knowledge formation around 'the human' wherein the seemingly unnatural is academically and politically required to be no more than abnormal, and therefore correctable. In short, as we illuminate in the second part of the book, pubertal monstrosity had no theoretical place nor power-knowledge function in the era of Reform.

Notes

1 Herewith an example: 'Elise P. was born on the 24 of March, 1942, as the first child of healthy parents. There are no known cases of pubertas praecox in the family; the mother menstruated since her 13th year' (Christensen 1947: 157).

2 During the first half of the 20th century, unsurprisingly, racial classifications were frequently at stake in medical engagements with precocious puberty and assumed the same plural, overlapping forms. For example, Ellis (1934: 1328) asserted that 'The patient is of Jewish parentage', while Cookston (1948: 90) reported on the case of 'A. L. K., a 3-year-old Negro girl'. In a 1941 study comparing the age of the onset of walking in precocious pubescent patients and 'normal' children, the author assured readers of the consistency of his framework as follows: 'In all cases included in the present survey the patient was a member of the white race and was born in the United States, Great Britain, France or Germany. In racial and national origin, therefore, the patients with *pubertas praecox* are comparable with the members of the normal groups' (Dennis 1941: 955, italics added).

3 The effect of diet on sexual development is shown in certain of the lower animals. The "neuter" larva of the bee is changed into a perfect female or "queen" by superior aliment alone.

4 Indeed, as the 1800s wore out and the new century progressed, the nutritional hypothesis remained as a compelling and intriguing problem to puberty scientists. In 1941, in her study interrogating the relation between child obesity and the timing of pubertal maturation, US paediatrician Hilde Bruch grappled with the question: 'Long-continued malnutrition during childhood results not alone in deficient weight but is associated also with marked statural retardation and delay in pubertal development. It is not unreasonable to suppose that persistent overnutrition has the opposite effect and is, at least in part, responsible for the rapid development of obese children' (Bruch 1941: 374). We shall reengage with her work (and critical views, in particular) in Chapter 8.

5 In his *Leçons d'Anatomie Comparée*, Cuvier claimed that 'one organ is at its highest degree of perfection in one species, while another reaches that same degree of perfection in a different species' (Curvier cit. Foucault 2002: 295). As feminist theorist Robyn Wiegman (1995: 31) writes, following Stepan, Cuvier's ideas 'underwrote claims throughout the nineteenth century for the permanency of racial characteristics, biological in origin, and connected to the organic coherence of the organism as a whole'.

6 For an excellent discussion on the use of metaphors around plant and human sexuality in the modern discourse of botany, see Londa Schiebinger (2004: 11–37).

7 From Foucault's angle, the contemporary 'interclass family model' was finally constituted through the double manoeuvring of two paramount and almost simultaneous historical movements, each organised around a specific sexual danger concerning the child: 'In one case [i.e. the anti-masturbation crusade], the child's sexuality is dangerous and calls for the coagulation of the family; in the other case [i.e. the campaign for the proper house], adult sexuality is thought to be dangerous [to the child] and calls instead for the optimal distribution of the family' (Foucault 2003b: 271).

8 Until at least the 1830s, the physiological association of menarcheal ages with those of the onset of menopause – and so the linkage of pubertal timing with the length of the fertility period – was widely postulated and accepted in medical science. By the dawn of that decade, as shown in Chapter 5, John Roberton troubled this assumption with his early hospital studies.

9 Recall that Rowlett's case is on an extremely early maturing girl – 'her hips and breasts began to grow rapidly in a few weeks after she was born, and at twelve months of age she began to menstruate' – whose reproductive capacity was ultimately attested by her pregnancy at age 10 (see Chapter 2).

Part 2

From biological to cultural monstrosities

Chapter 5

From the world of the naturalists to the first population studies

By the dawn of the 1800s, scientific inquiry into pubertal timing had become a hotbed for racialist articulations of pubescence and climate – particularly with regard to female sexual-reproductive development. Many medical men – often citing natural historians – asserted that the 'Tropical races' reached puberty strikingly earlier than the Central Europeans, and that the latter did not mature as amazingly late as the peoples from the colder regions of the world, such as the Scandinavians or the Eskimos. Within the 1830s–1840s, however, these understandings suffered a profound theoretical and methodological transformation.

In this chapter we explore the historical apparatus underpinning the early 19th-century medical world views of puberty and the inception of statistical norms concerning the coming of age in different 'races'. This apparatus, as we show, was co-shaped by three main strategic forces: the scientific demands of medical jurisprudence, the intertwined debates of scientific racism and scientific sexism, and the progressive movements of colonial reform, namely focused on slavery and the oppression of women outside the 'civilised' West.

Pubertal medicine is called into the court

Focusing on the British context, we start by looking into the judicial call for positive scientific knowledge of puberty. In a time of growing humanist concerns with the child, such knowledge became instrumental for the juridical system to be able to deal with a number of legal dilemmas and criminal matters. Scottish physician Anthony Todd Thomson will be our interlocutor here. Praised for his contributions in the fields of chemistry and pharmacy, he became the first professor of *materia medica* (i.e. the pharmacology of substances) and therapeutics at the University of London in 1828, two years after its foundation. In 1832, he was appointed professor of medical jurisprudence to that institution, being solely responsible for the course from 1837 until his death, in 1846. The 1834–5 sessions of this course appeared at that time in a series of issues of *The London Medical and Surgical Journal*.[1]

One of the main topics dealt with in these lectures was pubertal development, and more particularly 'the determination of the age of puberty: the legal questions depending upon this point being *extremely numerous*' (Thomson 1834a: 486, our emphasis). In introducing these questions, Thomson (1834b: 514) acknowledged some of the clinical instances of premature puberty recorded in previous years (e.g. White 1809; Cooper 1813; Breschet 1821). In doing so, he reiterated the conundrums raised within the medico-legal apparatus by the earliest reported cases of pubertal precocity, this is to say, by the child monster's power to upset the law (this is briefly tackled at the beginning of Chapter 2).

Marital laws and family disputes

In societies where marital life was the single legitimate outlet for many to escape parental powers and other social constraints, and marital arrangements allowed for families to ensure their socioeconomic prosperity, the age of marriage constituted an important legal affair. According to the law of England, young people could marry from the legal age of puberty: 12 years old for girls and 14 years old for boys. Children of prepubertal ages were considered '*non nubiles ad matrimonium vel ad procreandos liberos*' – i.e. unable to accomplish the marital duties of procreation (Thomson 1834b: 515). In Britain, however, both the cannon and the ecclesiastical law determined that marriage could be contracted as soon as the parties physically attained puberty, irrespective of their chronological age. This meant that girls and boys could get married before the ages of 12 and 14, respectively, provided that they were demonstrably pubescent and no longer infants – i.e. under 7 years of age. 'Thence', said Thomson, '[the attainment of puberty] may become an important inquiry, when non-age is plead in view of dissolving an early match, and one which can only be decided upon medical evidence' (p. 515). In cases of early marriages, in short, if doubts were raised as to either the age or the connubial (i.e. pubertal) status of any of the young parties – as in the case a precocious pubescent child under 7, yet of an older appearance – a bodily examination of their sexual maturity would be mandatory.

Pubertal prematurity also raised legal difficulties in disputes over family heritage. If a male individual claimed to be the legitimate heir to his father's estate but his mother gave birth to him at a very early age (hence not being considerably older than the son), the alleged 'non-age of his reputed mother' could be put in as a plea against him by another interested party (p. 516). In ascertaining its validity, Thomson argued, medical experts needed to consider that pregnancies were observed at very young ages – namely those reported in cases of female premature puberty – and that the age of menarche varied between populations according to climate. For example, it 'begins very early between the tropics, sometimes so early as eight, nine, and ten years of age'; whereas 'in Lapland and Norway, menstruation rarely occurs before the twenty-fourth year of age . . . and frequently only during summer' (Thomson 1834a: 486). Consequently, Thomson (1834b: 516) reminded his students that, 'as puberty is earlier in warm climates than in cold, women also become mothers sooner' – a 'fact' widely accepted at that time but 'proved' wrong by John Roberton, as seen later.

Criminal matters: rape and infanticide

Puberty science was also called for in many medico-legal examinations of survivors of sexual assault, a matter 'of great interest and importance, inasmuch as it involves the happiness and reputation of *woman*' (Thomson 1834c: 614, italics in original). Rape was legally defined as 'the *carnal* knowledge of a woman by force and against her will', which did not necessarily imply 'perfect penetration and seminal emission' but nonetheless presumed some level of vaginal penetration: 'there must be *penatratio*, or *res in re*' (Thomson 1834d: 641, italics in original). In the cases of rape of young girls, the 'carnal knowledge' of the victim was automatically criminalised if the child was not yet 10 years old, 'whether she consent or not'; but it would not constitute felony if the girl was above that age, 'unless it be against the will and consent of the child' (p. 644).

In the latter instances, signs of virginity loss and the state of the genitalia were to be especially considered in the examination of the rape charge: knowledge about female sexual physiognomy in terms of maturational stages, clinical conditions, and racial specificities, was therefore necessary. Particularly, medical witnesses should be aware of the genital 'firmness and fullness' characteristic of a pubescent 'healthy virgin', but also of the fact that such features could be absent in 'delicate and unhealthy young girls . . . without the slightest doubt attaching to their chastity' (p. 642). Also, 'if the female be not an European', examiners should not necessarily regard 'the enlargement of the nymphae' as a sign of virginity loss, for it was a constitutional feature found in 'the female of some warm climates, as the Moorish, the Mandingo, and the Hottentot women' (p. 642).

Thomson also cautioned against the possible dishonesty of the accusers, especially young women. For example, there could be the case of 'a girl who has brought a charge of rape', the accusation resulting from 'malice, or from a desire to revenge': hence the critical need of telling the virginal girl from those 'accustomed to sexual intercourse', and of keeping in mind that the absence of the hymen 'may result from the introduction of fingers and other instruments in the vagina' (p. 643).

As to young sexual offenders, boys under 14 were legally deemed non-pubescent and thus 'incapable' of committing rape; but, 'as you well know', Thomson suggested, there would be situations allowing for the crime to be perpetrated at earlier ages (p. 644). Hence, an examination of the genital maturation of the accused could be required, which called for a strictly physiological (non-chronological) understanding of pubertal development. Once 'proof of impotency' could rebut a charge of rape, moreover, expert witnesses should take into consideration that the testicles might not have descended into the scrotum 'and yet every other proof of virility be obvious' (Thomson 1834b: 514).

Thomson (1834e: 772) also expressed concerns about cases of infanticide – 'the murder of the child in the act of parturition, or immediately after it is born' – allegedly committed by young girls as an attempt to hide their pregnancies. If the accused was legally considered non-pubescent (i.e. under the age 12), her reproductive status had to be medically confirmed so as to render the prosecution valid and the punishment applicable.

Again, the perceived racial-environmental variations in age of puberty onset were to play a key role in determining whether a plea of 'non-age' was valid against a charge of infanticide. Thomson (1834f: 674) cautioned that, 'if the female ha[s] recently arrived from a tropical climate, she may become pregnant at the period at which she might have become a mother had she remained in her native country', that is, at a very young age. By the same token, a Norwegian in the same circumstances 'could scarcely be *justly* condemned on a charge of infanticide under twenty years of age' (Thomson 1834a: 487, his emphasis). This fabulous logic was premised on the idea that females moving to the more temperate regions of Europe 'still continue for a time under the influence of the climate from which they came; and thence, in criminal trials in which the question of female puberty is raised, the medical witness must always have reference to this fact' (p. 487).

Factory child labour and female pubescence

At the time of Thomson's lectures, the regulation of child factory labour in Britain was in the order of the day (see next chapter). A reformist movement rebelled against the dreadful work conditions to which children were subjected at the mills, let alone the very young ages at which they were employed. Some legal actions were taken after what is perhaps one of the most important documents in child legal history, the *Report of the Commissioners on the Employment of Children in Factories*, issued in 1833. The *Report* – co-signed by the British founding father of sanitary reform, Edwin Chadwick – led to the 1833 Factory Regulation Act. Henceforth, among other 'progressive' measures, the employment of children under 9 years of age in textile factories was criminalised. Those above the legal age had to undergo a medical inspection in order to certify whether they were sufficiently healthy for their age and fit for the job.

Regarding factory children's situation, Thomson voiced one single and rather paradoxical anxiety. While certain that '*great poverty* . . . and *a laborious life*' potentially delayed the onset of menarche, he was convinced – aligning with many others – that the 'low pitch of morality' and the high temperatures of the factory environment were causing young girls to sexually mature and become mothers too soon (Thomson 1834b: 513, his emphasis). This argument was analogous to the perceived powerful influence of warm climates in hastening pubescence. That 'truth' theoretically reappeared within the cotton mills of Glasgow and Manchester, although this time assuming the form of industrial heat and suggesting class-specific effects rather than racial ones. Following

Thomson's judicial rationality, if a working girl under 12 was accused of infanticide, the perceived triggers of puberty associated with factory life could legally sustain the charge and refute a plea of non-age in her defence.

Was Thomson's knowledge up-to-date?

Thomson's lectures reflect a thorough interweaving of medical expertise and judicial powers around pubescence. In the background of his case illustrations, there is a loud appeal: the fundamental task of a modern science of puberty was to give answers to the new social issues raised by the general problematic of sexual-reproductive prematurity.

In doing so, his lessons offer a good overview of pubertal medicine's state of the art in the early 1830s, which basically combined two theoretical traditions. First, Thomson voiced the same principles of ancient Greek humoral pathology, embraced and continued by the whole of Western medicine until well into the 19th century (see next chapter). Accordingly, 'a sanguine temperament' could accelerate the onset of menarche, together with 'nutritive diet, wine, the frequent use of the warm bath, dissipation, dancing, and whatever can excite the nervous energy' (Thomson 1834a: 513).

Second, and most notably, we find Thomson endorsing the same world views of pubertal timing conveyed by early writers and faithfully reprinted in medical texts until his time. Aligned with the mainstream opinion, he simply preached the environmental-racialist ideology pioneered by the celebrated Swiss physiologist, Albrecht von Haller (1708–77), and strongly continued by French naturalist Julien-Joseph Virey (1775–1846) some decades later.

In the following, using Virey as an emblematic representor of that environmental-racial regime concerning sexual-reproductive development, we illuminate its main premises: the warmer the region, the earlier puberty onsets; the later puberty onsets, the healthier and morally fitter an individual is. We show that this game of truth was embedded in a sexist and heteronormative medical philosophy intertwined with racist discourses that favoured colonial powers and were supportive of slavery. Finally, we argue that Virey's problematisation of early development is still set within the old framework of the monstrosity of nature.

Precocity and decay: pubertal timing as a scientific vocabulary of racism

Virey was known for his well-cited entries to a French medical encyclopaedia, *Dictionnaire des Sciences Médicales*, in several of which he spoke about the development of children during puberty. His views on the subject also appear outlined in his ostensibly racist *Histoire Naurelle du Genre Human* (first publish in 1801, followed by the 1824 extended version in two volumes on which we draw here).

Pernicious habits, heat, and the natural precocity of the nègre

Holding to both humoral medical ideas and modern naturalist conceptions, Virey understood that the onset of puberty resulted from the combined effect of biological, environmental, and psychological forces. In his view, puberty was triggered before the right time by the force of hot temperatures, sanguine and melancholic temperaments, nutritive diets in excess, the growing debauchery in cities as opposed to the simple and naïve life of the countryside, let alone hereditary predispositions and, of course, masturbation. 'Puberty onsets earlier due to moral precocity, the pernicious solitary pleasures which, in urging [*sollicitant*] the sexual organs prematurely, excite [énervent] youth' (Virey 1816: 560). He also asserted that just like some inappropriate dancing or reading activities, 'stimulating foods and spirits, in exciting the nervous system, the sensibility, in intensifying the circulation, hasten the vital movement and make the body develop with swift precocity' (p. 555).

According to almost everyone writing on the subject, heat was a major trigger of female pubescence. Likewise, Virey (1824a: 129) suggested that, 'if not the sole cause of precocity of [the onset of] the menstrual cycle, warm climate influences it a great deal'. Thomson (1834a: 486) also maintained that 'the influence of climate is more strikingly perceived in the puberty of girls than of boys'. This notion was obviously in agreement with the universal evidence that females mature sexually somewhat earlier than males everywhere. Virey (1817: 15) explained this phenomenon fairly simply: 'In general, the female sex arrives at puberty earlier than the male sex because the latter requires greater perfection and power than the former [to develop]'.

Following the observations offered in a host of traveller narratives and medical volumes, he also 'saw' the racial effects of climate upon the timing of sexual-reproductive maturity across the planet. 'In Eastern [*Oriental*] people, for example, who are pubescent at the age of eleven or twelve, the reproductive faculty ceases at the age of thirty, when [men] need the most powerful excitants to be able to perform the conjugal duty' (Virey 1815a: 474). Elsewhere he continued: '[Eastern] women also cease to menstruate at around that period [thirty years old]; all their beauty fades and withers from the earliest age, like some young flower whose root is struck by a deadly languor' (Virey 1824a: 127–8). The same applied to the women from the tropical regions: 'like the flowers of those countries, having barely bloomed in the morning, they soon wither with the ardour of the day' (p. 133). Overall, he maintained that populations generally reaching puberty at younger ages were doomed to an early decay; whereas those 'in whom puberty is slow and late conserve their vigour, their youth, and their generative forces until an advanced age' (p. 127).

Thus, climate seemed to produce variations in pubertal timing – but only to a certain extent. Virey believed that there was 'a [pubertal] nature proper to each race', irrespective of the universal influences of environment, nutrition, or temperament (p. 144). Accordingly, racial conformation would produce a discrete influence upon the timing of pubescence, and the reality of the slave trade offered evidence of that: 'In the negro race, even when the individuals are transported into climates more temperate than that of Africa . . . they reach puberty earlier than the white race . . . *which proves that the black race is naturally more precocious than ours*' (p. 134, our emphasis). The presumed sexual prematurity of the *nègre* was deeply embedded in Virey's belief that the fundamental biological structures of Whites and Blacks were too different to each other for these 'races' to belong to the same species of humans.

At the dawn of the 1800s, precisely at the same time that abolitionists achieved important milestones towards the abolishment of slavery, an unprecedented debate about the origin of the 'human races' exploded in Western scientific thought (see Stepan 1982). The monogenists, on the one side, maintained that all races derived from the same biological unity and constituted one single species, regardless of so many physical and moral differences observed by travellers, missionaries, or colonial doctors. For the polygenists, on the opposite side, racial variations were in many cases so strikingly wide that these could only be explained as resulting from distinct species. It goes without saying that the polygenist stance was bound to anti-abolition propaganda and claims for racial segregation.

Virey's arguments were clearly closer to the polygenist side (although he never explicitly branded himself as such). While pointing to the monkeys as the ancestors of all humankind, he found many flaws in 'the unity of the human species', criticising the views presented in its defence by physical anthropologists such as Johann Blumenbach and James Cowles Prichard (see Virey 1824a: 429–35). His 'limited polygenism', as historian Francisco Bethencourt (2013: 265) puts it, fundamentally opposed the 'white race' to the 'negro races' (the *noire* and, below them, the *noiratre*). According to Virey's classification based on facial angles, the latter formed a species of their own, having remained the closest to the apes in evolution.

From a long list of memorable statements, we quote a couple so as to portray the de-humanising character of his racist discourse. He maintained that 'the negro man is born an *imitator*, like the monkey; he recognises the intellectual superiority of the white, easily bares his slavery, [and] is rather carefree and lazy. Those habits announce . . . *soullessness*' (Virey 1824b: 4, our emphasis). Cranial shapes appeared to indicate so, for 'in the negro, the forehead recedes and the mouth advances, as if he were made to eat rather than to think [*réfléchir*]' – a trait comparable to 'the beasts' (pp. 41–2).

Despite such claims, he actually argued against the enslavement of the *nègre*, although in a rather condescending and careful manner:

> [T]hey are intemperate, debauched; be it, but what harm does it cause you? . . . Doubtless, in asking for the alleviation (*l'adoucissement*) of his misery, one is far from wishing to justify the horrible crimes that an unbridled

> license has made him to commit, although these may have been but the reprisals for what he had suffered; but, at least, why not make the destiny of these unfortunates bearable?
>
> (Virey 1824b: 64–5)

But let there be no mistake: from Virey's position, 'these unfortunates' were fated to powerlessness. 'The friends of the blacks', he scornfully argued, 'moved by philanthropic feelings that honour their hearts, took in charge the rehabilitation of the negro's genius' (p. 49). To him, they could praise Black people's intelligence as much as they liked. After all, the examples offered were but 'exceptions' to an inherently inferior intellect, 'so much so that the negro nations will not civilise themselves by themselves, as the white race did' (p. 55). Ultimately, Black people's 'uncivilised' cultures and enslavement were no more than the historical consequence of their biology; for 'nature . . . establishes the inequality of races and species' (p. 68). And yet again, Virey was not for racial segregation. According to his own eugenicist formula, 'the mixing of races is the true way of enhancing (*embellir*) the species', for it would 'compensate the lack (*défault*) of an individual with the excess of another' (Virey 1815b: 533).

New societies, old monsters

Virey's ambivalence represents a transitional discourse, inextricably bound to the political transformations through which his and other colonialist countries were going. As he wrote in his later work, 'the universal progresses of true philanthropy have led to the abolishment in several nations of the trade of those unfortunate' (Virey 1824b: 64). A renovated society with new 'free' citizens rose, bringing new racial concerns and discourses with it.

But, unlike his racist gaze, which kept an eye on the post-slavery world to come, his medical problematisation of early puberty would quickly become *démodé*. It is true that he articulated a modern vision of child development embedded in God-given heterosexist wisdom, based on which he foresaw the 'pubescent being' as a 'citizen of the future (*postérité*)', as opposed to the young child, who 'is of no sex, and belongs only to the present' (Virey 1824a: 111). Yet, Virey's deterministic stances on human nature did not permit him to set the problematic of sexual maturation outside the old framework of biological monstrosities. In his view, as shown above, pubertal precocity did not proclaim the 'posterity' of populations but rather the shortening of a procreative lifetime. Moreover, it caused the general decline of individuals, hence jeopardising humankind. When imagining an entire 'race' of early bloomers, he did not see anything other than subjects whose reproductive capacity would soon fail the vital order of nature: 'engender or die' (Virey 1817: 13). In the extreme, early puberty combined an excess of vigour with the announcement of death.

This discourse is actually made explicit by one of Virey's fellow contributors to the *Dictionnaire des Science Médicales*, writing on 'Puberté'. The author bluntly asserted (despite citing evidence showing otherwise) that precocious pubescence in very young children 'usually puts them into the grave at the natural age of puberty, meaning twelve or fourteen years' (Polinière 1820: 50). In this statement, the child monster appears in a twofold way: the confusion of maturity and immaturity as well as the mixture of life and death (see Chapter 2).

Although Virey never focused on such cases, he did pose the problem of developmental monstrosities, particularly treating of hermaphroditism, but also in his article on 'giants'. While pondering whether they had ever existed, to be sure, that text eventually served to assert the dullness and lack of stamina of the tall Germanic peoples, as opposed to the warlike character and brightness of the smaller and darker Europeans such as, of course, the French. Furthermore, the modern European 'giants' faced a fundamental health issue, which was at its heart similar to that of early pubescent people: 'the majority of the giants very soon become old, decayed, and die before the usual age of caducity' (Virey 1816: 568). Ultimately, within Virey's discursive regime, hermaphroditism, sexual precocity, and extreme growth entailed the contra-natural existence of human bodies whose monstrous development, in one way or another, undermined their own 'posterity'.

Puberty science between scientific racism and colonial reform

In this section, our main 'voice' is British surgeon John Roberton (1797–1876), the first main representor of a numerical and systematic study of pubertal timing. His life work destroyed old medical myths on pubescence, while opening avenues for the scientific production of new ones. He voiced powerful anti-racist concerns alongside fairly Eurocentric views, reflecting a historical move from an excluding and de-humanising racism to an inclusive and normalising one. He extensively denounced situations of sexual-reproductive oppression of young girls and women around the world. He did so at the price of making female subjects the main object of the modernised science he founded, and of launching the range of cultural anxieties currently comprised as 'the sexualisation of young girls'. He also advocated for the recognition of midwifery as a medical profession and scientific expertise in Britain and its colonial extensions. While sustaining the professionalisation of medical women, his claims reinforced the gendered divisions of labour within the emerging public health system. Indeed, he was a true social reformer of his time. He foresaw the role of a pubertal medicine in the moral, political, and legal endeavours towards a more humanist, 'civilised' world, resorting to statistical and ethnological research methods to sustain his biomedical arguments. In the end, his anti-racist and pro-women discourse was wrapped up with the glossiest sexism and the most patronising ethnocentrism.

Roberton's scientific and political standpoints

In his first extensive paper on female pubescence, Roberton summarised the state of knowledge on the subject and declared his general stance about it:

> The age of puberty, as indicated by the eruption of the menstrual secretion, or the age at which the aptitude for generation commences (for the two phenomena are regarded as occurring at the same period) is a point concerning which there exists little or no difference of opinion. Physiologists concur in teaching that the period [of menarche] is not uniform, but that it is influenced by many circumstances, as climate, constitution, and mode of living; that in warm climates it occurs often as early as the eighth or ninth year; in temperate climates is usually postponed to the thirteenth or fourteenth year; and in arctic regions to the nineteenth or twentieth.
>
> This opinion, which is general, appears to me to be in a great measure, if not entirely, erroneous. As the inquiry concerning the age of puberty is, for many reasons, of importance, I offer no apology for entering upon it. Besides, so precarious and unsettled is that department of physiology denominated *experimental*, that any attempt to place the little of the science which depends merely upon *observation* on a surer basis, deserves, even if it prove a failure, to be received with indulgence.
>
> (Roberton 1832: 227–8, italics in original)

The central figure of his criticism was Baron Haller, 'whose view has been implicitly and universally adopted' (Roberton 1845a: 160). Indeed, between the late 18th and the early 19th centuries, this well-cited physiologist, 'the great Haller', as called by Virey (1817: 3), was perhaps the most famous proponent of the above environmental hypothesis.

Roberton (1832: 228) was unmerciful about those writing before Haller, arguing that 'the notions of the most eminent of his predecessors . . . are so blended with fable as to merit little notice. Even the illustrious Boerhaave has assured us that there are whole nations whose women are destitute of the catamenia'. He also showed little respect for the analogical kind of reasoning endemic to naturalism, and more particularly to the repeated parallel between female pubescence and the ripening of fruits and flowers. 'Thus do we reason from analogy, – a mode of arriving at a conclusion which is a general favourite, and well may be, since, besides carrying with it a fair show of philosophy, it requires little appeal to facts' (p. 232). Briefly, it was evident to him that human beings reach reproductive maturity under whatever climate, whereas the same does not apply to every kind of vegetable. Besides, he contended, the indigenous flora of colder regions does not generally take longer to develop than that which is specific to southern regions.

As to the 'geographical scale' of puberty ages proposed by Haller and followers, Roberton stressed that it was largely underpinned by traveller and naturalist portraits, the majority of which suggesting gross generalisations (p. 232). For instance, he spoke of 'Mr Ward's elaborate and very learned' work, *Account of the Hindus*, in the following terms:

> [H]ad it been entitled "An Account of the Bengalee Hindus derived from Observations in the Neighbourhood of Sirampoor," it might have been correct enough, but to publish the work as a description of the Hindus in general, as its title would imply, was as unfair as it would be in a Hindu who, after residing some years at Naples, should give the result of his observations there as "An Account of the Christians".
>
> (Roberton 1845a: 158)

Roberton (1832: 236) delved into that kind of ethnographic literature, preferably by 'authors who have resided long among those of whom they write', demonstrating that alternative views also circulated among the narratives of travellers and natural historians. He found accounts of girls reaching puberty, being pregnant, and getting married at very early ages among the 'Artic peoples' and the 'northern tribes of Europe and Asia', for example, which did not agree with the presumed later onset of menarche in those parts of the globe. Regarding the seeming effect of climate upon body size, he mockingly used his peers' typical verbosity to point out that 'the pigmy Laplander and the gigantic Swede are found in the same latitude. If, therefore, cold affect the stature, it must operate in two diametrically opposed ways, in producing both giants and dwarfs' (p. 233).

Conversely, in women from Tropical Asia or in the 'African Negress', for example, early sexual maturation and premature sterility were expected. About the age of puberty, however, sources asserted that there was little or no difference between Europeans and those populations (Crawford cit. p. 240; Winterbottom cit. p. 244). Regarding their supposed early infertility, Roberton argued that, even if it were true, it would anyway be no proof of an earlier puberty but rather the result of women having become mothers in adolescence. In his own words, that assumption 'would perfectly coincide with, and tend to illustrate, an admitted physiological principle, with reference to our own countrywomen, that child-bearing commenced at a premature age, for example, under sixteen or eighteen, rarely continues throughout the whole of the natural period of female fertility' (p. 243).

Besides drawing from insufficient data, according to Roberton, other key factors would have led travellers and natural historians towards erroneous conclusions. At the outset, there was the problem of the nonexistence of registers among the 'barbarous nations', meaning that, 'when a writer pretends to fix the precise period of female puberty for any uncivilized race, it is to be regarded as at best but a probable conjecture' (p. 236). In addition, in his view, their accounts suggested two interconnected errors of analysis. First, early marriages would be too readily equated with early pubescence. He did not find it surprising, as they were '*so general in the east, and in other fertile tropical countries, where . . . wives, procured by purchase, are viewed as the goods and chattels, rather than as the companions and equals of the men*' (p. 246, his emphasis). Second, he thought that travellers wrongly equated precocious sexual behaviour with pubertal maturity. They would have been misled by the permissiveness of societies such as that of Hindustan, where most everything, he suggested, incited children to sex and its pleasures long before pubescence took shape.

> The nudity in which they live for the first seven or eight years; the loose conversation, tales, and songs to which they have to listen . . . their public and private monuments, on which nothing is ever represented but the most revolting obscenities . . . these are some, and but some, of the polluted sources from which the youthful imagination of the Hindu draws its imagery!
>
> (Roberton 1832: 248)

Although for Roberton none of this alone could trigger pubertal physiological changes, it would more commonly allow for early sexual intercourse, and consequently for occasions of pregnancy in girls whose pubescence appeared relatively earlier.

His undoing of Haller's 'geographical scale', thus, was strongly motivated by concerns with the social situation of women outside 'civilisation'. Drawing from a humanist stance infused with cultural and moral prejudice, he pointed to traditional systems that favoured forms of abuse and violence against women and children – marital norms in India being his favourite case. Furthermore, as seen above, he warned against the sexualisation of young girls, formulating it in a manner that fundamentally reappears in contemporary discourses about the impact of a 'hypersexualised' popular culture on children's development (see Chapter 1). Unsurprisingly, his ethnocentric brand of feminism called for a colonial apparatus of intervention, of which 'the institutions of Hinduism' figured as a principal target:

> [S]o vicious are they, that there can be no hope for India but in their destruction. A change to be effected not by force or by fraud, however; but in part by immediate prudent legislation, and at length completely by the introduction of that great source of beneficent innovation, unadulterated Christianity, with the arts, sciences, literature, and mental freedom that follow in its train.
>
> (Roberton 1846b: 64)

Given his reformist standpoints, he could not endorse the environmental-racial hypothesis of pubertal timing as still formulated by his medical peers. If nothing else, it rendered the practices he condemned as the natural outcome of a sexually precocious type of constitution endemic to specific climates – that was to say, to specific 'races'. As he posited in prophetical manner, 'such a fact must for ever militate against the benevolent hopes cherished by many of the best of mankind, that a bright day of moral renovation awaits the degraded myriads of the equinoctial world' (Roberton 1832: 251). Bluntly put, Haller's environmental formula did not go well with the mentality of colonial reform and its practical requirements. His theory would ultimately allow for political authorities to justify their lack of initiative concerning the abuses of women and children in colonial lands – not to mention the enslavement of Black people, as we discuss later in the chapter.

As a medical scientist, furthermore, Roberton's empiricism was in open conflict with a long tradition of knowledge on puberty based on flawed data collections and unsound theorisations. What, then, did he propose anew?

Roberton's hospital study

In 1829, two years after being appointed surgeon and obstetric supervisor to the Manchester Lying-in Hospital, Roberton conducted the first investigation on the age of menarche in Britain. This was the second earliest study of its kind, the first having been published by German physician Friedrich Benjamin Osiander, based on a sample of 137 hospital patients from the Göttingen Poliklinik (cf. Tanner 1981a: 293).

Roberton's method of data collection consisted of randomly asking the age of first menstruation to women entering the institution to give birth. The query, he made sure to clarify, was posed 'along with other questions usual on the occasion . . . so that it did not appear as if put out of curiosity or for a private end, but as one of the queries necessary to be answered in order to her admission as a patient' (Roberton 1832: 231, footnote). Needless to say, ethics around research participation and consent was something completely alien to Roberton (and to everyone at that time). His methodology was wholly invested in the accuracy and measurability of the data collected, 'rejecting the evidence of all [women] who evinced either a doubtful recollection of the fact in question, or answered with reluctance'. Regardless of its empirical limitations, so evident to today's medical statisticians, the gathering and use of recollection data on menarche would be extensively replicated in population studies of pubertal timing until at least the 1950s, when Dagmar C. Wilson and Ian Sutherland (1950) introduced the method of probit analysis into that field of research.[2]

Roberton's foremost aim was to represent a physiological phenomenon in its most natural and healthiest circumstances. Hence, he argued, his sample was composed of women generally in good sexual-reproductive condition. Their successful pregnancies were 'proof' of that, as well as 'their walking, in an advanced stage of gestation, from considerable distances to the hospital; the greater number being inhabitants of our widely extended and scattered suburbs'

(Roberton 1832: 230). In addition, only married women were included in the study, for, according to the medical morality of his time, pregnancies outside marriage suggested a non-normative sexual life which often led to venereal conditions and reproductive complications, hence possibly introducing a bias, as it were, in his results.

He was perfectly aware of the class-specific character of his sample, anticipating possible criticisms about it. If it was pointed out that he ought to extend his inquiry to 'a class of patients more respectable, and hence perhaps more credible, than that which furnishes the applicants to a public hospital', he assured readers that 'such has actually been the case' (p. 231). Inclusion criteria were perhaps one of the reasons why his first table comprising 326 women published in 1830 increased to a total of 450 two years later.[3] Presumably, at least some of the 124 instances added to the sample were collected in private clinics.

In any case, his point was not to discuss the time of menarche according to classes, but rather to prove the naturally wide distribution of ages at which menstruation would first occur in whatever class, nationality, or 'race'. Charting the results for either 326 or 450 women, he gave ages of menarche within a range of nine years – starting at 11 and finishing at 20. Like the former table, the latter presents a relatively regular increase of figures from the eleventh year (10 instances) to the fifteenth (97 instances), and a somewhat progressive decrease from the sixteenth year (76 instances) to the twentieth (four instances). Considering these results, he concluded:

> One very obvious corollary I would draw from this table, namely, that the natural period of puberty in women occurs in *a much more extended range of ages, and is more equally distributed throughout that range*, than authors have alleged.
>
> (Roberton 1832: 231, his emphasis)

Roberton also troubled the assertion that teenage pregnancies were responsible for the arrival of menopause before its perceived usual age (i.e. about 45 years). Indeed, as earlier quoted, he referred to this 'admitted physiological principle' in order to contend that the presumed earlier sterility of women from tropical regions was no real evidence of their earlier puberty, but rather most likely caused by their getting married and pregnant at very young ages. 'The earlier or later termination of child-bearing, therefore, in any country, will depend on the average age of marriage which there obtains' (p. 254). Yet, he wanted to test how generally applicable that principle was. Drawing on the voluminous records of the Manchester Lying-in Hospital, he suggested that the correlation between the period of first gestations and of menopause should not be regarded as a universal law but merely as a norm from which natural deviations were observed.

Roberton's innovative methods and statistical thinking gave scientific consistency to his biomedical and political premises. A decade later, however, he would find himself having to insist on the same conclusions:

> [T]hat puberty is a phenomenon which varies in different constitutions – as much a constitutional peculiarity, in fact, as the colour of the hair or the form of the face; that while in a great majority of instances it is arrived at in the fourteenth, fifteenth, and sixteenth years, in a number of constitutions it is several years earlier, and in others a few years later, the occurrence of the phenomenon extending through a range of about nine years.
> (Roberton 1842: 678)

Roberton's comparative population studies

Roberton was relentlessly determined to refute proverbial knowledge on pubertal timing, the persistence of which he ascribed to racial prejudice and a regretful lack of initiative within the medical profession – especially on the part of British physicians working in colonial lands. After years of waiting for responses from his colleagues to suggestions for collaboration, only to receive frustrating news, he turned to Christian missionaries (whose expertise he praised for combining religious teaching and a practical knowledge of medicine). In 1841, addressing two reverends responsible for the Moravian missions, he lamented in his letter that, 'if the intelligent missionary does not aid the physiologist in collecting information regarding the less known varieties of our race, help from other quarters is not likely to be obtained' (Roberton 1842: 679).

Over the 1840s, he managed to recruit a little army of missionaries, local commenters and fellow colleagues based overseas in order to establish his preliminary conclusions. Via this colonial network painstakingly established, he collected ethnological and quantitative data on menarcheal age within various populations: namely, 'the African Negress' (1842, 1848), the Hindu (1845a, 1845b, 1846a), the 'Esquimaux' (1845c), and the Portuguese from Madeira and other Southern Europeans (1846b).

In his letters asking for scientific partnership, he gave precise instructions as to how data were to be collected. Ages of menarche should be easily recalled by girls and confirmed by their mothers or other relatives, but any existing records such as the registers of female mission schools should also provide the study with valid information. He incited his collaborators to gather as much data as they could, though he eventually had to settle for great disparities in sample sizes. Nevertheless, when plotting the numbers afforded to him against the results of his hospital study, he remarked that the age distributions found at home and abroad were fairly similar – with one exception, as we show later.

Published in 1842, the first data set on Black women in the West Indies only presented 13 valid instances of menarche, mostly coming from Jamaica, to which Roberton added 64 instances collected in Barbados six years later. The total of 77 recollected ages of menarche averaged about 15 years and seven months. Given this result, the racialist assumption of Black people's earlier sexual maturation seemed pure nonsense to Roberton. The sample was meagre, but he believed that it would be enough for medical science to embrace his view. He was wrong, as we show in the next chapter.

As to the Eskimo from Labrador, a sample of 16 instances gave a mean age of about 15 years and 11 months. In order to make it comparable to the data gathered at home, Roberton selected the first 16 entries plotted by each of the three data collectors of his hospital study. Though the proportion of later bloomers appeared greater in Eskimo than in Manchester women, he cautioned against climatic or racial interpretations of this result and pointed to social factors. 'The retardation, if any, would perhaps be attributable to the same class of causes which, in the West Indies, was found to render instances of retarded menstruation not unfrequent in the negress', that is, poverty and disease (Roberton 1845c: 63).

The figures for Madeira, received in 1846, gave a mean age of about 15 years and five months. By then, Roberton (1845b) had already gathered a much larger sample of English women, this time composed of 2,169 instances, which comprised his Manchester hospital data with the cases collected by two colleagues in their London clinics. Comparatively, the mean age for Madeira (based on 228 instances) was about seven months later than that for England. He remarked that this difference would probably disappear if larger samples were provided from abroad, preferring to stress the identical manner in which ages appeared distributed on the comparative chart. He also highlighted that 'the maximum number of instances [i.e. the mode, in statistical terms] . . . is opposite the age of 15' in both the Portuguese and the English columns, thus troubling 'the notion – the old universally received opinion – that puberty is earlier in Madeira and the whole of the south of Europe than in our own country' (Roberton 1846b: 283).

'In a word', he concluded towards the end of that decade, 'the black peasant females of the West Indies, the peasantry of Madeira (of Portuguese origin), the Eskimo of Labrador, and the manufacturing females of Manchester, would appear to arrive at puberty about the same period of life, viz. the middle of the sixteenth year' (Roberton 1848: 76). However, the same did not seem to apply to Indian girls.

In 1845, Roberton received data on this population from three medical sources based in Calcutta, which he combined into one single table of 239 instances. He found a mean age of puberty onset of about 12½ years. Over the next year, provided with tables from Bombay and Bangalore by another medical source, he increased the sample to 540 instances, now averaging 13 years for the commencement of puberty. Following the report of an Indian medical scholar, he pondered whether some women could have given their early age of marriage as that of first menstruation, presumably confusing the blood produced by a ruptured hymen with menarche. According to that local observer, those who reported the first menstrual flux at ages 11 or 12 frequently stated that their catamenia had taken one year to 'recur', and only regularly henceforth (Gupta cit. Roberton 1845b). But, even admitting some erroneous recollections, it seemed that the female population of Hindustan was maturing considerably earlier than any other in the world. Roberton (1845a: 167) believed that the explanation for this phenomenon 'must probably be sought in race'.

From Virey's racial determinism to Roberton's sexual selection theory

In establishing a relationship between race and pubertal development, Roberton did so in a manner altogether different from that hitherto conveyed. Focused on the problem of pubertal timing, he never posed the question of human races in terms of their origin. In fact, we find no published evidence that he ever entered the monogeny-polygeny debate. For him, sexual prematurity was not a more or less fixed characteristic of some 'races', unlike what would be easily assumed by either side of that quarrel.[4] Instead, early puberty was the accidental result of a protracted and regular process of sexual selection within a population:

> When it is recollected that the consummation of marriage among the Hindus has taken place, at the latest on the arrival of puberty, during the lapse of more than three thousand years, and that the practice is sanctioned by ancient laws and consecrated by custom, it is easy to conceive that those females who were the latest in reaching puberty would be the least sought after for wives.
>
> (Roberton 1845a: 167)

In other words, Roberton suggested that Hindu marital arrangements allowed for a societal situation in which young girls who had reached puberty were generally preferred to those who had not. Insofar as the latter would continue unmarried, eventually having no progeny, their hereditary physiological traits such as their later sexual ripening would not pass on to the next generations. Hence, he hypothesised, given the 'preference on this ground in the selection of wives . . . Hindu women would gradually come to consist, in a proportion different from that in Europe, of such as by constitution are early nubile . . . [for] the peculiarity in question would be propagated, extended, and transmitted, and so a race distinguished by it would be produced' (p. 167).

By that time, to be sure, heredity was still a somewhat vague notion without any precise biological definition. Galton's biometrics and his eugenic project on the inheritance of mental faculties was yet to come, let alone the establishment of Mendelian genetics at the dawn of the 20th century (see Stepan 1982: 111–18). Nevertheless, quite ahead of his time, Roberton suggested that maturational differences between 'races' were the evolutionary result of social practices being maintained or changing over time, according to which some developmental conformations were more adaptive than others – and so more frequently transmitted through the processes of heredity.

Over two decades prior to Darwin's (1871) publication of his sexual selection theory, in short, Roberton drafted an explanatory model of early puberty – understood as a population phenomenon – based on the idea that racial variations in pubertal timing were the outcome of selective mechanisms concerning marriage and reproduction. In the history of puberty science, he is responsible for introducing the field to an evolutionary discourse of sexual selection, and to the modern notion that, as Ian Hacking (1990) would put it, nature itself is the product of chance.

From monstrous bodies to the monstrosities of culture

For Roberton, the most striking aspect about the results for Hindustan was not the greater frequency of instances of menarche under 11 years in comparison to the English table, but the significant proportion of Hindu women in whom the menses appeared at ages 12 and 13. In pointing it out, however, he was not really posing the problem of whether a population was averagely reaching puberty at a certain 'correct' age – that approach came a little later, as will be seen in the next chapter. Quite the contrary: his notion of normal pubertal timing equated with a wide and relatively balanced distribution of ages in any population. Ultimately, he advocated the 'graceful variety of nature', which he saw reflected in the figures for English women: 'Instead of being largely accumulated at particular ages, they are much more evenly spread out in certain proportions through a considerable number of years – from nine to twenty-one' (Roberton 1846a: 60).

Considering the 'deviation from the established harmony of nature' among the Hindu (i.e. the predominance of menarche at specific ages), he suggested that it was provoked, not by 'nature's laws', but rather by 'some absurd interference with those laws' eventually leading to 'monstrous results' (p. 61). Combining the modern language of statistics with evolutionary thinking around 'selection', his causal discourse on early puberty represents a crucial break between pubertal medicine and the monstrosity of nature paradigm. It opened up the study of pubertal timing concerning populations to a new twofold problem: monstrous sociocultural behaviour, and the abnormal sexual body. In Roberton's discursive framework, this is to say, there is no such thing as biological monstrosities, only cultural and behavioural ones. Unlike Virey, Roberton did not care for monstrous bodies. He did speak about them, but only to lament that, until just eight decades before, the single official site for medical publications in Britain 'was the annual volume of the Transactions of the Royal Society, where now and then might be found such cases as that of "a monstrous boy seen at Montpelier", or that of "a woman speaking without a tongue", or that of "a man who lived eighteen years on water", and such like' (Roberton 1846c: 317).

He also regretted that only recently had scientific midwifery been introduced in Great Britain, against the reluctant ignorance of many medical men. Virey argued the opposite. For him, any obstetric interference with the act of parturition was to be somehow punished by nature, so much so that not living according to its primordial calls and precepts explained why biological monstrosities were predominant among humans and domestic animals (see Virey 1817: 35, 56–7). Roberton (1846c: 308, 309) contended that 'it is an error, and a very gross one, to imagine that child-birth is generally safe and easy in countries where there is no obstetric science', maintaining that traditional 'Hindu midwifery . . . is destructive to life in a degree never paralleled' elsewhere. Finally, from his perspective, early development implied neither the reproductive decline of a population nor the precocious death of an individual. Rather, the phenomenon raised questions as to 'the social and domestic position of the female sex' in the British colonies, especially in India (p. 309).

Roberton's 'internal' racism

Within his academic and political views, we find no traces of Virey's racist portraits and ambivalent stance on slavery. Roberton simply despised analogies between the 'Negro' and the orangutan. To a natural historian of Jamaica for whom 'the amorous intercourse between them may be frequent', he replied with his usual irony: 'According to this singular hypothesis, the Mulatto son of a West Indian planter may be the grandson of a monkey' (Roberton 1832: 243–4, footnote). He insisted on the 'extremely pernicious' effect of such views upon race relations everywhere, which he deemed morally and politically problematic (Roberton 1842: 682). The prevailing situation of racial prejudice and abuse in colonised territories, he argued, 'is neither honourable to us as a nation, nor safe to the stability of our rule. The medical profession might do something towards remedying this state of ignorance and apathy' (Roberton 1845a: 168–9).

Clearly, his contention against racial discrimination and women's sexual abuse came at the expense of a great deal of ethnocentrism and entailed a colonialist impulse of reform. To be fair, whereas Virey spoke of the 'friends of the negro', Roberton presented himself as one, praising 'the native worth of our long wronged but now emancipated fellow-subjects of the negro race' (Roberton 1848: 76, footnote). However, while celebrating the intellectual brilliance of a medical observer from Bengal – an 'accomplished convert' to the Church of England – he figured that the 'Hindu mind' was overall distorted by 'immemorial [sexual and marital] customs, so monstrous and iniquitous' (Roberton 1846b: 63). Via Dr Allen Webb, Professor of the Calcutta Medical College, he suggested what were the most dramatic consequences of such customs:

> The result of this state of things is a fearful amount of crime. Perhaps no country on earth has immolated so many new-born infants as India, nor has any race of mankind more generally practised the abominable art of murdering children when yet in the womb of the mother. The art of producing abortion and all its long train of evils, at once subverting both the order of nature and the end of being, is but too openly practised even now.[5]
>
> (Webb cit. Roberton 1845b: 262)

Ultimately, Roberton's statistics served to show that governmental actions had to be taken in order to normalise such 'monstrous' cultural settings and, eventually, the sexual biology of women under oppression – that was to say, under any oppression other than colonialism and the Western style of patriarchy, of course.

Roberton's racial discourse represents a move from the de-humanising racism *à la* Virey to racism of a wholly new kind. To call it ethnocentric is perhaps too vague. In fact, we would argue, his ethnocentrism is not the core characteristic but only a surfacing theme of the new scientific racism he advocated. Looking into his ethnographic postcards from India, what we see is a constant game of oppositions between right and wrong marriage, good and bad sexuality, permissible and unacceptable amorous conduct, proper and filthy education of the young, 'civilised' and 'savage' treatment of women as the 'natural' child-bearers of any nation or community. Roberton's problematisations around early development point to a profound preoccupation, not with the unnatural body, but with the debased conduct of marital and reproductive affairs, and with the biological perpetuation of the abnormal effects of such debased conduct. His anxieties eventually spoke to, and are an early formulation of, what Foucault calls 'an internal racism':

> [A] racism against individuals who, as carriers of a condition, a stigmata, or any defect whatsoever, may more or less randomly transmit to their heirs the unpredictable consequences of the evil, or rather of the non-normal, that they carry within them.
>
> (Foucault 2003b: 316–17)

In other words, Roberton introduced puberty science to a corrective and monitoring type of racism that is tightly bound to the 19th-century coupled notions of abnormality and degeneration – a new problematic menacing the social body *from within* – which became endemic to present societies. His scientific racism was about preventing deviations among *any* population – deviation from what normal sexual-reproductive maturation should look like in a 'civilised' nation. His racism, in short, was about protecting the social body against itself. Rather than disqualifying and excluding, it was aimed at the rehabilitation and reintegration of 'others'.

This type of scientific racism, which is at the heart of Roberton's statistics on pubescence, is the counterpart of a broader transformation in power-knowledge. By 1830, with Roberton, a regime of truth heavily based on naturalist theorisations and eventual depictions of occasional observers was confronted with a regime of statistical findings and systematic reasoning. In the history of pubertal knowledge, in short, Roberton marks the shift 'from a technology of the truth-event to a technology of truth-findings' (Foucault 2006: 246). Henceforth, pubertal timing began being normalised. As we have shown in this chapter, this event took shape via the interweaving powers of a medical jurisprudence newly concerned with early puberty, changing scientific discourses on biological difference, and the political imperatives of a new humanist programme of reform.

While obviously drawing from specific disciplinary arrangements and respective concerns about puberty, the multiple practices and discourses forming this apparatus are bound up with what Foucault describes as 'a sort of grand inquisitorial parasitism', reaching its peak during the 1800s:

> There is a double movement of colonization: colonization in depth, which fed on the actions, bodies, and thoughts of the individuals, and then colonization at the level of territories and surfaces. . . . Truth is everywhere, and awaits us everywhere, at any place and at any time.
>
> (Foucault 2006: 246)

Roberton's 'internal racism' and colonialist preoccupations are an exemplary reflection of this knowledge imperative: to him, the truth of pubertal timing was to be scrutinised, quantified, and policed basically in all the places where his letters and study recommendations could reach. But his colonialist concerns represent only one part of the whole. As his 1830 initial study or Thomson's 1832 lectures illustrate, the truth of pubertal development was also to be found at home, namely inside hospitals and clinics, textile factories, working-class neighbourhoods, or the migrant communities living among the city population.

Alas, that truth had to be ascertained in the bodies of young people brought into the court, as Thomson taught his students. To be fair, as earlier noted, many of Thomson's assertions on the matter drew from early modern myths about the influence of race and environment on pubertal timing. In particular, he advised medical-legal experts to consider the supposed earlier pubescence of immigrant girls coming from the 'Tropics', namely in accusations of infanticide – lest these foreigners tricked the judicial system. But, according to him, experts were also to be aware of the puzzling condition of 'premature puberty' in case such a subject happened to get married before the legal age, for example, fooling the law once again. At the outset, thus, Thomson and Roberton shared the same 'internal racism': for them, puberty should be known in such a way that its truth could be serviceable in the protection of the society against all abnormality living within it, that is to say, against collective degeneracy.

In Chapter 6, we delve into the findings, causal theorisations, and methodological arguments of the first statisticians of pubertal timing. Within their academic contentions, on the one hand, and their concurrent worries about cultural 'evils', on the other, pubescence was consolidated as a biosocial phenomenon at the population level. On the basis of this modernised apparatus, and prominently fuelled by class-related concerns, an epidemiology of sexual development was born.

Notes

1 In advertising their forthcoming publication, the journal's founder and editor-in-chief, Dr Michael Ryan, asserted that 'this is the first course of Medical Jurisprudence ever published in the British dominions; and we are convinced that it will be productive of great benefit to the maintenance of the utility and dignity of the profession' (Ryan 1834: 345).

2 See, for a brief description, Tanner (1981a: 286–7).

3 For a more accessible source of his 1830 article, see its reprint in *The Boston Medical and Surgical Journal* (Roberton 1830).

4 Even the influential British monogenist, James Cowles Pritchard, although rejecting a strictly racialist explanation of differences in pubertal timing, replicated the established views of the maturational effects of climate upon the 'races' (see, for example, Pritchard 1836: 130–7). Years later, in Roberton's preface to his final monograph (where most of his work on puberty reappeared copy-pasted), he proudly acknowledged having changed Pritchard's mind: 'It was no small satisfaction to me that my opinions . . . were unreservedly adopted and publicly maintained by Dr Prichard some years before his death' (see Roberton 1851: xiii–ix).

5 Webb, who had importantly contributed with data to Roberton's research, publicly supported his views in his *Pathologia Indica*, quoted at length by Roberton (1845b) before its publication.

Chapter 6

The biosocial reconfigured

Puberty onset and the emergence of epidemiological risk

Between 1830 and the end of the 1840s, as previously seen, the medical world came up with new ways of thinking and researching about puberty. These were statistical in essence, endowed with the sanitary spirit of metropolitan and colonial reform and with the positivist belief in the neutrality and accuracy of numbers in revealing the truth of biological and social phenomena. During that period, as we continue showing in this chapter, the modernising of pubertal medicine took place on the basis of two interlinked surfaces of emergence. At an academic level, within the debates around the endogenous and exogenous triggers of sexual maturation, pubertal timing was at once deconstructed and reconfigured as a measurable biosocial object through the new epistemic powers of statistics. On a biopolitical plane, preoccupations with the 'uncivilised' coexisted with increasingly heightened anxieties about 'civilisation' and industrial advance. As we discuss, the problematisation of Western progress in relation to sexual-reproductive development enveloped three major concerns: the deteriorating circumstances of the working classes, the 'perils' of a new cosmopolitan education, and child labour. Within this knowledge apparatus, a new epidemiological discourse of pubertal risk was born.

Pubertal timing and 'the value of the numerical method'

Towards the mid-19th century, counting and measuring for statistical purposes had become a common affair in the modern administration of the nation-state. The practice gave rise to a constellation of new categories by which people were first identified, then quantified, and finally compared in terms of deviation from average values. Tables of all sorts flooded into the pages of scientific and governmental publications. Percentages and averaged figures were presented as providing diagnostic pictures of the social body for academic and political use. The topics under scrutiny were plentiful: heights and weights of military recruits, sanitary conditions in working-class neighbourhoods, criminals and delinquents arrested in a town, ages of employment in a factory district, admissions of pregnant women or sick children to a public hospital, to name a few.

A vast portion of these data furnished the rhetorical and programmatic needs of public health promotors and social hygienists, generally concerned with the incidence of crime and disease alongside the physical and moral situation of the poor. In this 'avalanche of printed numbers', as Ian Hacking (1990: 2–3) beautifully describes it, puberty was no exception.

A rehabilitated science of sexual-reproductive development promised to set pubertal knowledge free from biased analyses and crude generalisations by means of systematic inquiries and mathematical calculations. In Chapter 5, we drew extensively on the work of one of the great representors of this move and perhaps its main originator, John Roberton. In 1830, to sum up, he delivered the second earliest population study on the age of menarche ever published (reprinted in *The Boston Medical and Surgical Journal* in the same year), introducing the technique of retrospective data collection to English-reading medical audiences for the first time. The study reappeared in 1832 as part of a more elaborate and much longer version of the previous piece, where Roberton reiterated his stance: the notion that the onset of menstruation was conditioned by climate lacked empirical support. He thought it 'to be, indeed, rather a vulgar hypothesis than a physiological truth' (Roberton 1832: 251).

It was also in the early 1830s that the great Belgian astronomer and statistician, Adolphe Quetelet, undertook the earliest recorded cross-sectional population study of child growth (cf. Tanner 1981a: 125), which integrated his famous 1835 essay on *Social Physics* (*Physique Sociale*) – a term borrowed from Auguste Compte's sociological positivism.[1] This book was where, after a series of papers, Quetelet notably introduced to the human sciences what quickly became one of the most influential notions in modern statistics, 'the average man' (*l'homme moyen*).

What was this 'man'? Found in any race, any nation, any neighbourhood, 'the average man' was basically defined by the highest percentage value of whatever was being measured and its 'natural limits' of variation or, after Karl Pearson, the standard deviation. This abstract 'man' was an ideal arithmetical figure embodying the most regular attributes of any given population, their frequency distribution nearly always assuming the perfectly proportional form of a bell-shaped curve, or so Quetelet asserted.

Displaced from its academic application in astronomy and physics, the Normal curve (as the founder of eugenics, Francis Galton, later coined it) came to serve a wholly different and far more creative knowledge function. Instead of indicating the approximate position of a star or the probable error of its measurement, averages were now meant to say something essential about 'types' of people: something that indeed was an abstraction and yet 'objectively' pertained to them in a certain quantity or rate. Starting with his 'average man', as Hacking wrote, what Quetelet did was to fit the curve 'to biological and social phenomena where the mean is not a quantity at all, or better: *he transformed the mean into a real quantity*' (Hacking 1990: 107, his emphasis).

Although the first puberty scientists were ignorant of the mathematical niceties advanced by Quetelet – none of them had ever applied the Normal curve to their data – the same discursive rationality already permeated their treatment of numbers. When some Manchester or Paris doctor reported a mean age of menarche in the 1830s and the 1840s, they were not simply inferring from the age at which female pubescence most frequently commenced in a given group of women: in giving such figures, they ultimately meant to represent the whole of a population – men included. Those women, or the samples they constituted, figured *as* a 'race', a social or professional class, a country. Ultimately, they were to portray the 'average pubescent individual', as it were, of an entire nation.[2]

Compelled by the same statistical faith, as previously shown, several missionaries and physicians joined Roberton's endeavour over the 1840s, providing him with tables of menarcheal ages from abroad. He thought them sufficiently representative of various 'races' living under distinctive climates: the 'African Negress' (i.e. descendants of slaves brought to the West Indies), the Eskimo, the Hindu, the Greek, and the Portuguese from Madeira. In that decade, as also seen in Chapter 5, his Manchester hospital sample was largely supplemented by two other physicians, Dr Robert Lee and Professor Edward William Murphy, who set up similar inquiries in their London clinics. In 1845, their data and Roberton's 450 age recollections appeared compiled into a single corpus. The Manchester sample, almost entirely composed of 'manufacturing women', became part of a far more impressive table comprising 2,169 instances standing 'for England' (cf. Roberton 1845a: 165). Looking at these data and the reports from India, Roberton concluded that the earlier puberty of the Hindu was owing to degrading marital and sexual norms perpetuated over millennia.

In the same year, physician to King's College Hospital, William A. Guy (see 1845: 363–4), reported on 'the age of the first occurrence of the menstrual discharge in 1500 cases' (presumably English women either born or residing in London). His tables show a frequency distribution ranging from 8 to 25 years of age, with the percentage of cases being indicated for each year as well as for age groups of three years (i.e. 8–10, 11–13, and so on until 20 and upwards). Guy says nothing about the sample, but he clearly took his measurements seriously and, in one particular aspect, was more methodical than most early puberty scientists: as he clarified, he computed the recollected ages as ages-at-nearest-birthday, as the process became known in the more recent phraseology of anthropometric measurers.[3] Like Roberton had initially done, he dispensed with a mean for his sample. He summarised the tabulated results by describing the distribution of cases across the age range (8 to 25 years), highlighting the ages at which menarche occurred with greater and lesser frequency. The study, he said, was not meant to give any particular insights about pubertal physiology and timing. Rather, its foremost aim was to demonstrate 'the value of the numerical method, and the necessity and importance of large numbers of observations'. If nothing else, it offered 'the largest collection of observations hitherto made in this country' on the topic.

This numerical feat would soon be surpassed. In 1847, another Manchester doctor, James Whitehead (1848a), tabulated the ages of the first 'menstrual crisis' for a sample of working-class women and 'educated ladies' totalling 4,000 cases. His questions, as seen later, focused on the effects of factory work upon menarche and the frequency of disease at puberty in girls of different socio-professional classes.

The continental revanche: climates, latitudes, and 'the primitive power of race'

The first French statistics on menarche were published by Dr Marc d'Espine (1835a) who drew on hospital inquiries conducted by himself in Paris and by two colleagues in Toulon and Marseille. The results appeared in his 'Researches on Some of the Causes that Hasten or Delay Puberty', the first part of which dealt with climate – and was largely devoted to contradicting Roberton, the author of the single 'numerical work' he knew on the topic (p. 7).

In order to assess the influence of climate on menarche, D'Espine argued, one had to be certain about the geographical origin of all the women constituting the sample. He lamented that Roberton gave no such information, the implication being that Roberton's data were, perhaps, invalid for the purpose of his research. In other words, he might not have ascertained whether the hospital patients comprising his sample had all been raised in Manchester, or whether a number of them had actually come from different latitudes when they were sexually mature or about to become.

D'Espine (p. 15) also protested that Roberton had fallen victim of the same vice that he himself criticised in most writers before him: 'after having victoriously fought by means of statistics the errors committed . . . about his own country', he made claims about other nations simply based on scanty evidence provided by a small number of voyagers (or so D'Espine read in Roberton's argumentation). Ultimately, 'Roberton shall admit that he did not yet give us one single plausible proof in favour of his new idea, that climate does not exert any influence on the age of puberty' (p. 17).

What's more, Roberton had not reported a mean age for his samples (he only started doing so a decade later). His tables obviously showed the age at which the number of cases was maximal. But, for D'Espine, to refer to the modal age (*l'âge commun*) without specifying the mean age (*l'âge moyen*) was misleading: modes cannot reflect the whole age distribution; only mean ages would do for comparing populations living under different climates. With that goal in mind, he calculated means for Paris women (85 cases) and for Marseille and Toulon women combined (25 and 43 cases respectively). He did the same for the Manchester data as well as for Osiander's 1795 table which comprises 137 age recollections by hospital patients in Gottingen (the earliest retrospective data on puberty ever printed). For each data set, he also tabulated the modal age of menarche together with the percentage of women falling within the mode.

Incidentally, the first averages resulting from Roberton's study were printed in a French publication, where D'Espine basically described Roberton's method and thesis as fallacious. D'Espine (p. 9) found 'an almost mathematical relation' between the mean yearly temperatures of the five cities and the mean age of first menstruation reported for each of them. Contrary to the British doctor's claims, D'Espine suggested, Haller was not entirely wrong.

A decade later, the influential physician and alienist, Alexandre Brierre de Boismont, espoused the same view. He was, at the time, the most active French instigator of a positive, statistical study of pubertal timing.[4] In 1842, after more than a decade of research, he published his final monograph on menstruation in which he drew on a sample of 1,200 women observed in Paris. The data had been collected by himself and over a dozen colleagues in their public and private practices. He tabulated the 1,200 instances of menarche alongside those previously offered by D'Espine, Roberton, Osiander, and two different sources reporting in 1835 on women observed in Lyon (451 cases in total).

Boismont (1842: 3) applauded such 'recommendable doctors' for having realised that statistics were to provide the answers to their questions. But, like Guy, he was fond of large numbers. Besides the issues raised by D'Espine about Roberton's and Osiander's collections, Boismont stressed that all his predecessors had worked upon rather meagre samples which, furthermore, were unable to reflect class differences. Nevertheless, after calculating the mean age of menarche for the women born in Paris, he compared it with the means reported by D'Espine for Marseille and Toulon, Manchester, and Gottingen, plus the result for Lyon obtained via a certain doctor Bouchacourt (referring to 160 women whose geographical origin had been ascertained). Boismont's conclusion corroborated D'Espine's on the influence of climate and latitude.

This was also the opinion of Adam Raciborski (1844), a French-Polish physician also based in Paris who, like Boismont, had his work on female sexual-reproductive development sponsored by the *Académie Royale de Médecine*. Raciborski seconded the conclusions of most authors about temperature, which he considered the most important of all the exogenous factors. In comparing populations, he argued, the interactive effects of climate and locality outweighed the influence of 'secondary causes' like hereditary traits (p. 20), for he assumed that those individual differences would generally exist in the same proportion within the cities or countries under study.

Besides his own data collected from 200 hospital patients born in Paris, he also obtained figures from three collaborators from Norway (Dr Faye), Sweden (Dr Wistrand), and Poland (Dr Lebrun). The samples concerned, respectively, 100 hospital patients born in Skeen, 102 born in Stockholm, and 102 hospital patients seen in Warsaw.[5] He tabulated the mean age of menarche, the latitude, and the mean year temperature for the above four cities and those formerly reported on by D'Espine (Marseille, Toulon, Manchester, and Gottingen) and by Bouchacourt (Lyon). The variations in pubertal timing reflected nearly the same ratio as the variations in latitude: for each higher or lower latitude degree, the mean age accordingly decreased or increased by about a month and a few days. He also inferred that mean age differences were simultaneously caused and often accentuated by the meteorological conditions particular to each place.

Unlike Roberton, Raciborski (1844: 77) asserted that 'races uncontestably exert quite a great influence' upon pubertal timing, even though racial determinism, he argued, would fade away over time, to the point where 'the women of all races [living in the same country] no longer obey but to one single law, that of climate'. How did he get to this curious conclusion? Quite simply, based on a table compiled by Dr Lebrun, he compared the ages of menarche 'in 100 Jewish women and in 100 Catholics belonging to the Slav race' observed in Warsaw (p. 31). Proportionally, the onset of puberty occurred a few months earlier in the former than the latter. Raciborski's reasoning went like this: the Jewish communities had moved from Egypt and the Middle East to the colder regions of Poland almost 10 centuries previously; over this period, their timing of sexual maturation came to be nearly the same as that of the Slav population. Yet, as he thought the result also showed, those centuries had not been enough to completely eradicate 'the primitive power' of race (p. 33): whereas only one case of menstruation at age 13 was found among the Slav, 12 Jewish women had become pubescent at that age.

Interestingly, Raciborski cited Roberton's paper on the 'African Negress' published two years before. Despite the 'too small a number' of cases ('12 negresses') reported on by a missionary based in Jamaica, the table revealed the 'great deal of exaggeration on the part of travellers . . . about the epoch of puberty in the tropics' (p. 76). However, Raciborski was certainly not impressed with Roberton's thesis that early pubescence was imprinted on a 'race' by force of debased sexual and marital norms. Instead, he preferred to quote Virey's portrayal of early pregnancies and quick reproductive decay in warm latitudes, and to suggest a link (via French demographer Benoiston de Châteauneuf) between the number of births registered in a country and its climate: 'In Portugal 5,10 children are born per marriage; in Sweden only 3,62' (p. 25).

The continental disputes around Roberton's work were noted in a number of medical periodical publications, not only in Europe but also in the US. In a review by the influential *American Journal of the Medical Sciences* (1844: 438–9), it was argued that his 'conclusions are probably in a great measure true'. Nevertheless, the relation of climate and latitude to the attainment of sexual-reproductive maturity, according to the journal, 'appears to be proved by [Raciborski's] table' reporting on several European cities.

Towards the end of that decade, Whitehead (1848a: 102) praised Roberton's research for having exposed the fallacies of 'the opinion formerly and almost universally entertained respecting the very early puberty of some tropical races'. Nevertheless, he also didn't buy his countryman's whole argument:

> I am inclined to believe, notwithstanding the multitude of evils consequent upon the deplorably degraded social condition of uncivilized

> communities . . . that climate does, nevertheless, exercise considerable influence in determining an early sexual development in hot countries, although not perhaps to the extent that it was formerly believed to do.
>
> (Whitehead 1848a: 105)

Despite Roberton's efforts, though, racialist takes on pubertal timing would not fade away. In 1869, Quetelet read a statistical review paper on the age of menarche in different populations to his fellows of the Belgian Royal Academy of Sciences. It had been sent to him by Professor Adolphe Hannover, from Denmark, in order to be inserted in the second edition of *Physique Sociale* (although Quetelet regretted not having received it in time for printing). Hannover, a firm supporter of racial determinism, rebutted Roberton's proto-Darwinian ideas around sexual selection. Basically, he overturned Roberton's argument. To Hannover (cit. Quetelet 1869: 164), the earlier puberty of the Hindus was not caused by 'the custom adopted for thousands of years of marrying girl children; on the contrary, that custom is rather the consequence of women's prematurity'.

As late as in the mid-20th century, the coupled question of climate and race was far from being settled – as it still is today. By 1950, a decade before the dawn of a new post-colonial era, British paediatrician Richard Ellis published the results of his research on the 'Age of Puberty in the Tropics', conducted in Nigeria. They drew from recollection data obtained from 300 girls and on bodily examinations of 333 boys born in the country.[6] He introduced the article as follows:

> The belief is widely held that children mature earlier in tropical than in temperate climates. This view has not only been repeated by medical authorities but in some instances is reflected in local legislation relating to age of consent and marriage and to the protection of juvenile labour. . . . No statistical studies of boys [on this subject] appear to have been made.
>
> (Ellis 1950: 85)

Ellis contended that, in fact, 'most recent studies have lent general support to Mills's [1937] view that in a tropical climate the menarche is retarded rather than accelerated';[7] and yet, he cautiously admitted, 'it is clear that the available evidence is still rather meagre and much of it open to criticism' (p. 85).

According to his results, the Nigerian schoolgirls' mean age of menarche was slightly higher than that of an English control group. As for the schoolboys examined in the two countries, their maturational timing was about the same. His concluding remarks would have gladdened Roberton's heart. Particularly, he argued that 'the age of consent for an unmarried girl in Nigeria is at present 13 years, as compared with 16 years in Great Britain, whereas the mean age of menarche provides no support for this discrepancy' (p. 88). Hence, he suggested, protective legislative measures were required.

We reengage with Ellis in Chapter 8, particularly to explore his significant (and, perhaps, much forgotten) anthropometric work around clinical standards of pubertal growth and maturation.

Constitutional causes and the death of 'temperaments'

Drawing on his French data, D'Espine (1835a: 9) asserted that 'other causes concurrently exert their action with climate' with which he dealt in the second part of his article: namely, growing up in the city or the countryside as well as individual 'temperaments'.

As to the assessment of the latter, D'Espine (1835b: 304) encountered an important difficulty: 'Nothing is worst established than the traits by which we recognise each kind of temperament'. As he noted, temperaments were described using a host of categories and combinations between them – 'bilious, sanguine, nervous, nervous-bilious, lymphatic, nervous-sanguine, etc.' – which had for long been employed in medical texts and diagnostic practices (p. 305).[8] As the terminology suggests, they primarily served to profile individuals in terms of types of diseases and behavioural troubles to which they were prone. As everyone concurred, it seemed, certain physical traits should be considered in those classifications, namely eye, hair, and skin colour and body types. Yet, D'Espine regretted, the framework was altogether inconsistent, the criteria being ultimately left to the judgement of each doctor 'at the patient's own bed' (p. 304).

He 'thought the best was to decompose the question' and to analyse those traits one by one in relation to pubertal timing, 'giving everyone the freedom to include such and such element in [the definition of] such and such temperament' (p. 305). Based on the observations of women from Paris and Marseille (the only usable data for his purpose), he gave mean ages of menarche according to hair colour, eye colour, skin colour, and 'the degree of force of the constitution' (p. 307) – i.e. robust, average (*médiocre*), and skinny or delicate. This is to say, he detached these features from the panoply of temperaments with which they were clinically associated, rendering each of them as a *factor* autonomously influencing the time of pubescence. In other words, he transposed those physical traits from a diagnostic framework into a statistical analysis of norms and deviations. Quite simply, D'Espine dispensed with temperaments.

At the end he didn't say, "this or that temperament hastens or retards puberty"; he said that in women with this or that eye colour, this or that constitutional type, puberty onsets earlier or later. As such, though D'Espine 'could not say anything about the influence of the races' based on his data (1835a: 7), his analysis was left open to strictly racial inferences around sexual development. Just note his disclaimer on skin colour: 'I must say that, by *coloured*, I don't mean a skin infused with blood vessels, but rather a skin more or less furnished with pigment, which more or less diverges from the perfectly white colour' (D'Espine 1835b: 307, italics in original).

Boismont (1842: 37) also addressed the 'powerful action' of the temperaments, 'which ultimately are the expression' of an individual's psychophysiological functioning, or what he called 'organisation'. Like D'Espine, he found it very difficult to measure and establish their types, especially because a person's 'organisation' could change considerably over time. Yet, he did not let those difficulties stop him from applying such classifications and calculate the time of puberty accordingly. About his framework, however, the only thing he tells us is that he observed 'the external form that seems to us to summarise quite accurately the functional state of the individual' (p. 38) – meaning that whatever criteria he used remains a mystery. He reported the mean ages for a sample of 477 poor women categorised as lymphatic-sanguine, sanguine, lymphatic, and lymphatic-nervous.

Interestingly, Boismont met D'Espine halfway in terms of their analytical approach to temperaments, for he also decomposed the question of women's 'organisation' into discrete physical elements. He gave means for 746 women according to bodily constitution (robust, good, average, and delicate), and for 748 women according to hair colour (blond, light brown, and brown). The stronger the body and the darker the hair, it seemed, the earlier the menarche. In addition, he gave means for 284 subjects classed in terms of their stature (big or short, i.e. above or below 5 feet tall), concluding that the taller women reached puberty later than the shorter ones.

For Raciborski, temperaments and other endogenous elements played a fundamental role in the period of pubescence. Even though '[n]othing is more difficult than to justly appreciate the temperament' (Raciborski 1844: 62), he apparently found no problem in calculating the mean age of menarche in women of lymphatic, nervous, and sanguine-nervous types. Most importantly, he claimed, the constitutional type inherited from parents was a key determinant of their daughters' pubertal age. Drawing on 192 observations, his results lent support to D'Espine's and Boismont's conclusion. On average, the reproductive organs matured later in girls of a delicate constitution and earlier in those of a strong one – precisely the reverse of what Virey and others maintained a few decades before.

Regarding the seeming influence of stature on pubertal timing, however, Raciborski argued that most previous researchers had failed to consider a host of key factors influencing the onset of menstruation which, in turn, could importantly impact on growth itself. 'As a result, it has often been attributed to height what does not depend on it in any way' (p. 66). He suggested that such a view derived from the protracted theories of Ancient Greek medicine according to which menarche functioned to release the young female body from its plethoric state, that is, the excess of blood contained within it. Consequently, menstruation was supposed to start earlier in smaller women due to their perceived greater concentration of blood. He contended that, since both puberty and physical growth were actually affected by nutrition, living conditions, and the incidence of disease during one's development, stature could not be treated as independently causing an earlier or later menarche. Therefore, he simply dismissed attempting a statistical analysis of the influence of stature.

In fact, at the start of his research he had tested that hypothesis by conducting what we would call a pilot study: 180 hospital patients were 'very carefully measured' (p. 71) and classed as short (below 4 feet 4 inches), medium (between 4 feet 4 inches and 4 feet 9 inches), and tall (above 4 feet 9 inches). On average, the shorter the women, the later they reached puberty, precisely the opposite result to that provided by Boismont. Raciborski argued that the study should not be attached any significant value. Rather, it simply suggested how such inferences 'might easily abuse the power of statistics', each new sample possibly leading to incongruous outcomes (p. 72).

He extended the same critique to the statistical analysis of each of the physical traits associated with temperaments, a project which he deemed plainly fruitless: 'It is time for us to be convinced that there is no direct relationship between [those traits] and the time of puberty' (p. 64). To him, hair, eye, or skin colour alone could say nothing about sexual development; they could merely give an indication as to this or that psychophysiological disposition. And even so, although dark hair was usually ascribed to a nervous temperament, for example, it could also be found in a number of women of a lymphatic type. Ultimately, in his view, those inquiries produced 'no other effect than that of actually compromising the numerical method which has already raised, due to similar abuses, a very vigorous opposition against it. We have only to congratulate Mr Marc-d'Espine in this regard for having resisted such whims' (p. 64).

Temperaments disintegrated at the hands of the modern puberty scientists, not because they didn't endorse their clinical principles, but because they endeavoured to translate them into numbers. By the end of the 1800s, such notions had become simply too vague and difficult to handle for the likes of anthropometric researchers such as US growth scientist W. S. Christopher (we come back to him in the following chapter). In his 1904 paper on 'Types of Children' he painted the decline of a medical era, speaking of temperaments as follows:

> For many years – indeed, since the advent of the more exact scientific methods in medical research – it has been, to say the least, unfashionable to refer to "diatheses" and "temperaments." It is not difficult to find why these terms have dropped into disuse, and the reasons are good. Not only are the general terms themselves illy defined, but the attempts made to differentiate their subdivisions and parts are equally inchoate and confusing. They become, therefore, an easy refuge for inexact thinking, a condition obnoxious to modern medical methods.
>
> (Christopher 1904: 307)

Bluntly put, the old medical edifice of Greek humoral pathology began to crumble as soon as it was tentatively submitted to systematic quantification, of which D'Espine's efforts are an earliest illustration.

City life and the dangers of 'civilisation'

As to the 'influence of living in cities', D'Espine (1835b: 303–4) indicated the mean age of menarche for 66 city-born women and for the same number bred in very small towns and rural areas. On average, the onset of menstruation occurred about six months earlier in the former group. He found the result supportive of the generalised belief that the habits and moral environment endemic to city life – 'waking up late, the precocious development of the imagination', for example – precipitated puberty.

Drawing on the same problematic, Boismont broke his sample down (1,200 cases) and gave the mean age of menarche for the women from the countryside, towns, and the capital city, and for the women from the poor, the middle,[9] and the upper classes of Paris. Again, he reached D'Espine's conclusion on the different developmental outcomes of growing up in rural or urban localities.

In particular, Boismont (1842: 18) cautioned against the peculiar stimuli of 'civilisation' to which young girls were exposed in the great cities, especially in the middle and the upper classes – 'a fact that has long been recognised, but which had not hitherto been the object of so rigorous an analysis, of such a positive mathematical application'. He eloquently contended that the cosmopolitan *milieu* pushed female children – 'those young spirits already so suggestible' – into inappropriate occupations such as participating in high-society functions (*salons*), reading romances, watching theatre shows, or even listening to music: 'What things we would have to say about this purely intellectual education in which morality is but an accessory!' (p. 17). Unsurprisingly, he suggested, upper-class women were prone to nervous temperamental types: in 53 'ladies and dames' examined he predominantly found 'an extreme nervous hyper-excitability' which he deemed hereditary but also triggered by the inappropriate education they received (p. 45). Not only did it not equip girls for the demands of domestic labour, all those activities, he maintained, prematurely excited their nervous system which subsequently accelerated pubertal development.

To him, this 'fact' was perfectly evinced by his statistics. On average, women from the well-off classes of Paris reached puberty about 10 months earlier than those from the middle class, and about one year and three months earlier than the poorer women. Conversely, in the latter group there was a significant proportion in whom menstruation started as late as 16 or 17 years, which Boismont correlated with enduring deprivation, poor housing conditions without proper sanitation, and hard work. Beneath the sophistication of the city, under 'the crust of that civilisation', he exclaimed, 'an immense suffering population . . . resembles those withered plants that have never received the beneficial light of the sun' (p. 14).

Raciborski (1844: 45) also dealt with what he called the exogenous 'secondary modifiers' of pubertal timing, meaning the differences in diet, daily activities, and social education found within the city, and between Paris and the nearby villages. But, once again, he refrained from engaging with what he considered a rather complicated and often misleading statistical affair. In short, such analyses implied being certain about too big a number of variables, as researchers would say today, all of which were either unknown or unstated by most workers. 'One must never forget', he wrote in this regard, 'that the numerical method can very often lead into error rather than truth' (p. 36). Nevertheless, he believed that the quality of diet was to play a significant part in the delaying or hastening of girls' sexual ripening.

Even more emphatically, he conjectured about the extent to which the educational trends popularised among the upper classes put undue pressure on the 'nervous system, which seems to be the most direct instrument of the vital forces, and which presides to the development of all organs' (p. 39). Here, his attention was mainly devoted to the 'great influence of music upon the sensibility of the sexual organs', about which, he claimed, 'science is today in possession of incontestable facts' (p. 46). By facts, of course, he meant naturalist analogies. He quoted at length the curious experiment described by Fournier-Pescay in the *Dictionnaire des Science Médicales* in which an orchestra played live to a couple of young elephants, their trunks gently moving 'as if to inhale those amorous emanations' of the melodies (p. 48). To the observer's eyes, their 'sexual' behaviour appeared prematurely excited by the music, most notably that of the female, her approaching the male with 'sensuous touches' (Fournier-Pescay cit. p. 49).

Raciborski also warned about the highly suggestive power of amorous imageries 'upon the ovaries and in particular upon the interstitial movements of the Graaf follicles' (p. 51). Once more, he correlated this phenomenon with the earlier ages of menarche usually met in upper-class girls. In this regard, he cited Harvey's description of a caged female bird that laid an egg simply by watching two other birds coupling in another cage. By the same token, Raciborski suggested, 'nervous excitation or even imagination alone . . . might at least stimulate [ovarian] development. . . . The longer these excitations last and the more they are repeated, the more certain their effect will be' (p. 52). Conversely, countryside women appeared to reach reproductive maturity relatively later mainly because, following the celebrated Rousseau (cit. p. 41–2), 'the simplicity of their customs, of their imagination . . . makes their blood ferment later and render their temperament less precocious'.

A few years later, drawing on the problematic of girls' employment, Whitehead expressed very similar concerns. 'The prevailing diseases of educated females at the age of puberty', according to his statistics, 'are pre-eminently those of an hysterical character', the reason being, 'without doubt, to be found in the faulty system of education pursued at boarding schools':

> The mental faculties are called into premature activity, and tasked to a degree beyond their power of endurance, and the mind is crowded with a mass of matter under the fictitious denomination of accomplishments,

> which Nature never designed that it should entertain. . . . These are agencies to which the unlettered are entire strangers, or which they experience but seldom, and only to a very limited degree.
>
> (Whitehead 1848a: 95–6)

From the viewpoint of his scientific sexism, and as any medical man would argue at the time, the psychosomatic economy of maturing girls was altogether too frail and susceptible to be taxed with school work and the premature exhilarations provoked by (certain) readings.

Consequently, while also voicing racist views of 'the lax state of morals which prevails among the African and other equally ignorant and debased tribes, as well as in most southern countries', Whitehead pondered whether 'civilisation', as Roberton advocated, indeed was an effective counterforce against 'the undue excitement of the sexual passion' (pp. 103–4). As illustrated above, D'Espine, Boismont and Raciborski vigorously entertained the same critical discourse on the modernised West. Whereas Roberton construed 'civilisation' as the main remedy for debased customs and sexual deviancy, the above authors emphasised it as the source of many 'evils'. Embedded in this scientifically productive paradox, as we discuss next, there was the whole problematic of industrial progress and its dilemmatic social consequences.

Factory work and the rise of an epidemiology of child development

Until the dawn of the 19th century, child labour in agricultural and manufacturing work had ostensibly been considered unproblematic. Orphaned, abandoned, or 'incorrigible' poor children were often recruited in compulsory fashion and without any remuneration from early ages until reaching maturity. The use of their work was bluntly promoted by statesmen as an effective disciplining strategy against the 'dangerous' idleness of a mass of uneducated and aimless young people who should otherwise contribute to the economic growth of a nation (see Cunningham 1990, 1991).

From the early 1800s onwards, however, the employment of children in the growing textile districts of the industrialised West, especially in Britain, was increasingly represented as an 'evil' only comparable to enslavement. Henceforth, this problematic became a central tenant in political debates around social reform. Exploited by their employers and even their own parents, as it was frequently claimed, factory children were now regarded as defenceless subjects whose safeguard ought to be secured by the state (see Pinchbeck and Hewitt 1973).

As historian Per Bolin-Hort (1996) argues, concerns about the deterioration of patriarchal relations and the displacement of women from their domestic and mothering roles constituted a unifying and successful discourse of the British Factory Reform movement. The image of the suffering labouring child lacking parental protection was antagonistic to the family ideology popularised among the bourgeois and aristocratic circles, according to which childhood was a vulnerable period requiring permanent maternal care and guidance, while fathers were to be, ideally, the only household providers. Furthermore, following popular prejudices about the manufacturing classes, political reformers conveniently portrayed factories as hotbeds of immorality and unchaste behaviour to which no girl or woman should be exposed. Their proper place was, needless to say, at home.[10]

Factory environment and sexual prematurity

Illustrations of the appalling situation of children at the mills abounded in the reports of the various parliamentary committees and special commissions appointed to inquire into their work conditions. Unsurprisingly, such documents highlighted issues around the health and safety of labouring children. Given their protracted hours of work in crowded, insalubrious, and extremely heated rooms, the dangerous tasks they were meant to perform around heavy machinery, and the brutality they often endured at the hands of supervisors, factory work and its environment were seen as distorting children's physical and moral development (Bolin-Hort 1996).

Girls' sexual conduct and reproductive maturity, particularly, appeared to be incited by the unnatural and sexually deviant effects of factory heat. Recall the teachings of Professor Thomson from last chapter: 'In the cotton mills of Manchester and Glasgow, the girls are often mothers and display signs of puberty very early; a circumstance which has been justly ascribed, in part, to the high temperature of these establishments: but, probably, much is owing to the low pitch of morality in those places' (Thomson 1834b: 513).

The same concern was voiced – and indeed amplified – by official accounts of the factory situation such as those drafted by the 1832 Sadler's committee. This document is cited in an 1843 critical review article published in *The British and Foreign Medical Review* (*BFMR*) which deals with several medical books and governmental documents 'on the Influence of Manufacturers on Health' issued in Britain and France.

One of the medical experts quoted in Sadler's report (cit. *BFMR* 1843: 290), namely a certain Dr Hodgkin, maintained that working in textile factories caused 'premature puberty in the female, leading to most immoral consequences'. However, as the journal reviewers contended, 'the anticipations and positive averments of Mr. Sadler's witnesses' were necessarily at odds with Roberton's stance:

> Mr. Roberton . . . has clearly shown that the notion respecting the influence of temperature upon the period of puberty is at least *not proven*; and, further, that it is probable that the idea is a mere conclusion from the analogy of the vegetable world, having no sure basis whatever in direct

observation. It is, at any rate, quite certain, that the effect of factories in this respect has been inferred from considerations of this kind.

(*BFMR* 1843: 308, italics in original)

Since, according to Roberton, high temperatures did not accelerate girls' sexual maturation, how could factory heat produce that effect? It would not take long for Whitehead to corroborate Roberton's stance. Based on his own statistics, he found 'that, in this respect, mill employment has an effect the very opposite of that which is generally believed to have' (Whitehead 1848a: 89). Furthermore, he concluded that factory work was not, strictly speaking, a major problem to health. He was not the only one, as seen below.

Pubertal timing and the new science of growth: a missing link

In stark contrast with factory reformers' poignant statements, there were medical authors who, in a clear reaction to the 'factory problem', portrayed manufacturing labour in strikingly positive terms. Rather than a source of ill health, some maintained that it actually provided the young with a remedial and invigorating life. Such assertions prompted the *BFMR* (1843: 296) reviewers to mockingly exclaim, 'we are gladdened to the heart that modern advances in civilization . . . have, whilst enriching the capitalist, trebled and quadrupled the health and the happiness, and the bodily comforts of the most helpless of our fellow creatures!'

In the face of such contradictory arguments about factory work – a 'remedy' versus an 'evil' to health – the *BFMR* reviewers suggested that the whole discussion had been largely clouded by the imperatives of a cold and insensitive political economy, on the one side, and inflated reformist partisanship, on the other. Yet, they pointed to a few medical authorities who, led by 'the spirit of accurate and unprejudiced inquiry, have come to intermediate conclusions' (p. 297).

In France, commissioned by the Academy of Moral and Political Sciences, and with the collaboration of Benoiston de Châteneuf (quoted above), statistician Louis-René Villermé had recently published the results of their inquiry into 'the physical and moral conditions of the working classes'. Besides the modern idea of public health, Villermé is one of the main inventors of what later came to be called (after Paul Godin) epidemiological auxology, 'the use of growth data to search out, and later to define, sub-optimal conditions of health' (Tanner 1981a: 142). In his view, as the *BFMR* (1843) summed up, factory work could not be the only or even the main explanation for the greater incidence of illness among the labouring classes; rather, respiratory infections, consumption, or stunted growth were primarily caused by the pauper circumstances in which workers lived.

A very similar argument was presented in the 1840 report on the health conditions of manufacturing districts in England. It was drafted on behalf of the Poor Law commission by Edwin Chadwick, one of the main promoters of factory and sanitary reform in Britain. 'One most important result of such investigations', he wrote, 'would be to disabuse the popular mind of much prejudice against particular branches of industry arising from the belief that causes of ill health [which are] really accidental and removeable, and sometimes unconnected, are essentials to the employment itself' (Chadwick cit. *BFMR* 1843: 306). In his view, bluntly put, the problem was the industrial town rather than the factory per se.

It is unsurprising that the first epidemiological studies of human growth took place during the 1820s and 1830s, in a context of inflated state fears over the deteriorating lives of the poor and of increasingly medicalised programmes of social engineering. Amid the political and scientific polemics around the paradoxical outcomes of industrialisation, comparing the heights of growing bodies became an increasingly popular method for evaluating the impact of labour and other socioeconomic factors on the health of the new generations.

By the end of the 1820s, Villermé (1829) had published his seminal article on the height of French military recruits. At the start of the 1830s, in Belgium, Quetelet (1835) collected the measurements for his study on the rate of growth from birth to maturity (derived from an unstated number of boys and girls). In England, following Chadwick's instructions for factory inspections in 1833, similar measurements were taken by Samuel Stanley under the supervision of J. W. Cowell, and four years later by Leonard Horner, one of the most vocal figureheads of factory reform in the country (see Tanner 1981a: 147–61). Cowell and Stanley measured a total of 1,933 working-class children of both sexes in order to compare their heights according to their kind of employment. Horner, alarmed by the forging of child workers' birth certificates, conducted a considerably larger study among the young operatives in which heights were given for a total of over 16,000 girls and boys.

Recall that Quetelet's growth survey mentioned above was the earliest of its kind. The results were reprinted in his 1835 book on *Physique Sociale*, where he also cited Cowell's factory data and followed Villermé's concerns about the stunting impact of poverty on physical development. A few years later, the overtly racist Dr Robert Knox authored the English translation of the book, thus giving himself the opportunity to criticise Villermé's and Quetelet's environmental hypothesis in a couple of footnotes.[11]

These authors' statistics have been carefully described by Tanner (1981a). Regardless of Tanner's analytical whim to test whether their data correctly expressed the adolescent spurt, the first modern growth scientists had practically nothing to say about the coming of age. Even Quetelet's anthropometric dream, at least at the time of its inception, was as much devoted to human physical proportions as it was indifferent to pubertal phenomena. His 'average man' was the epitome of all that is beautiful or harmonious, the biosocial archetype of nature's imperious regularity. This was the rationality underpinning his measurements of heights and weights of the developing body (incidentally, he failed to mention anything about growth oscillations at puberty, his tables showing no age at which girls are taller than boys).

It was only in the late 1840s that an epidemiology of pubescence arose from within the coupled problematisations of child labour and the living conditions of working-class communities. As previously seen, the primary surface of emergence of a numerical knowledge on puberty was colonial reform and racialist scientific debates on the sexual development of different populations – often argued via, and intertwined with, climatological and geographical questions. Only with James Whitehead, as we now show, did the factory become part of the apparatus of a positive and systematic study of pubertal timing.

Factory work and girls' pubescence: the reverse 'truth'

For Whitehead, some of the official allegations concerning the impact of factory labour on health were 'far wide of the truth':

> It has been asserted for instance – and the assertion is quoted in every European country as referring to an absolute fact – that factory employment has a particular tendency to induce premature development of the sexual organs, and that a precocious womanhood is more frequently witnessed among the manufacturing population than among other classes of people. Until lately, I also entertained a similar belief, based, it must be confessed, upon the authority of others whose statements I now believe to have been advanced at random, or founded, at best, upon a very few isolated cases, altogether inadequate to a general conclusion. A more extended inquiry into the subject has convinced me of this popular fallacy.
>
> (Whitehead 1848a: 88–9)

He divided his sample of 4,000 hospital and private patients according to their occupation: five groups engaged with manufacturing activities, two groups did domestic work, and one last group was composed of 'educated ladies'. For each of them, he tabulated the mean age of menarche, taking note of the percentage of 'unfavourable cases', that is, the incidence of diseases (e.g. pleurisy and rheumatism) which he deemed were triggered by menstrual disorders, particularly the retardation or suppression of the menses.

Given the later pubescence found in the working-class groups, especially in the power-loom weavers, Whitehead concluded that their sexual development and health was not really affected by high temperatures. In fact, speaking to this question, he painted a rather benign picture of factory life which, sadly, tells us a great deal about those women's professional situation:

> I frequently meet with instances of females who have been employed from the age of nine or ten years, to the middle period of life, and for at least twelve hours daily, in an atmosphere seldom below eighty or eighty-five,

> and sometimes above a hundred degrees in temperature, without in any way suffering in health or bodily vigour. Many of them work during the whole period of pregnancy until within a few days of their confinement; and it is not at all rare to see a mother again pursuing her avocations, with apparent comfort and cheerfulness, by the time the infant she has given birth to has attained the age of twelve or fourteen days.
>
> (Whitehead 1848a: 91)

He did acknowledge having observed 'girls employed in the carding and spinning-rooms who appear completely to have lost their healthy constitutional tone long before the age of puberty arrives' (p. 93). But, to him, this did not merely result from their long workdays and the very hot and dusty atmosphere in which they laboured. Their medical problems were above all due to their housing conditions, 'a total disregard to cleanliness, and a badly regulated household economy', all of which he considered especially endemic 'to the Irish residents, of whom a large proportion of our female factory population consists' (p. 94).

However, in no working-class group were the ages of puberty lower, and the incidence of ill health greater, than in the 'educated ladies' – their 'prevailing diseases' being, as quoted above, 'hysterical' types of conduct. According to Whitehead's and so many others' clinical gaze, such disorders often accompanied the first menstrual 'crises', most notably in middle and upper-class adolescents. Hence his conclusion:

> An employment requiring moderate and regular exercise, especially if pursued in an open untainted atmosphere, is of the first importance. . . . In no class of people is the menstrual function so healthily performed as in those necessitated to earn the means of subsistence by personal exertion . . . while the converse of this is known to obtain with those in easy circumstances.
>
> (Whitehead 1848a: 96)

As late as in the early 20th century, as will be seen in the following chapter, this discourse on menstruation and its natural psychosomatic dangers to health continued playing a central part in medical campaigns against girls' schooling.

Whitehead vs Roberton: from a 'graceful variety' to the healthiest time of puberty

In a passage of his treatise, as noted by several medical journal reviewers, Whitehead spoke to 'a difference of about nine months' between his and Roberton's average results for their country:

> This disparity I can account for only on the supposition that his inquiries may possibly include a greater proportion of educated females than mine;

> the menstrual advent taking place, as was already shown, considerably earlier in these than among the labouring and uneducated classes.
>
> (Whitehead 1848a: 103)

Whitehead was wrong, as he admitted in a letter (Whitehead 1848b: 52) addressed to the Editor of the *Provincial Medical and Surgical Journal* (currently known as *British Medical Journal*). Most of Roberton's Manchester data derived from lower-class women, not 'educated females'. Their mean age of puberty was nearly the same as that reported by Whitehead for his entire data set, also collected in the same town.

When speaking of 'a difference of about nine months', moreover, he alluded to the average that Roberton had recently given for England based on 540 instances, which, as Whitehead came to realise, had been taken at random from the table comprising 'Mr. Roberton's personal enquiries, and those of Professor Murphy, of Dublin'. Roberton had reduced their total sample of 2,169 cases 'in order to [make] a more accurate comparison between England and India', as stated in the 'footnote suspended to the said table' which Whitehead regretted having 'formerly overlooked'.

In reinterpreting their disparate results, however, Whitehead hastily assumed that Murphy's numbers derived from Irish women. They didn't: his inquiries had been conducted among his London private clientele. Whitehead, who clearly didn't hold the Irish people in high regard, quickly jumped to a new conclusion. While implying a methodological critique, he appealed to Roberton's kind of scientific racism and, we venture, his sympathy:

> Perhaps it may with some reason be remarked in this place that statistical evidence derived from among the Irish in reference to this subject, cannot fairly be adduced in support of the average for England, since, whatever influence early sexual intercourse may have in promoting a precocious development of the sexual organs, has its full effect in the sister island; as no restriction, either conventional or legal, exists to prevent the earliest practicable connubial alliances among the lower orders.
>
> (Whitehead 1848b: 52)

In other words, if indeed sexual permissibility and early marriages caused entire nations to mature at younger ages, as Roberton asserted, then his sample 'for England' was biased once mixed with data obtained from the less 'civilised' Irish population. Roberton didn't take this misleading suggestion about his results well as Whitehead (1848c: 83) let us know in his second apologetic letter: his 'errors', he wrote, 'have caused some degree of pain to the gentleman referred to, Mr. Roberton, (as I am privately informed has been the case)'.

This anecdote reflects two completely different ways of engaging with the problematic of pubertal timing. Whitehead's inquiries were primarily focused on the incidence of menstrual disorders at puberty, hence his devotion to class differences among one single population, that is British women, rather than to racialist comparisons. Thus, at the outset, he coupled the question of the coming of age with the problem of disease. Roberton, rather, was interested in construing pubescence as a natural, non-pathological phenomenon. Its 'graceful variety', as shown in the last chapter, comprised a wide range of ages which was ideally to be found in whatever 'race'. To him, any greater incidence of early puberty was principally the outcome, not of illness, but of deviant socio-cultural settings conditioning hereditary mechanisms. In fact, strictly speaking, neither Roberton nor any of the earliest statisticians of pubertal timing ever posed the question of the healthiest or most 'favourable' age of puberty. But Whitehead did:

> Abstractly considered, the age best adapted for the favourable development of puberty, must be that at which the event most frequently occurs under ordinary circumstances; we accordingly find that at the ages of fifteen and sixteen years, the proportion of cases in which the change is accomplished with difficulty is considerably less than that in any other period of similar extent.
>
> (Whitehead 1848a: 62)

In other words, for Whitehead, the normal or 'ordinary' age of puberty is that at which the probability of disorders and illness is *the lowest*. This means that, in considering any particular community, there is no pubescence without some disease. This is not the same as saying that pubescence is a natural function which, nevertheless, might as well be the source of physiological and behavioural dangers. That was the clinical discourse of pubertal abnormality, as shown in previous chapters. Rather, according to Whitehead's statistics, to a greater or lesser extent, puberty is inescapably bound to ill health among any given female population. Thus, the 'ordinary' time of menarche *should be* 'the ages of fifteen and sixteen years', that is, when the frequency of disease was seemingly 'less than any other period'. In short, Whitehead introduced puberty science to an epidemiological notion of risk. More than a natural 'crisis', puberty was now becoming a risky stage of life virtually *for everyone* by means of statistical technology.

From Roberton in 1830 to Whitehead in the late 1840s, to sum up, there were two major transformations in the medical construction of pubertal knowledge and its regime of truth. First, notions around the biological and environmental triggers of pubescence were converted into numerical form, either giving rise to new kinds of reasoning around pubertal development, or ultimately reinforcing old ideas about sexual and racial difference. The early normalisation of pubertal timing provided medicine with a knowledge whose interventional power was based on the fact – on the statistically demonstrated fact – that the biological and the social shaped the developing body and mind. Parallel to this discursive formation, there was another major move in pubertal knowledge: from a descriptive to a prescriptive type of statistical discourse on pubertal timing. To be sure, Whitehead saw no particular clinical use for his findings (see the Conclusion to this book). Nevertheless, his epidemiological discourse is an early step towards the formulation of a norm or principle that would infuse practically the whole of medical and psychiatric science from the second half of the 1800s onwards: it is normal for puberty to be unhealthy. In response to this dangerous truth, as shall be seen in the last part of this book, a 'normal' body of pubescence would be produced – and continually reshaped until today.

In the next chapter, we continue tracing discourses of danger and risk from the viewpoints of pubertal medicine and psychiatry. Focusing on epidemiological and clinical work, we excavate the expansive apparatus within which, from the late 19th century to the early decades of the 20th, puberty was scientifically established as a healthy-unhealthy condition.

Notes

1 'They fought over various labels', as Hacking tells, 'such as "social mechanics" and "social physics". In each case the name apparently proposed by Comte for his historical epistemology was snapped up by Quetelet as a name for the statistical study of people (anathema to Comte). In desperation Comte invented the word "sociology", holding it to be so ugly that the statistical students of humankind would never deign to steal it. He was proven wrong once again' (Hacking 1990: 39–40).
2 In 1835, Marc d'Espine introduced his statistical work on menarcheal ages 'as a means to contemplate the influence of [certain] causes upon the development of puberty in that sex; and I wonder whether I can by analogy conclude that there is a similar influence on the puberty of the man' (D'Espine 1835a: 6). We come back to his studies later in this chapter.
3 'The ages stated', in Guy's own words, 'are the birthdays to which the first . . . appearance of the menses was nearest; thus, fifteen years will include all cases in which the menses appeared during the last six months of the fourteenth, and the first six months of the fifteenth year, and so of the other ages'.
4 He left us notable writings in criminal psychiatry and legal medicine, namely on a curious 'criminal' matter which was short-lived but copiously addressed by the sociological science of his time: 'suicidal madness' (Boismont 1856).
5 It is unclear in the original data whether these patients were born in that city.
6 Interestingly, Ellis (1950: 85) was careful to never explicitly indicate their 'race', stating otherwise that 'no European children were included. Although no attempt has been made to classify the children by tribes, the great majority were Yoraba and Ibo'.
7 See, for example, Ito (1942) and Kark (1943).
8 Writing several years later about temperaments in relation to menstruation, Whitehead (1848a: 64) put them in historical perspective. As he charmingly explained, they were the milestone of a 'system of medical philosophy which prevailed, with but little alteration for fifteen hundred years afterwards. [Hippocrates] considered the human body as constituted of certain humours . . . which, in their nature, were either hot, cold, dry, or moist. The equable distribution of these humours was considered necessary for maintaining the body in a temperate condition, or in health; hence the origin of the word Temperament'.
9 To be sure, Boismont did not speak of 'middle class' but of the *métis* (which literally means 'half-breed'): 'In the great capital cities there is a class of women who, by their

customs, their habits, their way of life, their organisation, separate from the population from which they come and approach, up to a certain point, the rich class'.

10 As Bolin-Hort (1996) notes, this discourse was entertained not only by politicians and clergymen but also by textile unionists who strived to gain parliamentary adherence to their main struggle, that is, the limiting of the work day to 10 hours for all factory employees. As a result, however, legislative actions could be solely endorsed for the regulation of child textile labour in 1833 and also, later on, for the protection of adult woman workers, namely with the 1842 Mines Act and the 1844 Factory Act, while leaving the demands of the male workforce politically unattended for several decades.

11 First, as to their reading of data on the heights of French men from two different regions, 'The translator is firmly persuaded that Dr Villermé and M. Quetelet, have failed to detect the real cause of difference of stature in those two departments: it is a question purely of race, and not of feeding or locality' (Quetelet 1842: 60). Second, Knox maintained, 'Quetelet has unaccountably omitted . . . the great cause productive of differences in stature of men and animals – to wit, difference in race or blood' (p. 61). However, this certainly did not mean that Quetelet was a strict supporter of environmental, non-racialist approaches. By the late 1860s, when he finally drew his attention to puberty, he found himself endorsing Hannorver's racist theorisation on differences in pubertal timing. As earlier noted, Quetelet gladly presented Hannover's article to his fellows of the Belgian Royal Academy of Sciences, only regretting that it had arrived too late for the new edition of his *Physique Sociale*.

Part 3

The surveillance of all

Chapter 7

A most dangerous *condition*

Puberty science and the surveillance of all

Between the late 19th and the mid-20th centuries, puberty science enormously expanded the field and the reach of its intervention: from the management of the few to the surveillance of all. In the final part of the book, starting with this chapter, we trace the coupled ways in which pubertal medicine's normalising power was generalised to all maturing subjects. This shift encompassed the clinical, pedagogical, and epidemiological establishment of normal puberty as dangerous, alongside the increasing involvement of institutions for the young in studies of growth and sexual development.

By the dawn of the 20th century, puberty figured in medical and psychiatric literatures as a decisive condition or stage of human development which, paradoxically, constituted a great deal of risk to the maturing child's health. Seen as a 'critical' turning-point in people's development as reproductive and social beings, pubescence was widely held as a powerful trigger of abnormality and disease. Booming towards the end of the 1800s, this discourse was actualised again and again in countless attempts to explain, prevent, and find remedy for a diverse range of conditions concerning youth.

As we show in this chapter, the 19th-century 'discovery' of pubertal morbidity – i.e. the association of pubescence with the onset of illness – played an important role in the theoretical and disciplinary workings of the medical sciences for several decades. In a continual game of clinical and epidemiological elaborations and re-codifications, the link between puberty and pathology was systematically evoked, particularly where psychiatry was concerned, until as late as the 1940s.

Puberty is a 'crisis'

The assumption of morbidity as endemic to sexual maturation is rooted in the idea that puberty entails a 'crisis' for the child (let alone parental life). This notion keeps reappearing, albeit in altered forms, in today's representations of adolescence and wherever there is talk about sexually developing children. Puberty is popularly deemed a profound and almost sudden transformation of body and behaviour – a 'revolution', to use a recurrent metaphor of 19th-century physiologists. This revolution, the takeover of the person by a new psychosomatic order, naturally gives rise to a crisis, and therefore to conflict. That is to say, teenagers are understood as normally undergoing a more or less difficult process of adjustments to a rapidly changing body and to a new realm of feelings, thoughts, and desires – a period of 'storm and stress', as is often repeated after Stanley Hall (1904). This is, bluntly put, the remaining discourse of the pubertal crisis, the practices and knowledges of which shall be traced throughout this chapter.

While historically connected to the very old notion of crisis inherited from the Ancient Greeks, the puberty-as-crisis discourse did not arise with them but rather around the mid-19th century, namely with Raciborski. This is not to say that he rejected the old notion or came up with a completely different substitute. On the contrary, as shall be seen, he reinvigorated the Hippocratic 'crisis' within a new problematic, furnishing it with a more encompassing kind of power. Before starting with him, thus, we shall briefly clarify the medical conception of crisis as it had prevailed, according to Foucault (see 2006: 242–8), from Hippocrates to the birth of modern physiology in the late 1700s, that is to say, for about 22 centuries.

The Hippocratic 'crisis'

In Hippocratic or Galenian medicine (the old medicine of the humours) 'crisis' is the moment at which any given condition is expected to either regress or transition into a chronic or deadly state. As Foucault puts it, 'when the crisis occurs, the disease breaks out in its truth. . . . Before the crisis the disease is one thing or another; it is nothing in truth. The crisis is the reality of the disease becoming truth' (p. 243). As such, it is also the event providing the doctor with a rationale to intervene. It was mostly around this event, as James Longrigg suggests, that the Hippocratic technique of the 'prognosis' was organised:

> Prognosis . . . was necessary to pick out the crucial signs and predict the critical periods of the disease so that appropriate action could be taken to restore health. Crises were believed to occur on what were termed 'critical days': diseases were supposed to reach a crisis on a fixed day (or on fixed days) after their commencement. . . . A crisis that occurred at a time other than on a critical day was believed to indicate the likelihood of a fatal outcome.
>
> (Longrigg 1998: 144)

Notwithstanding the predictive role of the prognostic activity, however, it was not really up to the doctor to *judge* the disease, that is to say, to determine whether the patient was to recover or not. This *judgment* – which is one translation of the original Greek term 'crisis' – was precisely the function of the crises and their natural rhythms, which were what the doctor should foresee and to which the whole medical action should conform.

In Hippocratic discourse, Foucault (2006: 242) also points out, crises are not simply, or actually not so much 'a moment in an evolution'; rather, they are 'quite precisely the moment of combat' between the body and its disease, 'or even the point at which the battle is decided'. In joining the battle, to be sure, 'the doctor does not cure, and it cannot even be said that he directly confronts the disease, since it is nature that confronts the disease': the doctor is far less an 'agent of a therapeutic intervention' than the 'manager', the facilitator of the body's victory over illness (p. 244). He must identify the cycle of crises particular to the condition, anticipate its critical moments, and carefully reinforce nature's movements so that the condition reaches a timely and complete crisis – and hopefully takes a favourable course thereafter. In the end, 'just as the disease comes up for judgement on the day of the crisis, so the doctor, in his role as a kind of arbitrator, is judged in turn by how he presides the combat' (p. 244).

This is, roughly, the power-knowledge frame of the medical notion of crisis as deployed until the 18th century, the main features of which were taken up in the modern conception of puberty as crisis: a truth-producing event; a combat resulting in the judgement of the condition; and an opportunity for the doctor to intervene by enabling nature's success.

A new 'hygiene' for the pubescent: the modern 'crisis' of puberty emerges

In Hippocratic medicine, just as there were diseases that reached a crisis on 'critical days' (e.g. on either even or odd days), there were also diseases that reached their 'critical' time at about the coming of age. Pubescence, and the menarche most notably, was believed to be a definitive temporal marker in the course of a number of childhood conditions, but also the underlying mechanism producing a beneficial crisis in such cases.[1]

As Raciborski (1844, 1868) indicates, the first appearance of the menses as well as their recurrence were overall regarded as a secretory function with a powerful remedial action. Cases of delayed menarche or menstrual suppression would potentially lead to a whole host of more or less injurious health problems, hence requiring prompt treatment. By the 1840s, Raciborski regretted that this premise had not yet been totally abandoned:

> Since menstruation is generally regarded as a function intended to eliminate something harmful or at least superfluous from the body, there is usually a great deal of concern about its arrival. . . . It would be vain to try to avoid this opinion: if it is perhaps not so clearly formulated in any modern book, it is at least the most faithful expression of the spirit that still presides over most of the therapeutic indications concerning the indispositions of young girls.
> (Raciborski 1844: 208–9)

At the end of the 1860s, Raciborski still found that this premise was well inculcated in medical practice and even more in popular beliefs. In his *Treatise on Menstruation*, he scornfully wrote: 'For want of having scrupulously followed the [progresses of] clinical teachings, many doctors, quite distinguished moreover, still attribute to the menstrual flux the marvellous virtue of being able to judge the diseases' (Raciborski 1868: 392). No wonder, he condescendingly argued, the menarche had remained the source of momentous anxiety to doctors and families: 'How not to worry about this physiological act, how not to seek to accelerate [its onset] . . . when it was considered a favourable crisis, capable of taking many previous morbid dispositions away?' (p. 500).

While a number of conditions – e.g. scrofula, anaemia, or chlorosis – were usually met in pubescent girls whose menses remained absent, it was obvious to him that neither could the delay be reasoned as their cause nor could the onset of menstruation be their remedy. On the contrary, he insisted, it is the progression of those conditions 'that after childhood retard the development of the Graff follicles, that stop them from reaching the degree of procreative maturation at the usual time, and consequently render the menstrual congestion impossible' (1844: 214).

Therefore, Raciborski warned against the uselessness and even counterproductive effect of what were called emmenagogue therapeutics employed to force the menstrual flow, namely 'through applications of leeches, irritating baths for the feet, the use of some exciting drinking infusions (*apozèmes*), etc., etc.; once again, there is nothing all those means can do if the Graff follicles are not yet conveniently disposed to ovulation (*la ponte*)' (p. 239). Physicians should rather apply themselves to diagnosing and treating what was after all the primary cause of the amenorrhea (the temporary absence of menses), lest they failed to save their patients.

For the same reason, Raciborski insisted that in cases of primary amenorrhea (the failure of menarche to occur) in adolescent girls who were otherwise healthy, 'one must not under any pretext provoke [the onset of] the menses, even if they are several years late according to the average age of their eruption' (p. 217). The only exceptions to this, in his view, were plethoric states in the which the menstrual congestion was arrested from reaching its haemorrhagic point despite the advanced maturational status of the patients. Only in such cases could the onset or the reestablishment of the menses restore health or, in Raciborski's words, 'judge the different morbid states' (e.g. infections) associated with their arrestment; consequently, he argued, only in those circumstances would the emmenagogue type of medication be effective (p. 218).[2]

To sum up his contention, doctors and parents should rather concern themselves with the all-encompassing changes of sexual-reproductive maturation (especially those implicating the nervous system) than being preoccupied with the arrival of the menstrual flux. The menses did not work as a 'critical' haemorrhage in most illnesses afflicting girls at puberty, nor did the menarche in any way play the role of a crisis in the progression of previous conditions or chronic ailments as formerly taught.

Boismont suggested otherwise, sanctioning and illustrating the curative crisis of the menarche. 'Certainly', he maintained, 'the general action of puberty is indisputable, but it is also evident that a lot of delicate, sickly, suffering young people, prey of more or less prolonged [and] sometimes serious diseases, seem to be reborn with the appearance of the menses' (Boismont 1842: 410). For Raciborski, instead, what indeed promoted the combat between nature and illness as well as the *judgment* of its outcome – i.e. the crisis – was the vital movement of pubescence concerning both sexes:

> The time of puberty is characterised by a great movement in the [bodily] economy; according to the circumstances in which one finds oneself at that time, the morbid dispositions, innate or contracted during childhood, may aggravate or be advantageously modified, if not completely disappear. It could be said that [puberty] constitutes a sort of court of appeal, where all the young subjects whose health has been compromised in childhood are definitively pronounced incurable or come out victorious. Let it be reasoned from this how important it is to watch over the moment of this transition.
>
> (Raciborski 1868: 279)

Here, clearly, the 'crisis' of puberty is still construed in reference to the temporality of illness and not yet to the temporality of human development itself. In other words, it is not yet the medical notion of pubertal crisis that emerged a little later in that century, as we show next. Yet, there is a stark difference between Raciborski's and the Hippocratic discourse of crisis, with the former remaining at the heart of the contemporary medicalisation of pubescence. For him, the crisis is not about an episodic moment, a discrete event, but rather an overall 'movement', that is to say, a *process*. As such, the kind of care and scrutiny it requires must not be circumscribed to the onset of observable bodily phenomena such as the menarche but rather extended over the whole pubertal 'transition'. The crisis of puberty, in short, is not just about one decisive combat or trial but rather a relatively long series of struggles and defences against disease: it is about a war.

'The most terrible scourge of that age', Raciborski claimed, 'though rarely mentioned in the treatises of pathology, is without doubt Onan's passion' (1844: 280).[3] In his view, onanism could be triggered by 'a primitive condition of the nervous system . . . or a congenital disposition of the genitals', or simply 'a vice of education' (p. 280). Whatever its 'cause', it exhausted the body's vital resources when it needed them the most, thereby rendering the child increasingly prone to ill health, particularly 'nervous affections' (1868: 333).[4]

As for 'treatments', in the case of girls found to masturbate as a result of 'excessive' genital growth, he maintained the following:

> The case is much more serious when this tyrannical passion is provoked by a particular disposition of the sexual organs, when the clitoris or the nymphs, for example, experience continual titillations as a result of their excessive development, when walking or the simple friction of these parts against the shirt or against the chair suffice to excite them. There is only one effective treatment in this case, it is the resection of these organs.
>
> (Raciborski 1844: 281)

In other words, where proper education and parental surveillance alone were unable to win the battle against onanism, additional medical means were to be deployed as a last resort which, while still incapable of curing the disease, could finally correct what was perceived as its exciting cause. To a great extent, this is to say, Raciborski could not defeat the diseases associated with puberty any more than the Hippocratic physician did; but, as his preventive techniques reflect, he did confront something that 19th-century medical sciences discovered: child and adolescent sexual abnormality.

Overall, Raciborski maintained that 'it is mostly the women . . . who require endless efforts to conveniently perform their mission in society'; hence, parents and family doctors should above all bear in mind the significance of girls' future reproductive roles and consequently turn the focus of attention to 'the development of the organs that will later be their instruments' (1844: 142). In addition, given the heightened impressionability of the female nervous system at puberty and its impact on sexual-reproductive maturation, one had to make sure 'that the intellectual faculties are not victim of too lively commotions; that sensitivity itself is not too excited and does not become the cause of other consecutive troubles, as evinced in [cases of] *hysteria*' (1868: 282, his emphasis).

In Raciborski's hygienic regime for the pubescent girl we find the model of what the medical technology of puberty as a crisis would become from the mid-19th century onwards, that is, the modern management of the pubertal war against disorder and disease. This war, mainly conducted via preventive and corrective strategies, followed a peculiar principle: the onset of a great variety of mental, nervous, and physical conditions in adolescents, in one way or another, is due to abnormal sexual maturation. During the challenging crisis of puberty, while preventing illness was the ultimate goal of the fight, doctors and families were engaged in monitoring and correcting behavioural and physical errors, deviations, defects – in a phrase, abnormalities of development – which risked undermining puberty's successful movement into maturity. In epistemological as well as practical terms, this is to say, in constantly alluding to pathological and moral dangers, the puberty-as-crisis discourse became a central technology in the modern medical and psychiatric war against sexual abnormality in the young.

Pubertal morbidity and the school apparatus

Around the mid-19th century, as suggested above, a type of problematisation and management of puberty took form in which pubertal development itself, given its perceived predisposition to abnormalities, figures as an exciting cause of ill health. This is, in short, Raciborski's model of 'crisis'. He spoke of 'a complete revolution in the [knowledge concerning the] physiology of menstruation, and . . . of its role in general pathology', thanks to which the old emmenagogue therapeutics were finally waning (1868: 500). Nevertheless, this 'revolution' did not mean a break with the Hippocratic conception and technique of the crisis, at least where puberty was concerned. Rather, it was revised and relaunched in Raciborski's hygienic regime, and given a more generalisable power, on the basis of modern physiology and the recent problematic of the abnormal. To him, the 'crisis' is still about a combat between the developing body and disease. As indicated above, however, instead of culminating in a singular physiological event, that combat needed to be watched over across the whole process of maturation towards sexual maturity, for that process naturally invites deviations, and therefore, pathology.

To some extent, as Foucault (2006) argues, the Hippocratic 'crisis' became epistemologically obsolete as soon as it was possible for doctors to demonstrate the truth of illness by tracing its origin inside the dead body and correlating a visible lesion to a set of symptoms. In this sense, there was no longer the need for something such as 'critical days' to accord truth to disease, for doctors would increasingly be able to point to the cause of disease, even if they were incapable of saving their patients. Likewise, the modern crisis of puberty would not be put to work in direct relation to the natural progression of this or that condition. From the 1870s onwards, it first and foremost referred to the temporality of pubertal development alone: the peculiar *tempo* of pubescence became a problem in and of itself. As such, the notion of puberty-as-crisis would have the power of referring to no condition and virtually all conditions at the same time, hence becoming applicable both to the sick and to the healthy, to everyone.

The first and most important codification of this knowledge is the statistical establishment of the growth acceleration at puberty – the forerunner of the so-called adolescent spurt – and its relation to the incidence of morbid conditions in youth. Growth (in height or weight, for example) and pubertal phenomena had hitherto remained strikingly apart from one another in population studies; the statistical demonstration of their correlation changed the whole game. The main stage of this crucial encounter was neither the hospital nor the factory but rather the school and educational institutions.

Pubertal growth and the discovery of the 'spurt'

It all started in 1872 with Henry Bowditch in the US, Luigi Pagliani in Italy, and Charles Roberts in England. At a meeting of the Boston Society of the Medical Sciences, Bowditch presented a diagram showing the rate of growth in height in 13 women and 12 men. They all belonged to the same family (probably his) and their measurements had been taken annually for the past 25 years. Though the paper would never be published, it was abstracted in *The Boston Medical and Surgical Journal* (1872: 434–5), later called the *New England Journal of Medicine*. Bowditch noted that boys were taller than girls at all ages until 12, when 'girls begin to grow faster than boys, and during the fourteenth year are about one inch taller than boys of the same age. . . . At fourteen and a half years of age boys again become the taller, girls having at this period very nearly completed their growth, while boys continue to grow rapidly till nineteen years of age'. He noted the striking disagreement between his and Quetelet's curves (see Chapter 7), the latter showing that 'girls are, at no period of their lives, taller than boys of the same age'.

Later in that decade, Bowditch conducted his massive cross-sectional survey in Boston state and private schools, the first and most cited report of which appeared in his *The Growth of Children* (Bowditch 1877). Mainly interested in the effects of race and environment on development, he measured male and female children of Irish-born and American-born parents. In his tables he saw once again the sex differences he had previously described, irrespective of race or life conditions. More exactly, he pointed to an increase in height velocity shortly before pubescence. Crossing his growth data with data on menarche from hospital records, he concluded that girls reach their prepubertal acceleration about two years prior to the onset of menstruation (though such an exact correlation between growth and pubescence in boys could not as yet be established).

By then, in Britain, the health of children and women working in textile factories remained a matter of great political concern (see Chapter 7). The 1872 Parliamentary Commission called for a comparative, large-scale examination of labouring children and working-class children not employed in factories. Body measurements were to be taken in schools located in or nearby factory districts (for school attendance was a legal imperative for children to work in the textile industry following the 1833 Act for the regulation of factory labour). Roberts was one of the medical inspectors appointed to conduct the survey. Drawing on these data, and contradicting Quetelet, he spoke of an increase in the rate of height growth 'with the accession of puberty', which he called 'pre-pubertic growth' (Roberts cit. Tanner 1981a: 179).

In 1872, Pagliani launched his first school survey – the earliest growth study to use a mixed (longitudinal and cross-sectional) method – the main focus being the impact of socioeconomic circumstances on physical development (see Tanner 1981a: 197–202). Over three years, he took measurements of upper-class schoolboys and of boys of a newly founded male boarding school for the orphaned and the abandoned. He also followed the growth of schoolgirls from well-off families and recorded ages of menarche. Between 1873 and 1876, in addition, he led a much larger survey in public and private institutions where a cross-sectional sample of measurements was collected. His results suggested a marked and quite regular growth acceleration at puberty in the two sexes. Given the data on menarche, in particular, he concluded similarly to Bowditch that girls attain their maximal height velocity about one to two years before the first menstruation. Quetelet's famous curve representing the growth of 'the average man' was once again disproved.

As Tanner (1981a: 201) points out, Bowditch entertained the idea that quick growth and sexual-reproductive maturation were 'antithetical processes', whereas Pagliani held that they were 'two manifestations of the same underlying influence'. The latter eventually prevailed.[5] In any case, their statistics as well as those of Roberts mark the end of Quetelet's paradigm. They espoused the auxological conception of growth spurt as a bodily event inextricably bound to pubertal development.

Growth acceleration: auxological and clinical problematisations

It did not take long for pubertal growth to become a central problematic in the epidemiology of development. During the last two decades of the 1800s, medical statisticians discussed whether the incidence of disease was greater shortly before pubescence, when growth was markedly slower, or rather during the pubertal acceleration. Again, the school was the space for scrutiny. This debate was described and commented upon in detail in an extensive review of modern growth science by Frederik Burk published in 1898 in Stanley Hall's recently founded periodical, *The American Journal of Psychology*.

In Switzerland, Adolphe Combe (cit. Burk 1898: 294) suggested an overall negative influence of growth acceleration upon health: 'Sickness increases with growth; in other words, the more a child grows, just so much the more is it inclined to disease. The periods of most accelerated growth represent, therefore, the periods during which the organism possesses the least power of resistance to disease'. On the other hand, Axel Key, in Sweden, argued that resistance to morbidity increased in the period of accelerated growth. 'The curve of disease (in boys)', he argued, 'reaches its first summit directly before, or, more correctly, at the beginning of the pubertal development' (Key cit. p. 290). In girls, however, the positive influence of rapid growth was not so evident, for in their case 'the curve of sickness reaches its first summit in the second pubertal year (the 13th), which is the year of accelerated increase in weight, and sinks thereafter very little' (Key cit. p. 292). In Denmark, Axel Hertel (cit. p. 293) similarly found that the highest incidence of disease 'is reached in the 12th or 13th year, directly at the threshold of the pubertal period'; nonetheless, drawing on his large school sample, he added that 'The strong physical development during this period is not able to lessen materially the percentage of sickness . . . [which] remains high in the case of both boys and girls'. In any case, within this nuanced and somewhat confusing debate,[6] the relation of pubertal growth to the onset and prevalence of illness became statistically established.

In the meantime, the numerical demonstration of puberty's accelerated development had flooded into the clinical arena, where the phenomenon was now often hypothesised as a causal background of conditions affecting youth. Again, the perceived sex differences in the tempo of reproductive maturation gave clinicians renewed reasons to position girls as at a greater risk than boys. As their growth was completed more quickly than boys, girls were perceived as naturally undergoing the changes of puberty in a more intense way, which was especially disturbing for both body and mind.

Drawing on 'The Etiology and Classification of the Anaemia of Puberty', Cosgrave (1888: 689–90) emphasised the rapidity of pubertal changes in girls. 'Professor Bowditch says that, up to 11 or 12, boys are, on the average, taller and heavier than girls; for the next two or three years girls have the advantage, whilst after 14 or 13 boys again excel in strength and height'. He also cited the recent work of German physiologist, Friedrich Wilhelm Beneke, 'who has shown that the annual increase in the heart and blood-vessels in girls up to puberty is 8 per cent., per annum, whilst during the establishment of menstruation it is 80 to 100 per cent. . . . There is no such rapid change in the male'.[7]

Cosgrave proposed a threefold classification of the 'anaemia of puberty'. There were the cases of 'anaemia of general malnutrition', in which the undernourished organism was unable to accomplish the additional demands of bodily maturation. Also, if the body underwent a hasty skeletal and muscular growth during the development of physiological functions, the organism could be perniciously overtaxed which would lead to 'anaemia of overgrowth'. Finally, the mesodermal action upon the formation of tissues and organs at puberty could be 'misdirected' and produce 'an excessive amount of reserve tissue', possibly leading to 'fatty anaemia' (p. 689). Overall, accelerated development was to blame.

Dealing with heart development at puberty, Pitt (1886: 1029) suggested as much. He spoke to 'the frequent occurrence of slight cardiac dilatation, and of the lack of reserve cardiac energy to meet emergencies, which I believe to be so common at this age, especially in those who have grown very rapidly'. He stressed the vulnerability of girls to cardiac conditions and subsequent weakness, quoting Beneke and Bowditch to support his view.

Lommel (cit. *The American Journal of the Medical Sciences* 1904: 168) offered a similar reasoning for the incidence of albuminuria (the abnormal presence of albumin in the urine, usually related to kidney disease) in pubescent children. What caused 'the albuminuria of puberty', he believed, were 'diseased circumstances' which resulted from the difficulties of the organism (especially the cardiac and vascular systems) to follow the general pace of growth and functional development.

Morbidity without *disease*: the auxological discovery of 'imbalance'

By the turn of that century, Christopher (1901) published his large epidemiological study on pubertal growth, based on the survey conducted in Chicago public schools between 1899 and 1900. In all, 6,259 children were measured for height (upright and sitting), weight, ergographic muscular endurance (except children under 5), strength of grip of both left and right hands, and 'vital capacity' (i.e. the volume of air exhaled).[8] Like others before him, he saw in his tables 'an exaltation of life processes at the pubertal period', especially in girls in whom that period was shorter; however, he proudly wrote, 'I am not aware of any other investigation which shows it to be true of so many physical measurements'(p. 693).

Christopher pushed the paediatric envelope of, to use his own phrase, 'pubertal morbidity'. In somewhat obscure anthropometric language, he contended: 'It is the great range of physical measurements of this period which permits of the existence in the child of an enormous lack of balance in the physical measurements, and it is *this condition* of lack of balance which gives rise to the morbid manifestations' (p. 693, our emphasis).

To him, this is to say, the problematic of pubertal growth was not simply about intensity and velocity. What was also at stake was the evidence that, at puberty, in striking contrast with the course of development during childhood, all the measurable indicators of growth showed a wide range of variation around their yearly mean values. While this range, Cristopher pointed out, 'must be considered normal', it also reflected simultaneous processes of intensified growth which would tend to generate unbalanced increments (e.g. between height and weight). In this 'condition', he found a principle of ill health: 'It is found associated, in a causal relation, with most of the morbid manifestations of puberty, particularly disturbed heart action, dilatation of the heart, fatigue, anemia, and some deformities, such as round shoulders and scoliosis, as well as many of the neuroses of the period'.

Christopher did not arrive to this conclusion – and this is perhaps the most radical event produced in his work – by assessing the average ages at which sickness was *de facto* more prevalent in the children examined, as Key or Hertel had done. He started off by computing an average pubescent body which, as his tables show, frequently and often significantly departs from what he called 'the normal average' (i.e. the mean value of a measurement for each year). In this regular irregularity of 'measurements' in the pubertal years, he saw multiple occasions for 'unbalanced growth'. 'In general', he finally concluded, 'it may be said that an important factor in pubertal morbidity is unbalanced physical development', which, he was careful to indicate, 'is physiologic', that is to say, not pathological in itself. He briefly described a few cases met in clinical context, but merely as an illustration of the causality he suggested.

Unlike the previous epidemiological auxologists, Christopher produced a probabilistic fact – morbidity rises at puberty – which was autonomous from the reality of disease itself. On the basis of the mathematical demonstration of 'unbalanced growth', there was no longer the need for the disease to be found in a given population for the danger of morbidity to be observable, demonstrable, and therefore true from an epidemiological standpoint. Henceforth, statistically speaking, risk existed in pubertal development alone.

Accordingly, Christopher outlined a 'plan for investigation of cases of physical unbalance' (p. 694): it called for the scrutiny of hereditary as well as exogenous factors such as nutrition and intellectual exertion, and of the measurements 'for which norms have been determined for comparison' (height, weight, endurance, vital capacity, etc.). The profound consequence of this discourse is that it enabled an entry-point into the clinical demand for standards of pubertal growth, and so an early step into the auxological production of the 'normal' pubescent body. But, for that part of the story, the reader will have to wait for the next chapter.

There is another, more obvious effect of Christopher's discovery in relation to the power-knowledge of pubertal medicine, as outlined in a short review of his paper: 'Dr. Christopher concludes that special medical supervision should be maintained over boys and girls during puberty and any disorders or anomalies of growth corrected as early as possible' (*The Lancet* 1901: 928).[9]

The pubertal war against disease had now to deal with a new and more uneasily manageable 'truth': it is normal for the growth of pubescent children to be unbalanced. The crisis of puberty reappeared within the body more forcefully than ever before. Puberty, Christopher maintained, 'is also a period of great individualization. It is a time when the weak fail and the able forge to the front' (1901: 693).

'Crises' and 'overpressure': beware of girls' schooling!

From the 1870s through to the 1890s there was a boom of 'pedagogical hygiene' aimed at the scientific optimisation of learning conditions, from classroom architecture and furniture to the duration of lessons and intervals between them. With it, anxieties about school 'overpressure' peaked in Europe as well as in the US (see Tanner 1981a: 189–90, 202–5). In the early 1900s, Edgar Darnall (1904: 292) exclaimed: 'Visit the female colleges and you will be impressed with the large numbers of pale-faced girls whose roseate blushes of youth have been chased away by nervous exhaustion born of the shadows of midnight toil'. The developmental problematic of child factory work moved into the schools – most notably those recently welcoming, or specifically for, female students.

Youth, the entire medical world seemed to agree, should be protected from a necessarily dangerous psychosexual development as well as an unnecessarily demanding school education. Pubescent girls were seen as being in greater danger than boys. Hertel's *Overpressure in High Schools in Denmark*, published in English in 1885, is a classic of the 19th-century problematisation of the school as a hotbed for the 'sickly'.[10] Drawing on his statistical results, he maintained:

> Thus girls have a strong predisposition to various diseases to start with, and it is therefore easy to understand that school routine and private tuition, which must affect girls even more potently than boys, soon induce various diseases, and especially anaemia, to assert themselves more strongly than

> before. More particularly during the years of puberty does sickness prevail to a great extent, at least one-half of the pupils being at this period more or less debilitated or ill.
>
> (Hertel 1885: 77)

'As for girls', he recommended, 'regular constant participation in household duties is both a useful and a healthy occupation', in addition to few hours spent at school (p. 192).

Around 1900, given the neurophysiological strain and menstrual anomalies (e.g. dysmenorrhea, amenorrhea, metrorrhagia, menorrhagia, anaemia) that sexually maturing girls were expected to experience, the prospect of regular school work overburdening them appeared sensible – and medically sophisticated. The perceived idiosyncrasies of female reproductive maturation, doctors believed, were bound to alarming states of nervousness and fatigue. Gynaecological science happily lent institutional support to a patriarchal campaign that basically shouted at parents: "Take your girls out of school!" Prevention against a 'dwarfed womanhood' ought to be secured, Darnall (1904: 292) instructed, 'by restricting the studies during the establishment of puberty, and if this cannot be done, by taking [girls] from school altogether until menstruation is established'. If not, the schoolgirl might well become 'highly cultured and shine in society, but her future husband will discover too late that he has married a large outfit of headaches, backaches, and spineaches instead of a woman fitted to take up the duties of life' (p. 292).

Interweaving with these anxieties, a more nuanced gendered medical pedagogy emerged. It called for the reorganisation of school activities according to the specific psychosomatic demands of female pubescence. These demands, it was contended by many medical men, were not being considered by the women responsible for teaching and supervising adolescent girls. In Britain, writing rather ambivalently about 'the so-called "high schools" for girls', a physician and professor of obstetrics at King's College took up the cry against 'co-education':

> I know of no large girl's school in which the absolute distinction which exists between boys and girls as regards the dominant menstrual function is systematically cared for and attended to. Indeed, the feeling of all schoolmistresses is distinctly antagonistic to such an admission. The contention is that there is no real difference between an adolescent male and female, that what is good for one is good for the other, and that such as there is is due to the evil customs of the past which have denied to women the ambitions and advantages open to men, and that this will disappear when a happier era is inaugurated.
>
> (Playfair 1895: 1409)

In the same breath, he made sure to assert he wrote 'in no spirit of opposition' to this movement of social change – despite its 'limitations which are essential because of the question of sex, which cannot be got over'.

In a time when feminists fought for the female population's right to school education, and women escaped domesticity by forging pedagogical positions in society,[11] a medical campaign shouted to the new girl schools' personnel: "Mind what you're doing to the future of our young women!" As happened since the mid-1800s in the industrialised West, on behalf of health and, of course, the nation, the crisis of puberty embedded a medical war against *certain* forms of progress (see Chapter 7).[12]

The psychiatric 'crisis': from asylum medicine to the war with oneself

In his lectures on *Psychiatric Power*, Foucault (2006: 248) illuminates the following: 'The birth of pathological anatomy and, at the same time, the appearance of a statistical medicine, of a medicine of large numbers – both the ascription of precise causality by the projection of the illness on a dead body and the possibility of inspecting a set of populations – provide the two major epistemological tools of nineteenth century medicine'. Thereafter, the Hippocratic technique and discourse of the crisis progressively became obsolete in medical sciences. However, and this is his main argument, the 'crisis' was kept alive in psychiatric practice, especially in asylum medicine concerned with hysteria, and more exactly in all the hysterical 'symptoms' provided on demand by the hysteric to such psychiatrists as Charcot. From the perspective of puberty science, as we now show, the continual relationship between 'crisis' and mental medicine took a more complex course, in which hysterical disorders were but one issue among many others.

The pubertal crisis and the onset of nervous and mental illness

In the late 1800s, there were a large number of patients whose doctors could hardly ameliorate their state or save them from death. More importantly, especially where illnesses of a mental or nervous kind were concerned – i.e. those affecting sensory-motor functions – it was not possible to ascribe an organic origin to many of them, to give them, so to say, a bodily truth. That was obviously the case with madness understood as delirium. But, to a great extent, it was also the case with a rather broad and grey area of conditions whose symptomatology was rather imprecise and, in many cases, overlapping: the neuroses.

In the absence of a real pathological body, 19th-century psychiatry resorted to the mythical body of heredity, captured by the inquisitorial activity of the clinician. The search for a tainted heredity across the patient's family history was 'a way of giving body to the illness at the very moment that this illness cannot be situated at the level of the individual body' (Foucault 2006: 271). Nervousness, alcoholism, sexual promiscuity, prostitution, and any kind of conduct deemed abnormal or socially dangerous was itself presumed to be a source of morbidity, being passed on to progeny in the stigmatic shape of mental and physical degeneration through hereditary mechanisms. The medical and moral past of a patient's relatives, in short, functioned as a predisposing pathological body. Heredity was the medical-psychiatric technology allowing for the past of mental and nervous illness to be 'revealed', just as the finding of a lesion would allow the history of a physiological condition to be tracked.

Around the same time that general physiology and auxological medicine suggested pubertal phenomena of growth acceleration and imbalance as a trigger of morbidity, psychiatry similarly 'found' that pubescence alone was an exciting source of behavioural problems, particularly in children predisposed to them. While still resorting to the fantastical body of heredity to render the *past* of mental illness intelligible – from the alcoholism of an uncle to the debauched youth of a mother – psychiatric diagnosis was now to refer to a truly physiological body as the *present stimulus* of a condition: the developing body of pubescence.

Once the onset of a number of neuroses was seen to occur during puberty, the correlation of neuroses and puberty became a key player in the symptomatologic and etiological description of such conditions. The year 1890 was prolific in the history of neuroses. In that year, Sir Andrew Clark (1890a, 1890b) offered 'The Barking Cough of Puberty'. His paper is an excellent example of how the power-knowledge of pubertal crisis worked in late 19th-century medical-psychiatric discourse.

After eloquently describing the physical, mental, and moral changes of puberty, he called attention to the pubertal 'peripheral changes' affecting the 'laryngeal area' (Clark 1890a: 1320). Talking to one of his various cases, he concluded:

> When, furthermore, we remember that for the most part the family and personal history of the patient is nervous . . . and that [the cough] disappears with, or shortly after, the complete evolution of sex, we cannot doubt – at least, I think, we cannot justly doubt – that this convulsion or barking cough of puberty (*cynobex hebetis pubertatis tussis canina*) is a malady of nervous origin, character, course, and issues.
>
> (p. 1320, italics added)

In short, Clark was able to assert the nervous nature of the condition and that, as he claimed, 'it has a well-defined individuality of its own' (p. 1320), by producing a symptomatology based on a predisposing heredity, on the one hand, and a 'critical' progression marked by the temporality of pubescence, on the other.

'Of local applications to the interior of the throat', he recommended an alleviating mixture containing 10% of either morphine or cocaine; but he admitted having found no treatment which was successful 'in shortening, to any great extent, the duration of the disease' (p. 1320). The best remedy to help these 'nervous' patients to overcome their state was, after all, proper pedagogy. As Clark prophetically wrote (about a cough!), 'we may help them to strive after self-effacement, to aim at some higher ideal than themselves, to find in labour strength, and through suffering tranquillity; and so, transfiguring their lives, to discover therein sacrifice instead of selfishness, and gladness instead of gloom' (p. 1321).

Here, the crisis is less a technique for the conduction of the body's struggle against illness than a technique for the struggle of the self against its own arrestment, that is to say, a technique allowing for the self to be healthily transformed. Besides a practice for managing disease, the crisis of puberty emerged as a medical technology for the mastery of the young self.

In the same year, the Physician-Superintendent of the Edinburgh Asylum for the Insane, Sir Thomas Smith Clouston, delivered his Morison Lectures on *The Neuroses of Development*. In his introduction, Clouston (1890: 3) claimed that brain pathology was 'intimately associated, hereditarily and functionally, with certain motor, sensory, and trophic neuroses incidental to the period of development' at which they most frequently occurred. 'When we carefully study some of these developmental disturbances', he promptly highlighted, 'we find them associated with and taking their character from the function of reproduction, which during adolescence is attaining its full strength'.

Besides Clark's 'barking cough', to which the lecturer devoted some time, Clouston argued that pubescence and adolescence brought out many other 'hereditary defects' such as epilepsy, hysteria, adolescent stupidity and adolescent insanity (let alone adolescent ugliness), perverted sexual instincts, perversion of the moral sense and volition, and unfounded aversion to relatives, to quote just a few (see p. 12).[13] In the end, he argued, there was only so much one could do to cure the neurotic or the convulsive besides circumscribing and managing bad heredity via hygienic measures. Yet he also maintained, 'if the physiologist can teach us exactly how the marvellous process of development proceeds normally and typically in all its stages . . . we shall be able to note when failures of normal development are beginning, and possibly to take measures *for the early combatting in some degree of such failures*' (p. 26, our emphasis).

Speaking to degenerative illnesses, he dealt with the very rare but equally dramatic onset of general paralysis at puberty, reporting two cases in detail. By then, this condition was already known to be caused by syphilis, a sexually contagious disease which is also congenitally transmissible to children. Clouston's 'developmental general paralysis' had the convenient disciplinary power of seemingly attesting to 19th-century psychiatry's claims about the ways of heredity – a promiscuous life *did* pass on its effects to the next generation in the form of a 'real' disease with well-delimited symptoms. However, the advent of penicillin treatment was yet to come and the infectious processes in the brain leading to the paralysis remained mysterious to the neurologist. Once again, thus, Clouston resorted to the rather speculative bodies of heredity and pubescence in order to explain the past and the present of the condition: 'It is quite clear that no correct generalization can be arrived at on the subject from these two cases, but they point strongly to a form of general paralysis due to hereditary syphilis as the predisposing cause, and to puberty as the exciting cause, with a neurotic heredity as an extra-predisposing cause' (p. 90).

Three years later, Wiglesworth (1893a, 1893b) reported a few more instances of 'developmental general paralysis' met in his and others' clinical work. Whereas the condition was usually associated to 'a time when the fresh vigour of youth has subsided', he warned that it 'may still claim its victims . . . at, or about, puberty' (Wiglesworth 1893a: 355–6). Every case was terminal (as illustrated by his appalling reports). Following Clouston, he ventured that a neuropathic or syphilitic predisposition could lead in these cases to paralysis by leaving the body unable 'to respond to the great calls upon the nervous system which the onset of puberty entails' (p. 365).

There was also acute insanity that was seen to establish itself in pubescent children, which was often conflated with Kraepelin's famous *dementia praecox*, the forerunner of schizophrenia (cf. Porter 1998: 512–13).[14] A reviewer of C. W. Burr's work on 'Insanity at Puberty' stated the following:

> Acute insanity also appears at puberty, and though rare, is sufficiently frequent to be of interest. . . . The treatment of insanity at puberty is largely preventive, such as proper education, avoidance of mental strain, teaching of self-control and clean morals. With more wisdom of parents insanity would decrease.
>
> (*The Journal of Nervous and Mental Disease* 1905: 752)

From a psychiatric standpoint, to sum up, the crisis of puberty was firmly in place by the dawn of the 20th century. And, as Burr suggested, proper parenting was increasingly demanded to avoid pubescent subjects' susceptibility to the onset of psychiatric conditions. More than ever, puberty's stormy enterprise required youngsters to find ways to control themselves, to master themselves, just as it called for parents to secure and even improve their role as carers, their 'wisdom'. The crisis of puberty was, in short, a technology of the self simultaneously imposed on children and adults: a technology of the good sexual child, and a technology of good parenting.

Hysteria, degeneration, and the instincts: the early 20th-century upgrade

Within the first two decades of the 1900s, progress in pathological physiology and the advent of endocrinology came to revolutionise medical and psychiatric views of sexual-reproductive maturation. As a result, the dangerousness of the pubertal crisis was recoded and amplified.

A most curious consequence of that knowledge revolution was the medical requalification of the hysteric young woman. Her attacks or 'crises' famously recorded by Charcot and often induced under hypnosis in front of his students had raised many eyebrows in the field.[15] Thirty years later, the adolescent girl's hysteria resurged as 'pubertal neurasthenia', as outlined by Macnaughton-Jones (1913). Regretting the abusive employment of such words as 'hysteric' and 'neurotic', he contended:

> The misery and unhappiness that have accrued to sensitive women through the misuse of these terms cannot be computed, and is all the more serious since the ignorant lay mind has become familiar with and places an entirely wrong interpretation on them. And so the girl or woman with uncontrollable sensations and feelings is regarded as a *malade imaginaire*, as fanciful of aches and pains – and said generally to be "nervous" – while all the time there are actual physiological anomalies of function or pathological states of the sexual organs which require to be treated and rectified.
>
> (Macnaughton-Jones 1913: 879)

'Pubertal neurasthenia' was perhaps difficult to articulate by 'the ignorant lay mind'; but the symptoms described by the author remained, after all, quite familiar. Besides the complaints of headache or fatigue, there were 'the more purely psychic, morbid imaginings and causeless apprehensions, fanciful ailments, groundless resentments and dislike of relatives or friends, unconquerable erotic impulses, and religious fervour and obsessions' (p. 880). Furthermore, as it turns out, the condition was found in pubescent girls without demonstrable genital or reproductive medical problems. Once such causes were dismissed, the therapeutic action to be taken was to inquire into 'the girl's moral, intellectual, and physical hygiene' (p. 881).

A decade later, drawing on the hypothesised influence of the ductless glands upon psychic life and development, Alfred Gordon still viewed hysteria as a typical condition of pubescence and adolescence. 'During puberty', he postulated, 'these glands by reason of a very active circulation are more apt to modify the mode of feeling and therefore of acting' (Gordon 1923: 74). Hence, he suggested that all hysterical phenomena 'are morbid manifestations to which an adolescent is particularly predisposed' (p. 75).[16]

Endocrinology as well as the rise of Mendelian genetics also threw a whole new light over the more disturbing mental pathologies affecting young people – namely, paralytic insanity and the so-called *dementia praecox*. Three decades after Clouston, the prominent physician and well-known figure of the eugenic movement in Britain, Sir Frederick Mott, offered his Morrison Lectures on 'The Psychopathology of Puberty and Adolescence'.

> The subject I have chosen is one that a previous lecturer illuminated; needless to say, I refer to the late Sir Thomas Clouston, one of the great pioneers

> in psychiatry. . . . Our knowledge of the functions of the reproductive endocrine system was only in its infancy. . . . Since then Edinburgh, by the investigations of its illustrious professor of physiology, Sir Edward Sharper Schafer and his pupils, have laid the foundation of endocrinology – a subject that has revolutionised our ideas of medicine, and which promises to illuminate the darkness of many diseases, including those of the mind.
>
> (Mott 1921: 279)

Drawing on post-mortem microscopic observations of testes and ovaries of general paralytics, Mott spoke of a regressive atrophy in both sexes and suggested an association of this process with the onset of the disease. He reported very similar results in relation to cases of congenital diseases such as imbecility, idiocy, and *dementia praecox*, which seemed to indicate a morbid principle common to all.

In Mott's attempt to answer the question, 'Why should this degeneration of the germ-cells come on in adolescence?', the Galtonian spirit endemic to those days strikingly emerged in his analysis: 'If the subject be approached from an evolutional point of view, we may consider that Nature, unmindful of the preservation of the individual and mindful only of the preservation of the species by survival of the fittest, would, by bringing on in adolescence a regressive atrophy of the reproductive organs, stop procreation of a degenerate stock' (p. 297).

It is true that, by the time of Mott's lectures, the 19th-century conception of degeneration was a bad souvenir of psychiatrists' ignorance about heredity. However, as his talk also illustrates, the notion had not vanished from psychiatric discourse. It had been reformed with genetic and molecular knowledge, and charged with evolutionary meanings taken up from the stance of eugenics – i.e. the problematic of race decay.[17]

The 'degenerates' were the young carriers of their family's madness and unsound morality, all of which manifested in the body and the behaviour of the child. That is what degeneration initially meant for Morel (cf. Foucault 2006: 223) and for Clouston two decades later. In the late 1800s, reflecting the criminological and anthropometric trends of his time, Clouston found the physical correlate of mental degeneracy in the shape of his patients' palates (see Clouston 1890: 42–53). By the early 20th century, the new science of genetics discredited such articulations. Accordingly, Mott 'showed' the physiological signs of degeneration to his audience, no longer in any anatomical stigmata (as Clouston, Lombroso, or many others did), but in what he saw as endocrinal and cellular processes of 'regression'. These processes reproduced, at the individual level, nature's selective exclusion of the mentally unfit, or so he claimed.

From the psychiatric standpoint of puberty-as-crisis, the notion of degeneration thoroughly intertwined with that of the instincts – the latter having ultimately had a longer life in mental medicine than the former (cf. Foucault 2006: 222). For the 19th-century psychiatrist, even if proper insanity was not at stake, the 'degenerates' had inherited the abnormal instincts of their parents.

In the early 20th century, just like degeneration, the sexual instincts were re-articulated anew.

Starting with Freud's *Three Essays*, most notably, the problematic of the sexual instincts at puberty was reformulated on the basis of a recently found body chemistry. At that time, Stanley Hall (Bowditch's former student at Harvard University) published his *Adolescence*, becoming the last great proponent of the 'ontology-recapitulates-phylogeny' theory, i.e. the evolution of the child into maturity reproduces the evolution of the species from the 'savage' to the 'civilised'.[18] Henceforth, the normalisation of adolescents' sexual conduct and roles was upgraded according to a game of endocrinal and evolutionary truths. Again, Mott's lectures serve as an exemplary illustration:

> With the onset of puberty and the maturation of the reproductive organs, the sexual hormones pass into the blood and impress on the body not only the visible sexual characters distinctive of male and female, but they reinforce in every cell of the body the predominant male or female characters, thus endowing the whole complex organism with an innately determined capacity not only to act and feel in a particular manner characteristic of the sex, but also to perceive the object upon which the action and feeling are directed in order to accomplish the supreme biological end – reproduction, and the preservation of the species.
>
> (Mott 1921: 289)

Pubescence exalted the instincts and established their sovereignty over the self. But, given the perceived unruliness and difficulty in mastering the sexual instincts in adolescence, these instincts could easily deviate from their *normal* orientation. Needless to say, Mott's immediate anxieties were about queer 'tendencies' in the young (p. 298) – the famous gender and sexual 'inversions' addressed by the British powerhouse of sexual psychology, Havelock Ellis.

Alongside such 'health' issues, instinctual abnormality at puberty brought another, perhaps even more compelling, level of concern to the crisis of puberty: the onset of criminal behaviour.

The 'defective' and 'maladjusted': pubertal crisis and the war against delinquency

In the late 19th, early 20th centuries, alongside more serious mental illnesses, paediatric psychiatry was equally concerned with the onset of conditions in which insanity or deliria were merely episodic or not at all present. Among such cases, thus, we encounter the great family of the 'manias'. Based on such authorities as Maudsley and Morel as well as his own observations, French psychiatrist Albert Mairet (cit. *The Journal of Nervous and Mental Disease* 1889: 775) talked of the 'mania of puberty'. To him, pubescence 'has in itself a great pathogenic importance toward the development of this mental disturbance.

The process may take a normal, physiological course or a severe, pathological one', either resulting in 'temporary cessation of mental development', or assuming a catatonic, choreatic, impulsive, or hysteric form.

Rather than producing a permanent loss of consciousness, of touch with reality, manias and similar disorders affected the maturing child's intellectual and 'moral' faculties. They were, bluntly put, diseases of the will.[19] While certainly less debilitating to the individual, they proved far more menacing to the society. The psychiatric surveillance of puberty, as Burr and others suggested, was to pay special attention to this class of issues:

> Dr. Burr states that he considers everybody somewhat unbalanced at the age of puberty, but that only the weaklings develop mental disease. What is probably the most common type of this period is seldom seen in asylums, and has been but little studied. It consists in a mild general impairment – dementia is too severe a word, but it seriously affects the future life of the individual. In another type there is gross moral aberration in addition to the mental deficiency (which may be slight). Many of the criminal class are of this type.
> (*The Journal of Nervous and Mental Disease* 1905: 752)

By then, for instance, criminal psychiatrists entertained the problem of 'Pyromania, a Psychosis of Puberty', as offered in a review published by *The Lancet* (1905: 583–4). According to the original French article's author, Dr Raoul Leroy, 'True cases of pyromania manifest themselves for the first time at the period of puberty'. Referring to the trial case of a 15-year-old girl as a typical example, he concluded 'that the morbid heredity in both paternal and maternal sides resulted in a brain liable to disorder and readily provoked to morbid impulse (in this case pyromania) on the occurrence of the stress of puberty, a critical time in mental development'.

Overall, as Italian psychiatrist Antonio Marro argued in a 1907 paper reviewed by Hamilton Marr, 'Manifestations of [behavioural] abnormality originate generally very early in puberty. . . . The infractions of family discipline open the way to outrages against social law, and this epoch may be considered as the beginning of the criminality of man' (Marr 1910: 134, 135).[20] The sex differences impressed upon boys and girls by the instincts, according to Marro, seemed well demonstrated in their offences: girls 'excel boys only in one category of the active faults – sins of the tongue' (p. 133).

Charles Gibbs, in a 1923 paper on *dementia praecox*, cited Marro's extensive volume on puberty written in 1900 as an up-to-date reading. Contrary to former medical views, Marro (cit. Gibbs 1923: 127) recognised that a 'lack of development of moral and affective faculties' did not imply mental retardation. Also, he correlated the onset of psychopathic behaviour in adolescents with 'unevenness of physical development' and metabolic anomalies involving the internal secretions at puberty, all of which, Gibbs asserted, were being found in 'delinquent or otherwise psychopathic individuals' (p. 127).

By then, Gordon (1923: 74–5) voiced very similar views and anxieties. 'From a practical standpoint', he maintained, 'the chief feature of the crisis in puberty is the continuous endeavor on the part of the adolescent to adjust oneself to the new physiological and psychic forces. Should the adjustment fail, neuroses and psychoses will ensue'. Notwithstanding the gravity of such diseases, he contended that the 'problem of greater magnitude' concerned the so-called 'mental defectives', starting with their incapacity to 'struggle against passions' at puberty and quickly escalating towards 'criminality in all its forms'.

From Marro to Gordon or Gibbs, juvenile delinquency was primarily about an abnormal or a 'lack of development' (either physical or mental or both), not illness. Rather than truly pathological, young delinquents were no more than 'mental defectives', the 'retarded' and the 'maladjusted', as usually termed in those decades, incapable of taking control over their will – i.e. their instincts. 'The most essential features of the psychopathic personality are considered to involve emotions and sentiments and instinctual behavior' (Gibbs 1923: 127). This was all the more alarming since most of these 'defectives' would escape the only remedy that could somehow rescue them from decay: pedagogy. Failing at school, either due to retarded learning or pure unwillingness, they eventually dropped out. 'Petty and serious crimes committed by this large army of juvenile delinquents', as Gordon (1923: 75) put it, 'are a matter of common knowledge'.

Marginal to the school or the workplace, the delinquent was a character inevitably trapped within the medico-legal space of the psychiatric ward. Predominantly a male figure in the first decades of the 20th century, the delinquent's objectification took shape within the walls of state correctional institutions. In 1939, drawing on his clinical observation at the Adolescent Ward of a New York psychiatric hospital, Frank Curran offered an overview of the panoply of issues at stake in what he saw as the erratic, unacceptable, and dangerous nature of the delinquent boy. His text on 'Psychotherapeutic Problems of Puberty' shows the historical model of abnormality as theorised by Foucault (2003b) fully in place: the sexual pervert, the criminal monster, and the incorrigible child appear superimposed on the same young, institutionalised individual.[21] In particular, Currans' case analyses stressed that juvenile delinquency and sexual abnormality were partly caused by a deficient psychological support from infancy to adolescence, especially due to an absent or unsound parental attachment.[22]

But, to be sure, as Gordon (1923) suggested, any child could succumb to the psychosomatic toil of pubescence and become a delinquent. In the end, the 'maladjusted' did not need to be 'dull', neurotic, or even suffer from the lack of proper parental attachment that Curran stressed. Maladjustment and delinquency ultimately resulted from the triumph of the primitive forces of the past, that is to say childhood, over the civilised forces of the future, that is to say adulthood. Quite simply, they resulted from a 'crisis' that somehow had gone wrong, which, according to what Gordon saw as the 'Neurological Manifestations of Puberty', seemed fairly likely to happen:

> The coming man or woman cannot readily abandon the traits of the passing childhood. There is naturally a struggle. Natural tendencies are now more in evidence, they may become perverted, exalted or abolished according to whether the combat between the infantile forces and the new requirements ends in favor of one or the other. Frequently this great physiological crisis precipitates mental and nervous disorders if the predisposition is neuropathic. In normal condition we frequently witness a very manifest change of character; the individual may become reserved or authoritative. There may be euphorism or depression.
>
> (Gordon 1923: 74–5)

For Gordon, the 'combat' is no longer between nature and disease, as it mainly was for a physiologist like Raciborski (1868) or a psychiatrist like Clouston (1890). Here, what is finally in question is a war between the normal maturing self and certain 'natural tendencies', that is to say, between nature and itself. 'The problem', as put by one of Hall's disciples, 'is largely to strengthen the volitional powers before the onset of puberty. Only a strong will can guide the human bark through the storm and stress of adolescence' (Terman 1905: 182). The psychiatric pubertal crisis of the 20th century essentially became, as Joseph Lander put in 1942, 'The Pubertal Struggle Against the Instincts'. Writing in markedly psychoanalytic key, he painted that struggle as follows:

> With the advent of puberty the sleeping lion awakens. . . . This new strength of the instincts, as we know, derives from the enormous accession of energy as the gonads begin to function at puberty. The former peace no longer prevails. . . . The youngster is suddenly immersed in war. . . . It is because the balance of power is upset in this fashion, because of the sudden re-emergence of all the old disturbers of the peace [e.g. masturbatory drives], that puberty and early adolescence are such stormy times, when severe new problems appear, and old problems become intensely aggravated.
>
> (Lander 1942: 457)

For the psychoanalytic Lander, the instincts were very much the same as they were for any 19th-century psychiatrist – i.e. something 'whose existence is natural, but which is abnormal in its anarchical functioning, which is abnormal when is not mastered or repressed' (Foucault 2006: 222). Those instincts were still the great instigators of the 'storm' of adolescence as announced by Hall, already infused with sexual chemistry by then. But, in Lander's Freudian framework, the pubertal crisis does not call for a complete suppression of the child's deviant behaviour. On behalf of the same fight against adolescent disorder and maladjustment that greatly preoccupied Hall or Marro, but unlike what they advised, *some* masturbation, disregard for parents' dislikes, or neurotic manifestations should be deemed acceptable, even curative. For, as Lander put it, such 'pubertal peculiarities' worked 'as safety valves which drain off enough energy to prevent more catastrophic explosions' (1942: 460).

Clearly, on the one hand, Lander's views were grounded in a relatively recent sexual psychology, Ellis and Freud being its great founders, which provided a new understanding of child sexual development.[23] Particularly, it called for the de-stigmatising of masturbation in the young, and so for the recognition of something so hardly and seldom conceived of in 19th-century medicine: child sexual pleasure. On the other hand, this realisation came at the expense of the 'finding' that such pleasures, if carelessly allowed or managed, were also the foundation of socially unfit or, even worse, dangerous minds. Speaking to the psychiatric profession, Lander concluded:

> Our job is *not* to restore them to a state of normality; it is our job to erect internalized barriers against delinquency. . . . Intensive sociological and educational measures directed toward [the primary-school] period can strengthen these children emotionally and give them the tools they will need to help them ride out the storm that lies ahead at puberty.
>
> (Lander 1942: 461, his emphasis)

On the basis of the adolescent 'maladjusted' and 'delinquent', as Lander illustrates, preventive surveillance against pubertal abnormality was to be a lengthy affair, preferably starting as early as in the first school years. The problem of criminality had never seemed so ubiquitous; puberty science proved more necessary than ever.

From about the mid-1800s onwards, as outlined in this chapter, the puberty-as-crisis discourse no longer entailed the management of, and possible recovery from, actual illnesses, but rather a preventive war primarily against abnormal sexual development. Within that period, puberty was clinically and epidemiologically deemed a necessarily intense, even unbalanced, process of psychosomatic transformation. In other words, this 'critical' process was both the bearer and the trigger of abnormal or disordered developmental phenomena, thus rendering body and mind vulnerable to the onset of a myriad of conditions. In the course of the hundred years following Raciborski's 'crisis', in physiological and mental medicine, in short, puberty was systematically demonstrated as a healthy-unhealthy condition.

Alongside this discursive formation, we shall show in the next chapter, a concurrent event took place. While clinicians and medical statisticians suggested that "it is natural for puberty to be abnormal", a new medical object emerged: the normal pubertal body. On the basis of this ideal as well as volatile body, doctors, and health researchers strived towards an effective supervision of pubescence, and sensible and accurate interventions upon its developmental disorders. In doing so, as discussed in the following, the medical profession also encountered the complications of diagnosing and treating abnormal, yet non-pathological, pubescent bodies.

Notes

1 'Most childhood conditions reach a crisis', it is taught in *Aphorisms*, 'some in fourteen days, some in seven months, some in seven years at the approach of puberty. But those that persist among boys and do not cease around puberty, or, in the case of girls, at the onset of menstruation, are likely to become chronic' (Hippocrates cit. Longrigg 1998: 111).

2 Treatments combined, among other techniques, iodine preparations aiming to accelerate the blood circulation, bleedings through small lanceted cuts on the legs or arms, and the application of leeches on the upper thighs and the vulva 'to combat the local plethora and conduct the blood of the internal sexual organs out' (Raciborski 1844: 226). In any case, the doctor's role in dealing with amenorrhea was that of managing nature's movement, not curing a disease.

3 In mentioning 'Onan's passion', Raciborski simply refers to masturbation, not coitus interruptus.

4 Unlike the more traditional medical views on the subject, Raciborski believed that onanism was the effect rather than the cause of mental as well as sensory-motor illnesses. In any case, one thing seemed certain according to him and doctors of his time: masturbation, especially in the young, was not at all motivated by pleasure!

5 'Nowadays we see the growth spurt as actually part of the finalization of reproductive function, an adaptive secondary sex character' (Tanner 1981a: 192).

6 So much so that Combe managed to read Key's and Hertel's writings 'under some misapprehension . . . as supporting his view', as Burk (1898: 295) notes.

7 Imbued with the evolutionist spirit that grew at that time, Cosgrave attempted to explain sex differences in child growth in a way that reminds us of John Roberton's pre-Darwin hypothesis of early puberty based on the selection of young wives (see Chapter 6): 'It is probable that the rapid development of the female is to be found in sexual selection. Men generally choose wives younger than themselves, and so women who are early sexually mature are most likely to be married and have offspring. In time this ought to cause a rapid maturity, and the general tendency would be emphasised in the offspring of mothers who were married young' (Cosgrave 1888: 689).

8 For a description of his methodology and measuring instruments, see Christopher (1900).

9 To be fair, Christopher never explicitly came to these conclusions although the implications could be gleaned from his work.

10 'By "sickly" I mean *unsound children, who suffer from chronic complaints, but who are, nevertheless, able to attend school regularly* . . . [T]hey ought to be called cases of *unsound* or *abnormal* health' (Hertel 1885: 16–17, his emphasis).

11 For a genealogy of the figure of the woman teacher in *fin de siècle* Britain, see Maria Tamboukou (2003).

12 In the 1920s, in Britain, Dr Alice Sanderson Clow and other members of the Medical Women's Federation still struggled to introduce non-stigmatising medical languages and views concerning girls' puberty and menstruation (see Strange 2000).

13 He gave particular attention to adolescent insanity, especially to the more serious stage of 'secondary dementia' of the disease, which he defined as a 'postponed idiocy'. It was mostly prevalent in the last five years of adolescence (complete at 25 in Clouston's periodisation), during which time the brain cortex became fully functional in his view. The recovery from the disease, he suggested, was somehow bound to, or at least coincident with, the final stage of development of the reproductive body and mind.

14 By the 1920s, Alfred Gordon (1923: 75) still suggested: 'Installation of puberty is one of the most potent factors which facilitate the formation not only of neuroses but also of psychoses. Dementia precox [sic] occupies the most conspicuous place among all'.

15 During his Morison Lectures, Clouston (1890: 110) scornfully commented on Charcot's demonstrations of 'hystero-epilepsy' at the Sâlpetrière hospital: 'This is not the place to enter on the vexed question, but I have had many adolescents, partly insane, partly hysterical, and all most liable to "suggestion", whom I am convinced I could in a short time have made into about as good subjects of hystero-epilepsy as any of the Salpêtrière cases by a few cliniques before students'. For a delightful history of Charcot's hospital practices and the struggles of the hysteric within the asylum, see Foucault (2006).

16 Speaking of epilepsy 10 years after, and stressing the importance of any knowledge 'which even in the remotest way may assist in the elucidation of such a baffling problem', Gordon (1933: 929) also noted the chronological coincidence between the convulsive attacks and the so-called critical periods of female reproductive life.

17 'Unfortunately', Mott (1921: 302) disturbingly argued, 'during the Great War these neuro-potentially unsound persons, of the great numbers of whom the pensions bill the Nation is paying is the best proof, were not fit for the frontline, and were not therefore killed off to anything like the degree that the A1 physically and mentally sound men were'.

18 See Stephen Jay Gould's (1977) outstanding history of recapitulation theories.

19 Mariana Valverde (1998) historicises this theme in relation to alcoholism.

20 For example, Marro (cit. Sullivan 1912: 525) reported a case of 'Automatic Parricidal Impulse in Puberty'. A boy 'without special hereditary taint' and with no apparent reason had attempted to strangle his mother. Marro concluded that 'the impulsive automatism shown by the patient was an exaggerated manifestation of the physiological instability of puberty'.

21 'Nick referred from Children's Court in October 1937, and his companion Ben admitted shooting at a street car with a stolen gun, killing a female passenger. . . . In Bellevue, Nick and Ben attempted sex play with each other as well as with other patients. Nick insisted on feminine roles in the dramatic activities; on the ward he wore rouge and hair ribbons, asked other boys to kiss him and treat him sexually as if he were a girl. . . . Prolonged psychoanalysis while institutionalized, similar to that advocated by Alexander and Healy, might be attempted but it is my belief he will continue to be a social menace and should be incarcerated indefinitely' (Curran 1939: 511).

22 It goes without saying, parent-child bonds were constituted as central objects of study and problematisation in the contemporary psychology of child development. For an outstanding critique of conceptions of attachment and 'correct' parental care as elaborated and put to work in developmental psychological research, see Erica Burman (1994: 65–104).

23 During the 1910s, this approach was being endorsed in well-known English medical periodicals. See, for example, *The British Medical Journal* (1911) on 'Puberty and the Neuro-Psychic System'.

Chapter 8

The birth of the 'normal' pubertal body (and its dilemmas)

At a meeting of the American Academy of Pediatrics held in 1941, Lawrence Frank presented his 'General Considerations on Certain Problems of Puberty and Adolescence'. He probably left some of his audience disappointed with what turned out to be more of a manifesto about the problems of paediatric science itself: he called for the recognition that children arrive to maturity in different engines – his metaphor – each of them travelling at a particular speed. For about a century, medicine had painstakingly tried to standardise a developing body against which all sickness and deviation could be assessed. Now, paediatrics was finding out that this body could also trouble the health and social expectations for which it had been created, that is, young people's safe journey into a proper adulthood. In a phrase, Frank spoke of 'the tyranny of the norm':

> We cannot expect the individual boy and girl to meet these requirements effectively if in our various programs and practices in the home, in the school, the clinic and hospital, and in the youth organizations and elsewhere, we persistently deny the basic, ineradicable differences among individuals and impose upon them the tyranny of the norm.
>
> (Frank 1941: 299)

In this chapter, we explore the knowledge apparatus through which the new paediatric science of the 20th century produced the 'normal' body of pubescence and adolescence, from the early forging of growth standards to the normalising of sexual development at the hormonal level. Engaging with a network of anthropometric, metabolic, and endocrinal views of the pubescent body, we trace the rise of a risk-oriented clinical regime for the surveillance and correction of sexual abnormality in the young. Within this regime of new technologies and new dilemmas around the normal and the abnormal, as we finally show, the 'constitutional' type of pubertal precocity was formulated. Thus, we end the chapter by coming back to where it all started: the precocious little monster.

Pubertal standards and 'physiological age'

In the 1891 *Annual Report of the State Board of Health of Massachusetts*, Henry Bowditch published 'The Growth of Children Studied by Galton's Percentile Grades'. Resorting to his 1877 data (measurements of 24,500 children; see Chapter 8), he presented a number of charts according to the percentile system introduced by Galton in the 1870s (cf. Tanner 1981a: 183).[1] Bowditch offered three graphical arrangements: height plotted against percentile by yearly age group; age plotted against percentile by height group (in inches); and height plotted against age by percentile, in which both sexes can be represented – the latter having become the model of most contemporary growth charts (see Cole 2012). Looking into these, one could say "at age 14, about 65% of boys (i.e. the 65th percentile) measure nearly 55 inches"; but, based on the same system, the doctor could also tell the parent, for example, "your daughter has the same height as about 87% of the female population of the same age, meaning she's *perfectly normal*". In short, Bowditch offered the first growth tables serviceable to modern clinical work.

The pubertal growth spurt was clearly represented his charts. In particular, Bowditch remarked that the growth curves remained fairly symmetrical until age 10 in girls and age 12 in boys. In other words, the taller children gained as much height as the smaller children of the same age, the yearly increments being Normally distributed around the mean during that period at each year of age. Then the curves moved towards the higher values, thus becoming asymmetrical, the reverse asymmetry happening at ages 14 and 16 in girls and boys, respectively. His conclusion: 'The pre-pubertal period of growth acceleration . . . occurs at an earlier age in large than in small children' (Bowditch cit. Tanner 1981a: 195); which basically meant that taller children seemed to reach puberty earlier. This argument was the key contribution of Bowditch's later study, as Burk (1898) indicated; yet, there was a problem in his logic.[2]

By 1895, the much-celebrated anthropologist and growth scientist, Franz Boas,[3] already disputed the argument's applicability, for, as Burk paraphrased, 'the small child of one age may be the large child of the next age' (1898: 307). Also, and most importantly, Bowditch did not realise what Boas explained years later. If the curves became asymmetrical, it was because *all* the children entering puberty at its earliest average age, *regardless of their size*, necessarily made the height distribution skew.

Consequently, besides the three quantities represented in Bowditch's tables – ages per annum, centile grades (5th, 10th, 20th, and so on until the 95th), and a growth measure – an additional factor ought to be considered: the timing of pubescence itself. An accurate measurement required the tempo of children's body growth (measured in height or weight gains, for example) to be correlated, not simply with their ages, but also their different rates of maturation. Boas statistically demonstrated that there is a temporality of development which is independent of individuals' chronological ageing. In other words, he discovered the so-called 'physiological age'.

How, then, does one measure children by taking their maturity status into consideration? Obviously, by including some bodily criteria of sexual maturation such as breast or pubic hair growth (the so-called secondary sex characters). In quantifying development statistically, how can one use those features? Quite simply, by grading them, that is to say, by forging standards. As we shall show next, the emergence of 'physiological age' is a foundational episode in the modern history of developmental medicine, especially in the epidemiological invention of the 'normal' pubertal body.

Growth standards and 'maturity-grading' criteria

The great French representor of anthropometric school surveillance, Paul Godin – who coined the term *auxologie* – started his surveys in the 1890s.[4] For several years, he followed the growth of over 200 boys (aged from 13 to 14 at the start of the study). He took 129 measurements of these boys – from face and head to feet – every six months, and rated them for 46 bodily features such as facial hair, eye shape, and skin colour. Furthermore – this being Godin's main innovation – he classified their pubertal development according to pubic and auxiliary hair, each comprising five grades. Despite his longitudinal data collection, however, he treated the data cross-sectionally, and, to be sure, Boas' complex statistical arguments were rather alien to him.[5] Yet, he was the first auxologist correlating pubescence and body growth empirically. In practical terms, thus, his ratings were an earliest step toward the medical construction of growth standards according to maturational criteria.

In Britain, it was an important 20th-century puberty and growth scientist who made the earliest and most consistent calls for a maturity-grading system in the construction of pubertal standards. This scientist was not Tanner but rather Richard W. B. Ellis, whose various contributions, surprisingly, are not mentioned once in Tanner's exceptionally detailed history of growth science (see next chapter).

In the US, following Boas' influence, maturity-grading criteria had already been employed by growth scientists, most notably by US psychologists Bird T. Baldwin (e.g. 1921) and Frank K. Shuttleworth (e.g. 1937). As to his own country, Ellis complained as late as the 1940s that the significance of employing such criteria in clinical and research contexts was yet to be recognised. Addressing the Section of Endocrinology of the Royal Society of Medicine, he insisted on 'the importance of grading on a maturity basis in addition to age when dealing with children from 9 years onwards' in growth studies and assessments (Ellis 1948a: 343). His argument was that the traditional height and weight curves smoothed out variations in the maturational status of children of the same age. Hence, these curves were misleading when clinicians compared them to individual cases. More exactly, because the traditional height and weight tables failed to indicate the standard deviation for each point on the curves, 'the range of normality' could not be taken into consideration in clinical settings: ultimately, 'no true allowance can be made for the individual body-build' (Ellis 1947: 282).

Moreover, he found that there was practically no proper data on the onset and development of pubescence to work with anthropometrically. Medical ignorance was greatest in regard to boys, the reason being, in his view, 'the absence of a clearly defined point such as the onset of menstruation, which can be retrospectively determined' (p. 282). Notwithstanding its statistical utility, he also stressed, the age of menarche 'does not necessarily correspond with the onset of ovulation, and has indeed tended to obscure the fact that puberty is actually a period of transition from childhood to adolescence rather than a single fixed point' (1946: 181). The clinically minded Ellis maintained:

> Any assessment of maturity of the individual child should therefore include not only the clinical examination and measurement, but also radiological examination. To these should be added the essay of oestrogen, androgen, and gonadotrophic hormonal excretion, though here the practical difficulties at present make this line of investigation of limited application.
>
> (Ellis 1947: 275)

Indeed, he was no old-school child measurer, and carefully weighed the value of 'certain crude generalisations with regard to general shape' drawn from anthropometric research (p. 270). Nonetheless, he praised the maturity-grading criteria for having allowed insightful views, namely on the relationship between maturational tempo and adult height. According to recent research, girls with a comparatively late menarche appeared to become taller by the end of adolescence than those menstruating earlier. As for boys, data on an analogous relationship was 'remarkably scanty' (p. 281).

In 1946, Ellis published his first cross-sectional study on pubertal growth based on a British sample of boys.[6] It was conducted in two different schools, the boys in 'School A' coming from foster-homes. Since the boys, to use his words, 'derived from somewhat different stock', he treated the two series separately. 'School A', he indicated, 'was exceptionally well suited for a controlled experiment of this type' (1946: 141). Besides diet and environment, he referred to the convenient fact that these boys had been measured annually since school entrance at age 5. In total, his sample comprised 208 children, from ages 12 to 16. Besides being measured for height and weight, they were examined for a number of pubertal signs, namely pubic, facial, auxiliary, and body hair as well as size and shape of genitalia. Ellis gave each feature different ratings of maturity: pubic hair, for example, was rated from P1 to P5 (like Godin had done). For each of these features, then, he grouped their ratings according to three main maturational statuses: 'non-pubescent', 'pubescent', and 'adolescent'.[7]

His results suggested that, on average, boys maturing earlier were taller and heavier than those of the same age group who matured later. He remarked that these differences could actually be traced as far back as at least the sixth year (according to the records available for School A). 'This does not of course imply', Ellis (1947: 281) carefully maintained, 'that [late maturing children] will be smaller in adult life' (as Pagliani, unlike Bowditch, already pointed out in the 1870s).

In the follow-up to his first study, Ellis (see 1947, 1948b) took height, weight, and leg-length measurements of 154 boys from the previous series of 208. Again, he assessed their maturational development according to the gradings described above. In addition, in order to test the correlation between growth and maturity more consistently, he endeavoured to study whether the age of onset of male pubescence was related to its duration. For that he examined 662 boys – 561 aged 9 to 17 from the two schools plus 101 adolescents aged 14 to 18 from two Edinburgh residential houses for working boys.

The data suggested that boys reaching puberty earlier were the latest to become adolescents. Even more significantly, the curves showed a wide-ranging duration of pubescence which he depicted in a clever chart.[8] In the end, he insisted: 'Since the age-range of onset of pubescence and of adolescence may show a variation of several years in different individuals it is emphasized that composite growth curves based on chronological age will tend to smooth out these characteristic patterns which depend on physiological rather than on chronological age' (1948b: 25).

Ellis made his case for the adoption of a maturity-grading system on the basis of three main arguments. First, the system allowed for a more accurate comparison between populations under similar experimental conditions than previously. As such, it would also permit determination of 'whether the age-onset of puberty is significantly affected by nutrition, latitude, and social environment as well as by the genetic factors which can be assumed to operate' (1948a: 348). Second, the recognition of differences in physiological age regardless of chronological age would make for better legal protection of child labour and a more effective regulation of the period of compulsory school attendance than had been in place. Likewise, Ellis called for the grouping of school classes by age as well as physical maturity. Last, as suggested above, he worried about the lack of maturational standards in routine clinical practice. This had the dangerous effect of narrowing what the notion of 'normal' puberty meant. Eventually, it led to problematic therapeutic decisions (see below).

Metabolic standards and maturation

The first half of the 20th century also saw the first attempts to standardise the 'normal' workings of young male and female bodies, particularly in view of their nutritional and clinical needs. As early as 1910, there was a clear call: 'Normal standards of organic efficiency are needed for the growing child, for the guidance of physicians in the treatment of disease, and also for the use of those who direct the physical and intellectual activities of normal children' (McCurdy cit. Richey 1931: 1281).

By the end of that decade, US physicians Fritz Talbot (1919) and Francis Benedict (1919) published the first conclusions of their large study, initiated by Talbot in 1911. Praising Talbot as a 'rare case' in medical research, Benedict (1919: 109) spoke of his mentor's endeavour with regard to the normal body as follows:

> Dr. Talbot early recognized the importance of not entering into the more attractive field of the study of abnormal and pathological conditions but realized that the greatest service, not only to physiology and pediatrics but, indeed, to pathology, could best be rendered by a careful survey of . . . perfectly normal children measured under such conditions as to make the results perfectly comparable, other things being equal, with the energy requirements of sick children.

Talbot and Benedict's results, however, could not, in their view, be generalisable. To clinicians' misfortune, as Benedict pointed out, they had demonstrated no law as to caloric needs according to age and weight. If anything, they disproved the utility of nutritional standards based on the weight-for-age index (rather than weight-for-height as advocated by Holt; cf. Benedict, p. 118). Obviously, Benedict argued, their curves indicated general trends. Yet, 'the deviations of the individual points are so great as to rule out immediately all claim to a regularity in [the] relationship between heat production and age . . . that can fairly be designated as a physiological law' (p. 132).

Nevertheless, the data suggested a steady lowering in metabolic rate from early childhood to puberty, without apparent changes with the onset of pubertal development:

> No obvious tendency for a deviation of the line [indicating metabolic rate] is noted at or about the age of puberty with either boys or girls. In both methods of computation for comparative purposes, i.e., per kilogram of body-weight or per square meter of body-surface, the curves are characterized by exceedingly low values during the first week, a rapid rise at about one or two years, and then a steady decline to 14 or 15 years, beyond which our observations do not extend.
>
> (Benedict 1919: 127–32)

Talbot and Benedict's conclusion was at odds with that recently offered by Du Bois, whose measurements on boy scouts suggested significant changes in basal metabolism[9] at puberty (cf. Nakagawa 1937). Over a decade later, US paediatricians Anne Topper and Hannah Mulier (1932) supported this view. They acknowledged Talbot's 1921 publication of normal standards for children, while reminding the reader that, according to Talbot himself, 'the metabolism during puberty will have to be studied further before any standards may be accepted' (Talbot cit. Topper and Mulier 1932: 327).

Topper and Mulier followed the basal metabolic rates of 38 children aged from 10 to 16 for a period ranging from one to four years. Their data showed 'a definite increase in metabolism before and during puberty, followed by a fall after puberty is established' (p. 328). They highlighted that the rise 'coincides with physiologic age rather than with chronological age, and occurs earlier in girls than in boys, coincident with their earlier pubescence' (p. 336). Their reasoning concerning this phenomenon was strongly anchored in the recent knowledge – and musical metaphors – of endocrinology:

> There is an awakening of the sexual life [at puberty]. All these changes are associated with a greater activity of the endocrine glands. Perhaps at this time, as Biedl suggested, the thyroid gland "if not the conductor, is at least the first violin of the incretory concert," and this may account for the increased basal metabolism found at this time.
>
> (Topper and Mulier 1932: 335)

As to guidelines for clinical use, however, their view was not promising: 'As there seems to be an individual variation in the height and duration of the increased metabolism, it makes the adoption of normal standards difficult for this important age period' (p. 336).[10]

By 1940, nutritional and metabolic standards for sexually maturing children were still an epidemiological priority. In that year, US physician Joseph Johnston entertained a possible relationship between metabolic phenomena and the incidence of tuberculosis, which remained a worrying epidemic. Aligning with the general opinion in the field, he claimed that 'an alteration in metabolism at this period might play a role in the activation of a hitherto latent lesion, and it has made desirable more information on the nutritional requirement in this seemingly critical age period' (Johnston 1940: 287). His hospital research focused on the cases of six female adolescents under treatment. He found 'that sexual maturation in the girls studied carried with it a depression in the retention of calcium and nitrogen', which he hypothesised as a contributing factor to the development of tuberculosis.

Standards for the growing cardiovascular system were also necessary, particularly for surgical and diagnostic reasons. In 1931, Dr Herman Richey published his study, conducted in the US, on the normal variations of blood pressure at puberty. Within the previous two decades, multiple attempts had been made to standardise measuring techniques and to establish normal blood pressure values of children and adolescents. However, as he remarked, only seldom had researchers 'considered the arterial system in its relation to physical growth and physiologic maturity' (Richey 1931: 1281).

He drew on measurements of 'Jewish and non-Jewish' schoolboys and schoolgirls aged 5 to 19.[11] In all, the sample comprised 1,147 subjects for whose blood pressure he tabulated the means, standard deviations, and coefficients of variation. He then correlated these figures with the measurements taken for growth (e.g. height, weight, ossification ratio) and maturity (graded according to ages of first menstruation and, in boys' case, Godin's ratings for auxiliary hair). He concluded: 'The differences of children as to precocity of sexual maturation are reflected in the behaviour of the blood pressures'.

As Richey's and the above authors' work illustrate, pubertal development had infiltrated all paediatric physiology, all its measuring techniques, and basically its analyses of all the chemical and muscular systems which keep the heart beating and the human organism alive. With the advent of 'physiological age', puberty had spread all over the interior of the body.

From statistics to the clinic: theoretical and ethical complications

Drawing on his data, Richey (1931: 1315) refuted ongoing assumptions about the pace of pubertal development by stressing the following:

> Puberty is not established by a sudden change. The first menstruation, a widely used criterion for puberty in girls, occurs suddenly of necessity, but is the result of the growth and development of years. The growth probably is characteristic of all parts of the body, including the skeletal, muscular, glandular and arterial systems. The evidence presented in this study indicates that children who mature early have higher pressures than the less precocious for several years before the onset of puberty.

Accordingly, he concluded the paper talking of the 'extravagant claims that have been made' about the rapidity and intensity of adolescent growth (p. 1330). As seen above, similar remarks were made by several authors such as Ellis or Topper and Mulier, and indeed most puberty and growth scientists of the first half of the 1900s. Such erroneous views, Richey asserted, resulted from the simple fact that pubertal changes were perceived as taking form within a relatively short period, especially in earlier maturing children.

Indeed, until the late 1800s, medicine had been unable to capture a timing of sexual growth whose realisation did not rely on the onset of menstruation, the growth of facial hair, mammary enlargement, and the like. That is to say, the conception of maturation depended on the visible, the stigmatic. Doctors simply couldn't *see* development, and sexual development most notably, extending beyond the age limits imposed by vision upon their clinical gaze.

From the 1910s onwards, to some extent, paediatric science dispensed with vision as an instrument for the surveillance of the abnormal and the pathological, which Foucault famously saw at work in the modern hospital and the panoptic prison. Henceforth, strictly speaking, it is no longer through the visible but rather the microscopic that sexual maturation is objectified, and its dangers substantiated, in paediatric discourse. 'Puberty', as Richey could now demonstrate, 'is established through a long period of development, the time required varying from ten to eighteen years' (p. 1330). The scientific advent of physiological age provided the doctor-family apparatus around young people with a new and more extensive technology of surveillance over their bodies and selves: a microscopic, molecular kind of panopticism.

In rethinking sexual-reproductive development in this way, paediatric researchers opened up the field to a whole new series of troubles. To start with, they reencountered – in a rather forceful manner – the very limits of their methods whenever there were measurements to be taken. The better the means of experimental control, the greater the awareness of the possibility for errors. Even more frustrating, in applying the complicated statistical techniques developed by such people as Galton and Boas, they kept finding that the regularity they needed so much to establish seemed, in most cases, harder and harder to demonstrate. In the end, leading specialists concurred, pubertal physiological phenomena were too irregular, too wide-ranging to be circumscribed within precise 'normal' limits. That was the practical conclusion of the metabolic studies reviewed above, for example, or Ellis's anthropometric project.

Alas, in discovering that development runs to its own rhythm and according to complex and unstable chemical balances, paediatric researchers also discovered the ethical dilemmas around the relationship between the management of risk and the decision to recommend therapy. Given that pubertal physiological imbalances or deviations from 'normal' values were medically suggested as natural and yet the *possible* indicators or triggers of disease, clinicians were in the delicate position of having to choose between promptly intervening or, instead, assuming the risk of not treating their patients.

For example, drawing on their results, Topper and Mulier (1932) argued for doctors to consider maturational signs when dealing with high metabolic rates in adolescent patients – particularly girls presenting overactivity of the thyroid gland, which in such cases, they stressed, was a non-pathological and passing condition.

From the viewpoint of Johnston's concerns, things looked somewhat different. Based on the study described above, he suggested that pubescence naturally entails changes in the normal metabolic balance which could debilitate the adolescent girl. In clinical practice, he cautioned, as doctors oftentimes observed that 'this physiologic tendency becomes pathologic', and given his and Moroney's recent findings 'on the relation of thyroid to the retention of calcium, it would seem logical not to dismiss these deviations expectantly but to treat them' (Johnston 1940: 287).

Ellis (1947: 282), in his turn, pointing to the temporal variation of pubescence, contended: 'Even a more general recognition of the physiological range of age of onset of puberty would avoid many normal boys receiving endocrine therapy unnecessarily'.

In one way or another, and motivated by different and sometimes even conflicting medical standpoints, these and other physicians pondered as to whether bodily correction was indicated. In other words, as we shall explore next, they raised a fundamental question that has been haunting pubertal medicine ever since: when is the clinician to intervene?

Children-to-be-corrected: new 'problems', new dilemmas

By the early 1910s, a Manchester physician gave 'A Note on Some Developmental Errors of Puberty'. The issue, he said, was not unfamiliar to clinicians, but it was still strikingly absent from medical textbooks. In that spirit, he maintained:

> It is clear that the [female reproductive] organs may be formed normally in utero, but that the changes which occur at puberty may be abnormal.
>
> There must, therefore, be developmental errors of puberty. The suggestion now made is that this should be recognized and taught. . . . The abnormality is generally on the side of under-development rather than on that of overgrowth; but there are cases of hypertrophy at puberty affecting, for example, the labia minora, the clitoris, and the breasts.
>
> (Fothergill 1912: 1121)

The medical discourse on bodily 'errors', as shown in the previous chapter, had been elaborated upon since Raciborski and others. Over the first half of the 20th century, such 'errors' were remade by a whole new network of experimental research methodologies and techniques of medical surveillance. A body appeared within this network that has since then been at the heart of virtually all concerns of paediatric science: the endocrinal body.

The rise of endocrinology and the death of child monstrosity

Endocrinology did not start off as a science concerned with development into maturity. Its birth was partly fuelled by the 'problem' of old age and chemical hopes of 'rejuvenation'. In 1889, French physiologist Brown-Séquard reported to his fellows of the Paris Biological Society on a game-changing experiment. He had injected himself with testicle extracts of guinea pigs and dogs. The effect, he proclaimed, was almost miraculous. At age 72, he promptly felt a boost in mental and bodily vigour. He attributed it 'to the action of an internal secretion', as T. E. Hammond (1926: 55) sceptically told the British Royal Society years later when speaking to the function of the testes at puberty.[12]

Indeed, 'organo-therapy' was a short-lived moment in clinical history. Nevertheless, it left its traces in puberty science. Reporting on his case of pubertal precocity in a 'female cretin', Wellesley Kendle (1905: 246) announced that the girl 'has now been on thyroid extract for six months, and has made immense progress'. Both her 'cretinism' and her sexual precocity, to the clinician's astonishment, were progressively disappearing. Fifteen years later, T. C. Graves (1920: 1134–5) indicated that a boy suffering from 'hystero-epilepsy, associated with delayed puberty, was . . . successfully treated with testicular extract'. But, although inclined to believe that 'a real psychotherapeutic effect' had taken place, he acknowledged: 'The therapeutic value by oral administration of extracts of organs having internal secretions (apart from the thyroid and pituitary) has been the subject of scepticism on the part of some pharmacologists, and at best they have been regarded as having only a psychotherapeutic value as placebos'. They were right.

Around 1900, Austrian physician Eugene Steinach staged his foundational experiments on sexual physiology. He was also in the business of rejuvenation; and, as Hammond (1926: 56) critically put it, 'Steinach considered that old age was due to lessened activity in the testes'. Yet, his vision went far beyond the 'cure' of ageing. As Anne Fausto-Sterling (see 2000: 158–69) beautifully shows, his work marks the birth of a hormonal theory of sex and gender differences. By then, many already believed that the so-called sex glands somehow contributed to those differences. Steinach took the stance even further: 'In Steinach's hands, hormones themselves acquired masculine and feminine characteristics. Sex became chemical, and body chemistry became sexed' (p. 158). In 1910, experimenting on rats and guinea pigs, Steinach found the 'sex-specific' hormonal power of the ovaries and testes. He called them 'the puberty glands'.[13]

Since then, via the so called 'sex hormones', all organs became connected to sex and gender truths on a molecular level, even organs with no sexual-reproductive roles.[14] Body hair, for example, came to be described as having a 'male' or a 'female distribution' according to an understanding of body hair growth based on hormonal chemistry. Overall, the endocrinological idea of 'sexual antagonism' gave rise to the medical invention of new sexual boundaries between and within subjects.[15] Such views necessarily had a momentous impact on modern paediatric science, especially where puberty was at stake. To start with, the old monstrosity framework of sexual precocity fell apart, as two reports by Ellis illustrate.

In the 1930s, before devoting himself to anthropometric studies, Ellis was clearly interested in clinical research on puberty, particularly conditions such as pubertal precocity and obesity. In 1934, on behalf of a colleague, he reported to the Royal Society on the case of a precocious pubescent boy aged 5. The examination record read:

> Pubic hair of female distribution is present, and the genitalia correspond to those of an adolescent boy of 14 or 15. No other abnormalities found. Prostatic massage produced a bead of prostatic fluid but there have been no emissions [of semen] or frequent erections. . . . Urine: Nothing abnormal found. . . . Skiagram of skull: No evidence of abnormality of pituitary or

> pineal glands. . . . The left adrenal gland was removed by the lumbar route, the patient making an uneventful recovery.
>
> (Ellis 1934: 1328)

Once the examination of the removed gland showed no tumour-like formation, and the skull no abnormality from radiological evidence (as the quote states), Ellis concluded by saying, 'at present the causation of the precocity remains obscure' (p. 1329). Indeed, after a century of clinical research and many surgical explorations, the condition remained puzzling. However, Ellis' report reflects an important changing moment in medical discourse. On a theoretical level, what used to be unnatural, the aberrant manifestation of maturity in a child, had become the product of chemical imbalances.

For Ellis and every physiologist, it was certain that it could be caused by tumours in such 'sexual' organs as the brain or the adrenals – or by something as yet inexplicable which, to their great embarrassment, did not seem pathological. On the level of power, we no longer find the authoritarian intimacy that 19th-century doctors had established with the precocious child's anatomy and behaviour. The monitoring of 'night emissions', erections, menses, or pubic hair growth, gave way to routine hospital practices such as prostatic massages and precise chemical measurements. The old vigilance of the child's 'prematurity', with all its moral inconveniences for both doctors and parents, was abandoned on behalf of a discursively ascetic clinical *protocol*.

In the following year, Ellis (1935: 1071–3) presented another case report, this time on a patient with 'Precocious Puberty and Pseudohermaphroditism'. 'D. B., aged 9 years, was brought up as a girl until three years old, and since then as a boy'. At age 4, the 'girl' had been observed to have a 'penis . . . of good size' as well as hair on the pubis and perineum. However, no testicles in the scrotum or inguinal canals were present. The child subsequently was hospitalised and 'the reconstruction of the urethra was completed by successive operations during the next eighteen months'. We learn from the discussion of the case that another fellow physician, Dr Cockayne, disapproved of the sex-assignment previously made. He had seen the child at age 6 'after the first plastic surgery, and had no hesitation in saying that she was a girl masculinized' due to abnormalities in the suprarenal cortex that he deemed congenital.

The patient's first physical signs of pubertal precocity came to be confirmed at age 8, when the 'boy' underwent a prematurely swift body development. To the doctor's gaze, however, this child's pubescence assumed peculiar traits:

> He has many feminine characteristics and interests. . . . His voice is unbroken, but is feminine rather than childish. . . . There is a little hair on the upper lip, and a considerable growth of hair in the axillae, and on the perineum and pubis, where it is beginning to assume the masculine distribution (fig. 2).
>
> (Ellis 1935: 1071, 1072)

The premature advent of puberty had come to confirm and reinforce the child's hermaphroditic condition, that is to say, the sexual antagonism found in both the body and the conduct of the 'boy'.

In short, this child embodied the undue mixture of maturity and immaturity as well as the confusion of the sexes. The clinician expressed this disconcerting confusion very clearly:

> The penis (? clitoris) [sic] is small for the degree of physical development; the reconstructed urethra reaches nearly to the base of the cleft glans. . . . The scrotum (? labia) is not pendulous, but is rugose. . . . Testicles are not present in canal or scrotum, but no uterus or ovaries can be palpated. No tumour is felt in either loin.
>
> (Ellis 1935: 1072)

The child was a 'pseudohermaphrodite' for, as Dr Frederick Parkes Weber put, 'true hermaphroditism' implied the presence of both testes and ovaries, the latter being absent in the 'boy'. Although there was no evidence of a pathological origin, we learn from the doctor's discussion that new surgical interventions were taken into careful consideration to confirm the diagnosis. However, Dr Cockayne pointed out, 'as it was too late to make her into a normal girl, it was thought better to do nothing except to make the hypertrophied clitoris more like a penis'. That is to say, the best was to surgically re-remake the 'boy' as *masculine* as possible.

This case is extremely interesting for various reasons. First, while showing the rare clinical encounter of the two great medical monsters of the 19th century in the same young body – the precocious and the hermaphroditic – it also shows that sexual monstrosity fragmented within the new physiological truth of the abnormal. Also, it documents a very important genealogical event: the history of pubertal precocity intertwines with the history of the intersex. Although Ellis and his colleagues had no theoretical framework underpinning it, a new practice around what came to be known as intersexuality was born. In a couple of decades, US paediatrician John Money would create the famous clinical protocol for the 'treatment' of intersexuality – internationally adopted until the present. It was premised on the rather 'social constructionist' theory that sex differences in behaviour were not predetermined by the biological sex and only started to engender at some point during infancy. From his perspective, it seemed reasonable to correct the 'ambiguous' genitalia of intersex infants as quickly as possible and educate them according to the assigned sex, making sure they conformed to the social expectations of masculinity and femininity. Money called these 'gender roles'.[16]

As to precocity, the pubescent child monster would just vanish completely in the following decade, as shown later in this chapter.

New subjects to correct (or not!)

As earlier argued, within the whole mystique around internal secretions, on the one hand, and experimental work on sexual chemistry, on the other, the endocrinal body emerged by the early 1900s. This chemically sexual body, as we now show, quickly became a central object in the practices and discourses of the modern paediatric science of that century, as well as one of its main technologies of power. However, the production and reproduction of that body from a paediatric viewpoint also brought a myriad of new problems into the field. We say 'problems' in a double sense. First, they refer to clinicians' problematisations of certain bodily phenomena which, although not deemed pathological in themselves, could somehow provoke sickness. Second, they refer to doctor's diagnostic dilemmas and ethical troubles in prescribing treatments for something that is an abnormality, an error, but not an illness. Confronted with a body physiologically unstable by nature, whose chemical behaviour is hard to predict, doctors engaged in a debate on the uses and abuses of their own correctional power upon the young.

One of those problems, and a most notable one in the first half of the 20th century, concerned 'undescended' or 'maldescended' testes at puberty, also known as cryptorchidism. In his 1939 address to the Section of Urology of the British Royal Society, Dr Poole Wilson offered a detailed and profusely illustrated paper on 'The Treatment of the Incompletely Descended Testis'. His stance is made clear from the start: 'Operative treatment may be safely carried out at any age after 3 years and should be completed before puberty. The optimum period is between 8 and 11 years' (Wilson 1939: 969). He also prescribed the new pharmaceutical technologies of correction, although far less enthusiastically than some of his peers: 'The use of gonadotrophic hormones as a means of inducing descent has also been introduced and far-reaching claims have been made for their efficiency' (p. 970). As to simply waiting for the testis to descend, he maintained:

> Cabot has whimsically described this method as "watchful waiting". For the attainment of full development it is probably essential the testis should be in the scrotum by the onset of puberty. Inasmuch as pubescent changes become apparent as early as 11 years this is the latest date to which "watchful waiting" can be safely carried out.
>
> (Wilson 1939: 973)

Otherwise, what were the risks of skipping treatment? 'The external genitalia in normal children and adults', he was careful to assert, 'show a wide range of development. Even so, if a large series of cryptorchids [i.e. boys with the condition] is observed, a small proportion of them will exhibit genitalia which are excessively diminutive. These children, in addition, commonly show either obesity, stunting of stature or other signs of hormonal deficiency'.

True, Wilson associated cryptorchidism with other endocrine-related conditions about which there was ongoing and often contentious discussion – namely obesity (see below). But, for a great part, and according to what most literature offered, the problems presented by an undescended testis were about shortness and genital size. The treatment was, in a word, cosmetic.[17]

Surgical interventions in the prepubertal years were a standard practice since the dawn of the century, starting with Bevan's description of his first operation. However, he noted that several professionals had recently published opposite views. One of them was another British physician, R. E. Smith (1939: 1), who in the same year argued as follows: 'At the present time, surgery and endocrine therapy are active lines of treatment. However, there is an increasing tendency to trust to spontaneous descent at puberty, and the object of this paper is to justify that policy in particular cases'. After almost a decade of observations, he remarked that in all the boys in whom the testes had eventually descended, 'the success would have been attributed to hormone therapy if they had received this treatment' (p. 12). The idea that 'operation was always necessary, as was generally taught and practised in my own medical school', should be abandoned (p. 3). Evoking the same endocrinal body that sustained Wilson's opinion, Smith contended: 'Puberty is in all probability a time when there is an excess of gonadotropic hormones circulating in the blood. . . . If this is so, then physicians should develop patience and avoid hormone as well as surgical treatment' (p. 12).

By then, as noted above, the link between obesity and sexual development had become an important medical issue. US paediatrician Frederic William Schlutz (1941) pondered, like most doctors did, 'What to Do about The Fat Child at Puberty'. He questioned the significance of hormonal factors in juvenile and adolescent obesity, and whether endocrine dysfunctions did play a main causative role:

> It is a popular conception among the lay public, especially educators, and a large part of our profession that they do. There is a growing conviction among those who have given much study to this problem that hormonal influences play a minor role in the development of obesity and have been overemphasized altogether too much.
>
> (Schlutz 1941: 376)

Rather than hormones, he suggested that overprotective mothering usually offered a better explanation in all the instances where organic degeneration or neoplastic changes were ruled out – which seemed to constitute the most cases.

In the same year, German-born paediatric psychiatrist Hilde Bruch complained as follows:

> In recent years there has been published a flood of enthusiastic reports about the remarkable results of glandular injections on the puberal [sic] development

> of obese children. Such reports seem to presuppose that without treatment no development, or only a delayed and abnormal one, would take place. Uncritical and without adequate controls, such reports are misleading.
>
> (Bruch 1941: 365)

Such interventions were generally prescribed under the premise that obesity in the young was caused by hypofunction of the thyroid or pituitary glands, which led to retardation of growth and sexual development. According to her findings, however, earlier pubescence 'is the rule for obese girls and is not uncommon for obese boys' (p. 373). Based on her sample of 200 cases as well as the recent growth data published by Boas and others, she concluded: 'Since obese children show acceleration rather than retardation of the growth processes, it is not logical to explain the obesity as resulting from deficient function of these glands. The need for endocrine therapy thus loses all factual support'; in the end, puberty 'will occur just as impressively if the patients are not subjected to long-continued, and exceedingly expensive, glandular treatment' (p. 374). Her remarks date from the early 1940s; but they could have been written by a host of paediatric researchers of the present (see Chapter 1).

Reviewing old monsters

By the mid-1940s, in a short article on 'Precocious Female Puberty' published in *The British Medical Journal* (1945: 268–9), an author contended:

> If every physician were first to say to himself: "It depends what you mean by 'precocious'", many an infant belly would remain unscarred. That there is a great variation in the time of onset of puberty among perfectly healthy girls is obvious. It is not so obvious at what stage it is justifiable to believe that the onset is early or late enough to warrant a search for a cause. Climate and race are certainly factors to be considered. . . . Are we justified in regarding as deviations from health even such extreme cases as that of Lina Medina, the Peruvian girl who began to menstruate at 7½ months and created a world's record by giving birth to a child when only 5 years and 8 months old?

From the outset, the doctor offered the same kind of problematisation illustrated above – i.e. in what circumstances and under which limits is the doctor to intervene on the abnormal. That is to say, just as many clinicians as well as medical statisticians, he questioned when abnormality is to become pathological.

But, as the second part of the quote shows, that was not all. While speaking to the absolutely exceptional, the author posed an older and equally fundamental medical problem, the answer to which would define the whole programme of contemporary sexual paediatrics. Bluntly put, the question was this: in view of our current knowledge, is medicine to keep regarding precocious pubescent children as monsters? Or better, aren't we now able to clearly separate abnormality from monstrosity on the basis of our medical theories and practices?

Since the dawn of that century (if not a few decades earlier), the same array of questions had been put – most notably in the fields of psychiatry and anthropometric psychology. Writing in Stanley Hall's journal, Lewis M. Terman (1905) articulated a similar critique:

> The general sense is that precocity means development in advance of some assumed norm. But as to what this norm should be, there is no agreement. Many who talk of precocity do not even realize that the assumption of some such norm is necessary. . . . To designate a quality or character as "abnormal" is, in the popular mind, to condemn it. Hence children of unusually rapid development have sometimes been called "monsters".
>
> (Terman 1905: 145, 147)

Furthermore, there was already a clear association of old developmental 'monstrosities' with the new pathological knowledge of the sexual-reproductive organs. In particular, the link between tumours and precocious puberty had been established. For instance, Terman referred to a case cited by Marro – an 'often quoted example' – concerning a 5-year-old boy found to suffer from a tumour in a testicle. Once it was removed, normality returned:

> By 9½ years he had acquired all the striking secondary sexual characters of mind and body which come with true puberty, even to the change of voice. On removal of the tumor, the voice became childish again and all the other marks of sexual maturity disappeared.
>
> (Terman 1905: 180)

In 1924, the doctors present at a meeting of the British Royal Society attempted to explain the perplexing puberty of a 3-year-old girl otherwise healthy according to the examination (Hutchison 1924: 8–9). They suspected that her condition was the effect of an ovarian steroid hypersecretion resulting from a tumour or a simple neoplasm in one of the ovaries. Hence, they all agreed, surgical exploration and treatment (i.e. laparotomy and unilateral ovariotomy) was the right decision. 'Unfortunately this procedure had been refused by the parents'. Within the 1920s–40s, in several other cases, clinicians indeed found that their patients' precocity was due to tumours or other abnormalities (e.g. hyperplasia) of the ovaries or the suprarenal cortex.[18] Dr Parkes Weber, perhaps inspired by early doctors' encounters with the child monster, called the latter condition '*infantile Hercules type* of suprarenal cortical tumour' (cf. Rodgers 1935: 38, our emphasis).

Weber was a frequent and chief voice in the discussions of reports on precocious puberty presented to the Royal Society in those decades.[19] In debating the above 1924 case, he already spoke of another type of pubertal precocity, 'the "pineal syndrome", which had also been called "macro-genito-somia praecox"' (cf. Hutchison 1924: 9). Given the enormous difficulty and risks of brain surgery in those years, it was only a bit later that physicians proved the link between pubertal precocity and tumours of the pineal gland and of the hypothalamus. Post-mortem analyses allowed for an early gaze. Speaking to the unsolvable case of a 3-year-old boy reported by T. S. Rodgers, one of his fellows entertained the likelihood of a pineal tumour and cited the following account:

> Two laparotomies had been performed [on a boy] and the adrenals had been found to be normal in size. At death, which was due to rheumatic endocarditis, the causative lesion of the pubertas praecox was found to be a tumour – the size of a pea and composed of nerve cells and fibres – in the region of the corpora mamillaria, pressing on the floor of the third ventricle.
>
> (Rodgers 1935: 661)

By the 1940s, the etiological types of pubertal precocity appeared clearly demarcated: 'pineal precocity' and 'hypophyseal precocity' – the latter caused by hypothalamic lesions affecting the hypophysis' hormonal activity – as opposed to the cases where the problem was found in the adrenals, defined as 'adreno-genitalism' or 'gonadal precocity' (see Lloyd, Lobotsky and Morley 1950). The 'premature puberty' of the 1800s was gone. Today's pathological classifications of 'precocious puberty' were born.

'Constitutional' precocity: the problematic of 'true' early development emerges

Needless to say, there were many unsolved questions about these conditions and experimental difficulties to overcome. In particular, despite the many important insights about the effects of brain steroid secretions on sexual growth, the relation of pineal and hypothalamic tumours to the precocious onset of pubescence could be demonstrated but not fully grasped:

> The causation of sexual precocity in 'pineal' tumours remains a physiological mystery, but the puzzle may be solved when the functions of the mid-brain are better understood and more information on neuro-endocrine linkage is available.
>
> (Neale 1938: 247)

> In the present state of knowledge it is exceedingly difficult to answer the question, how a tumor of the hypothalamus can produce an acceleration of body growth and genital development . . . presumably by increased secretion of gonadotropic and somatotropic hormones [by the hypophysis].
>
> (Stotijn and Nauta 1950: 220)

Even more troubling for the medical mind, there was a significant proportion of patients – even infants – in whom no tumours or malign neoplastic formations were found. That seemed to be the case of a 12-month-old girl seen by Ellis (1937: 13–14). In discussing the report, Dr Parkes Weber, who was not the catchiest name-giver, proposed that such instances 'should be termed "macrogenitosomia in females, without virilism and with precocious menstruation"'. Yet, despite no evidence of pathology, he pondered the presence of an ovarian granulosa-cell tumour. Indeed, a follicular cyst was later found and removed but its examination showed 'no definite tumour'.

As early as in 1932, in his volume on *Die Pubertät*, physiologist Rudolf Neurath talked of a 'genuine, primary, or constitutional' type of pubertal precocity (cf. Uddenberg 1944: 310). Besides the Swedish paediatrician quoted here, nobody else seems to have noticed it, or explored the hypothesis more thoroughly. As Gunborg Uddenberg argued in 1944, it was 'for the time being *terra incognita*' (p. 311, italics in original). Clinical engagements with the condition were still fairly focused on the pathological. In that same year, however, a game-changing event took place.

US paediatrician Emil Novak (1944), a colleague of John Money at the Johns Hopkins Hospital, found that in 60,000 gynaecologic admissions to that institution over 60 years, only one instance of precocity due to a granulosa-cell tumour had been recorded. Also, he found no cases in which the condition was demonstrably associated with a tumour of the pituitary. Unlike what clinical observation and practice suggested in its drift towards pathological causes, Novak demonstrated that the vast majority of precocious pubescent girls were not cases of ill health. Like Neurath, he called this type 'constitutional'. The news spread in no time:

> The constitutional element is one which has been neglected by many workers. . . . It seems impossible to escape the conclusion that the response of a girl's tissues to oestrogenic stimulation is, as Novak has put it, part of "an underlying foreordained sex pattern innate in the human mechanism and having its source in the chromosomes themselves." If this is so we must expect to find wide variations in the age of onset of puberty in the absence of any discoverable endocrine cause.
>
> (*The British Medical Journal* 1945: 268)

A flurry of clinical reports and reviews mentioning or focusing on Novak's new classification resulted. By the end of that decade, US paediatrician Lyman W. Mason introduced his study on the subject as follows:

> The cases presented herewith emphasize what has been expressed by several others, and particularly stressed by Novak, that, except for the relatively rare instance, precocious puberty in the female is just what the name would imply, i.e., the development of pubertal changes *at an earlier*

> *time than usual, these changes being based upon the same physiologic processes in the various endocrine glands as are at work during puberty which occurs at the usual time.*
>
> (Mason 1949: 730, our emphasis)

As Mason so clearly expresses, medicine had finally discovered that 'normal' and 'abnormal' pubescent children shared precisely the same physiological mechanisms, having only different maturational timings. From Novak onwards, the study of precocious puberty became, quite simply, the study of puberty itself. The whole contemporary problematic of 'early puberty' was set.

Novak is for puberty science what Money is in the history of gender: both of them killed the old medical sexual monsters. But, like Money did with intersexuality, Novak opened up his field to a new series of medical encounters with abnormality in the child. Hereafter, there is no longer the need to tell the monstrous from the abnormal, for Novak demonstrated that there is no monstrosity whatsoever. Now, the fundamental problem confronting paediatric science about pubertal timing concerns a border that is far more subtle, slippery, and troublesome to establish for both diagnostic and theoretical reasons: when normality stops and abnormality begins. The dispute is still ongoing today (see Chapter 1 and Conclusion).

Jørgen Flamand Christensen (1947), following in Novak's footsteps, offered a review of the different aetiologies of the condition as well as his own 'Account of a Case of the Constitutional Type in a Three-Year-Old Girl'. He spoke to the latter classification as follows:

> [T]he condition is called an abnormality rather than a disease [given that] . . . the children, except for their abnormal development, thrive as normal individuals, without morbid symptoms and with normal duration of life. . . . The rapid growth stops, however, at the age of 10 or 11 years, and such 'giant children' become short as adults. . . . Novak is of the opinion that this type, which he designates 'constitutional', is the most common type of pubertas praecox . . . Novak agrees with Feydit in that the 'child-mothers' who are sometimes mentioned as freaks in the older literature, belong to this type.
>
> (Christensen 1947: 168–9)

The 'gigantic' child that medicine had construed in the 18th and 19th centuries (see Chapter 2) re-emerged in Christensen's discourse only to become both a natural and an abnormal little child, statistically found to have a much greater frequency than formerly supposed. As his statements also illustrate, the 'problem' of early pubescent girls' shortness (due to the early maturation of the skeleton), as presently asserted in paediatrics, took form following Novak's views. Christensen did not spend any time on the matter of final height. But, to be fair, GnRH analogue-based treatment was several decades away and doctors could do nothing about the issue (see the following chapter). Rather, he emphasised that 'the psychic habitus of such children often bears the empress of their *anomaly*, some of them being sexually aggressive, a condition which naturally is dangerous in a child whose somatic development is that of an adult, but whose psychic development and experience, although being good for her age, does not correspond to her appearance at all' (p. 171, our emphasis). Similar views were expressed, after Novak's findings, in *The British Medical Journal* (1945: 269):

> The prognosis of the constitutional type of precocity is good. The girls grow into normal adults, except for a tendency to stunting of the long bones due to early union of the epiphyses. Their psychological management may be difficult, and it must be remembered that they ovulate and may, like the young girl of Peru, become pregnant.

While alarmingly suggesting the risk of very early pregnancies, none of the above authors explicitly posed the obvious and overwhelmingly distressing possibility of child sexual abuse in such instances. In a case discussion, however, one of Ellis' fellows of the Royal Society raised the issue: 'Dr. T. D. Rolleston emphasized the liability of cases of precocious puberty to precocious maternity and alluded to a case . . . of a girl aged 3 years "who was gradually deflowered by a friend of the house" and gave birth to a normal child at the age of 7 years' (Ellis 1937: 14).

In view of this set of behavioural and social risks raised by the 'constitutional' discourse of precocity, that is to say, by the early or very early developing child, what could the doctor and the parent do? Speaking to his own case, Christensen (1947: 171–2) argued:

> This girl, fortunately, has a home which is capable of lending her adequate protection and guidance through the difficult and trying years until the other children of her age catch up with her, and one can only hope that she will be able, when grown up, to lead a normal life in spite of having had no normal childhood.

Rather than unnatural, to sum up, precocious puberty became a completely natural 'anomaly'. As such, however, it was deemed a hazard to the patient, her family, and the social body. Any early developing child, especially a young girl, could grow into a deviant or maladjusted adult, unable 'to lead a normal life' – in short, a moral monster. Henceforth, the mixture of maturity and immaturity no longer entails a biological monstrosity but rather the risk of dysfunctional, even monstrous behaviours provoked by a precocious body, waiting to manifest themselves in the child and even those around her. By then, as Christensen's 'clinical' advice suggests, the only remedy available to prevent such dangers was, in a word, pedagogy. Parents, as shown throughout this chapter, were certainly supported by a completely new medical apparatus of surveillance. But, for the time being, it all came down to psychosocial management starting at home and the school.

In a few decades, however, clinicians would actually be intervening upon early maturing bodies for *possible* health problems. In other words, it wouldn't take too long for paediatric medicine to diagnose and treat its patients, not for sickness, not even for present disorders, but rather for risk and risk alone. That will be the story of our concluding chapter.

Notes

1 Galton came up with the method in his first biometric studies of growth, and more particularly the natural inheritance of *tallness*. For a discussion of his statistical work and inventiveness, see Hacking (1990).
2 His reasoning, as Tanner (cf. 1981a: 195) points out, suggests that he didn't interpret the curves cross-sectionally but rather as if they represented longitudinal data.
3 Tanner (1981a) offers an excellent and passionate description of Boas' statistical endeavour. For a discussion of Boas' important dispute of scientific racist arguments on genetics and the brain, see Stepan (1982).
4 See Tanner (1981a: 223–8) for an overview of Godin's work. For a detailed description of his methodology and aims, see Godin (1920).
5 Years later, when Boas had popularised the notion of physiological age, Godin (1920: 21) talked of 'the somatic individuality of the child'.
6 By then, he had already undertaken (during the winter of 1944–5) his study on the growth of Belgian children during and after the German occupation (see Ellis 1945).
7 By 'puberty', Ellis (1947: 273) basically meant the period from the first appearance of the secondary sex characters to the onset of ovulation or spermatogenesis, when 'adolescence' started its march towards full physical and reproductive maturity.
8 It shows two percentage lines, one for the 'non-pubescent' (i.e. those right before puberty) and another for the 'non-adolescent' (i.e. those right before adolescence) in each year of age (from 9 to 18). In between them one can see the variable length of the pubescent period started at different ages represented by a darkened area.
9 'By "basal metabolism" is meant the minimum metabolism necessary to maintain life with the patient at complete muscular repose, and, if possible, without any food in the stomach. It was impossible, however, to study the younger patients without food' (Talbot 1919: 229).
10 Years later, after reviewing all epidemiological data on the matter available by then, Japanese physician Itsiro Nakagawa (1937: 992) wrote: 'The question of metabolism just prior to and just after puberty has not yet been settled'. Based on a sample of 24 children and a methodology similar to that of Topper and Mulier – the only existing short-term longitudinal study of the matter – Nakagawa corroborated their general conclusion: 'The increase in the total heat production is one of the many physiologic manifestations of pubescence and probably occurs in preparation for the physical changes at puberty' (p. 999).
11 Despite drawing on a kind of scientific racism that was still trendy in medical research during those years, he quickly came to the conclusion he had nothing to say about race differences based on his data. It goes without saying, like many around that time, he conceived of a 'Jewish race' which did not include his notion of 'whiteness'.
12 As Hammond (1926: 55) remarked joining the critical chorus, 'it is obvious that suggestion played a large part in his experience, since these results have not been obtained by others'.

13 By the mid-1920s, the existence and possible action of a testicular internal secretion, still referred to by some as the 'puberty gland', was still in dispute (see, for example, *The British Medical Journal* 1924).
14 For an outstanding archival history of 'sex hormones', see Nelly Oudshoorn (1994). Also, see Fausto-Sterling (2000: 146–205).
15 On the basis of this framework, the constructionist character of 'sex' and 'gender' inescapably announced itself: against his own ideology, quite paradoxically, Steinach's experiments also showed that sexual differences could be literally engendered.
16 For histories and compelling critiques of the medical construction and management of intersexuality, see, for example, Fausto-Sterling (1993, 1995, 2000: 30–114), Bernice Hausman (1995: 72–109), and Susan Kessler (1990, 1998).
17 We are saying nothing he didn't incidentally suggest himself: 'Most of the investigations following orchidopexy have commented *only* on the position and subsequent development of the testes and for these there is no doubt that cosmetic results may be perfect. The occurrence of spermatogenesis is, however, the crucial test' (Wilson 1939: 972, our emphasis).
18 Such cases are documented, for example, in Gunborg Uddenberg's (1944) clinical review article 'On Pubertas Praecox'.
19 He published a trifling book called *Endocrine Tumours, and Other Essays* in 1936, on which a reviewer from *The Journal of the American Medical Association* (1936: 2259) commented: 'Any one interested in endocrine tumors should not be misled by the title, for a discussion of this subject occupies but thirty pages in the book and contains nothing new or worth while. . . . This book should have been distributed privately to the author's sympathetic friends'.

Chapter 9

Conclusion

Puberty in crisis

Beginning with the problematic of sexual-reproductive precocity, modern puberty science took shape along two main interweaving lines of transformation. Initiated at the dawn of the 1800s, the first movement was the shift from the monstrous to the abnormal individual in medical discourses on pubertal prematurity. Starting a little later, the second movement encompasses the insertion of puberty's power-knowledge into the modern government of populations: from the control of the few to the surveillance of all. True, the clinical assessment and management of disorder and disease, on the one hand, and the epidemiological techniques of risk prevention, on the other, follow different rationalities and historical conditions. However, from the 1830s–40s onwards, these two forms of medical reasoning have constantly interacted with each other in pubertal medicine, either in pubertal growth statistics or in clinicians' encounters with young patients. Henceforth, puberty progressively moved from being a state of health into being a 'state of risk'.

In our concluding chapter, while briefly redrawing these lines, we start by reviewing clinical and epidemiological constructions of pubescent children as subjects 'at risk' and 'to-be-corrected' up to the 1940s. Then, we resume the genealogy where we left it (i.e. 1950), focusing on Tanner's momentous contributions to the field. First, we look into the ways in which the so-called Tanner Scale of pubertal development was constructed and put to work. Our focus here is on how Tanner and associates took the theoretical and technical question of growth and maturational standards further, inviting anthropometric vigilance into the clinic more forcefully than ever before. Second, we engage with Tanner's statistical construction of a downward secular trend in pubertal timing since the 19th century, showing how his invention allowed for a whole scholarship to develop around it, and for a new discourse to emerge: puberty itself is going through a crisis! Finally, going back to Novak's 'constitutional' precocity, we trace the emergence of today's clinical corrective technology of early development. According to its current politics, healthy children should be submitted to treatments as a form of risk prevention. After discussing the ethical and epistemic complications fuelling the ongoing crisis of puberty science, we conclude with a reflection on our present as construed in paediatric and epidemiologic discourses on pubertal timing.

Catching up: from monsters, to abnormals, to everyone else

We ended Chapter 6 with Whitehead's (1848a) statistics on the age of menarche in different social classes in Britain. His work, as we argued, marks the birth of an epidemiological conception of risk in pubertal medicine: in no class or profession was there pubescence without some incidence of disease. Yet, he saw no direct clinical use for his results:

> It is not presumed that the facts now stated are susceptible of any very important practical application, as regards the treatment of disease. In a statistical point of view, however, they may be considered as not devoid of interest, especially as being a means of directing attention to any particular branch of labour which is proved to be less salubrious than another, and thus leading to the adoption of measures calculated to mitigate its injurious tendency.
>
> (Whitehead 1848a: 90)

Unlike the seminal works of Roberton (published between 1830 and 1850), Boismont (1842), or Raciborski (1844), Whitehead's statistical discourse rendered puberty inescapably risky to health. But, in the end, all these medical researchers aimed at some kind of socio-political intervention. Whitehead focused on factory employment and the sanitary conditions of the working classes; Roberton, fuelled by a new scientific racism and an ethnocentric style of social justice, pushed for colonial reforms; Boismont and Raciborski, based on their tabulated modes and means, problematised the medical and societal effects of industrialisation and the new cosmopolitan lifestyles.

On the clinical side, doctors were finding that the 'real' dangers concerning pubertal child monsters were behavioural rather than biological. From old medical mythologies to early 1800s textbooks, these little 'giants' figured as basically doomed to a very short life; their remarkable bodies proclaimed a premature death. By the 1820s–30s, clinical encounters with such children raised a new set of problems, all of which spoke to the notion of sexual instincts and impulsive conduct. Here, thus, the question was not merely about the patients' survival towards a healthy adulthood, but also whether they would conform to a reproductive and morally sound maturity.

As soon as the precocious onset of sexual behaviour was pondered in early clinical accounts on the condition, two distinctively gendered problematics appeared. In boys, there was the risk of onanism and involuntary losses of semen with all their fabulous consequences for the child's physical and moral health. In girls, far more disquieting than the peculiar manifestations of 'modesty', or even masturbation, there was the monstrous prospect of "children giving birth to children". As shown in Chapter 8, the sexual instincts and their intrinsic troubles provided one of the most successful technologies for the paediatric production of 'risk' until well into the 20th century.

Towards the mid-1800s, in short, family doctors rediscovered the little biological monster as a child prone to behavioural monstrosities. At the same time, the new statisticians of puberty correlated early maturation with sociocultural settings of 'monstrous' or 'evil' consequences. Roberton and several colonial doctors saw these in the traditional Hindu marital systems. Boismont, Raciborski, and Whitehead spoke with equal fervour about the horribly sexualising education of girls in the big cities, especially among the middle and upper classes.

Crises, corrections, and the 'normal' body

In the 1800s, 'abnormal' pubescent bodies were already submitted to normalising treatments. With Raciborski's (1844) clinical programme for the 'crisis' of puberty, female onanism could be clinically 'fixed': "just provide me with a lancet", he would say. Less than a century later, physicians said the same about pubescent boys' 'undescended' testicles and the genitalia of intersex children. Yet, when treating either early or very early instances of puberty, clinicians could only prescribe parental scrutiny and some form of pedagogical rectification when necessary. As for the correction of the precocious body, doctors would remain powerless for some time.

Until late in the 19th century, in short, two rather different frameworks coexisted within the clinical apparatus of pubertal precocity. The framework of monstrosity functioned through the old power of pathology and dealt with the insurmountable impossibility of curing the unnatural. The framework of behavioural abnormality conveyed the newer rationality of the instincts, hence allowing for the normalisation of precocious pubescent children's attitudes and imaginations. But, in the end, neither of these technologies of power – monstrosity and abnormality – could call for techniques of correction and surveillance other than parental control and school education.

While there were no treatments to offer to these children's parents, puberty's surveillance was enhanced and standardised. Over the last quarter of the 19th century, the relationship of sexual maturation and physical growth became established in anthropometric research, and more exactly in the bodies of many working, school, and institutionalised children. With this encounter, the 'crisis' of puberty – one of the most successful technologies of risk in medical history – was recoded and its power amplified. On the basis of growth 'acceleration' and 'imbalance', from Key in the 1870s to Christopher around 1900, scientists asserted that puberty was dangerous in and of itself. 'Pubertal morbidity' became a mathematical reality.

Such views circulated widely in clinical arenas, promptly translating into gendered anxieties about the 'stormy' ages of adolescence, as shown in Chapter 7. Similar concerns rose from within the asylum (e.g. Clouston 1890) and, later on, within the psychiatric ward for delinquent boys (e.g. Curran 1939). Ultimately, by the 1940s, pubertal development figured in mainstream journals of general and mental medicine as something for parents and educators to take very seriously: without proper 'attachments' and continual care, socially offensive and criminal conduct (e.g. homosexuality) were to be expected with the arrival of puberty.

Alongside the medical formulation of the puberty-as-crisis discourse, the normal pubertal body was also taking shape in medical sciences. By the late 1800s, Bowditch produced the first charts applicable to clinical growth surveillance in reference to a 'normal' population: in a word, to be used as standards. While clearly pointing to a growth spurt, he failed to understand its chronological relation with the tempo of maturation itself. Boas promptly saw Bowditch's methodological problem (see Chapter 8), subsequently demonstrating the role of 'physiological age' in growth measurements as well as the importance of producing them longitudinally rather than cross-sectionally.

The quest for clinical standards had begun. By the 1920s, auxologists tentatively proposed pubertal growth norms (e.g. weight-for-height) while acknowledging the inevitable variations existing between their standards and those offered by other authorities (see, for example, Veeder and Rholfing 1927). Like Pagliani or Bowditch in the 1870s–80s, measurers continued staging their data collections in schools as well as institutions for disadvantaged young people. They usually found in both cases accessible 'clinical material', as often put in those days, besides optimal experimental conditions.

In 1937, for example, following Boas' maturational-longitudinal framework, Dr Gustav Nylin outlined the 'normal' sequence of the onset of pubertal characteristics in pubescent girls. The 12 research participants are described as follows: 'They were inmates for the State Institute for the Blind . . . and were most of them suffering from congenital eye defects, but they were chosen because their physical and psychical status was otherwise as nearly as possible normal' (*The Lancet* 1936: 269). For several decades, youth institutions would continue being the main sites for puberty and growth scientists to stage their research endeavours, as we shall see in this chapter.

New technologies, new dilemmas

By the 1930s, the notion of physiological age infused the standpoints and methodologies of most anthropometric and physiological attempts to standardise the pubertal body, allowing for a new intricated network of physical and molecular measurements. That network provided parents with a different kind of technology of child surveillance, which conveniently dispensed with the difficulties and moral embarrassments of the old expert examinations and domestic control schemas concerning sexual precocity.[1] At the same time, however, that new network of knowledge also troubled the notion of normalness itself, hence raising a new set of dilemmas for the physician and the auxologist to deal with.

In the 1930s, Richard Ellis witnessed the embarrassing medical difficulties of correcting the 'hermaphroditic' genitalia of a precocious pubescent 'boy' (formerly a 'girl', before a set of surgical procedures were performed). In several other cases, he was also confronted with the task of reasoning and treating the seemingly healthy precocious pubescent body. In the 1940s, Novak illuminated what puberty science had hitherto neglected: the most frequent type of precocity is not pathological; it is 'constitutional'. With no tumour or neoplasm to remove, those children – mostly girls – were prescribed careful psychosocial management, especially during the first school years (i.e. until the bodily differences between the precocious and the 'normal' children started disappearing with arrival of the pubertal years).

During that decade, Ellis changed gears and joined the anthropometric run for pubertal and adolescent growth standards. Along the way, he graded the sexual maturation of a few hundred male and female schoolchildren in Britain and Nigeria (see Chapter 6). In 1950, he published their mean and median ages of puberty onset (also quoting the British school data recently given by a couple of authors). On average, neither the boys nor the girls of the Nigerian series developed earlier than their British contemporaries. The results were clearly unsupportive of the old medical belief, still in dispute by then, that children reached puberty earlier in the 'Tropics'.

As late as 1947–8, Ellis still argued for the general recognition that 'normal' pubescence takes shape within a wide-ranging period, according to each child's 'physiological' timing. Acknowledging it in clinical settings, as quoted in Chapter 9, 'would avoid many normal boys receiving endocrine therapy unnecessarily. This is particularly true of fat boys', he added, 'who are too frequently diagnosed as suffering from adiposogenital dystrophy, when the obesity is primarily exogenous and when puberty will occur normally without adventitious aid' (Ellis 1947: 282). Hilde Bruch (1941), as also shown in Chapter 9, similarly worried about hormonal treatments for obesity being overprescribed to adolescent girls.

Ellis also argued that the introduction of some simple maturity-grading system in routine medical examinations would permit the formulation of more accurate and sensible norms for clinical and academic use. In other words, he envisioned standards against which the patient could be assessed not only in terms of size – as in the traditional cross-sectionally derived charts – but also as to the rate of growth. Ellis was neither a longitudinal measurer nor a statistical genius, nor was he in love with anthropometry; he probably didn't realise the technical complexity of creating the type of standards for which he aimed. He never saw his clinical dream come true, dying in 1966, precisely the year when such standards were published for the first time by Tanner and colleagues.

Standards and bio-history (according to Tanner)

By the mid-20th century, Tanner's brilliant academic career had taken off. In 1952, Tanner reviewed the two main strategies used in constructing growth curves – i.e. the centile and standard deviation systems – and the types of standards that one can achieve with them, namely for the size (or distance) and tempo (or velocity) of growth. In resetting the whole question concerning the uses and limits of standards, he promptly pointed to the anthropometric and clinical conundrums of defining 'abnormal':

> The point of any standard of whatever sort is to enable the physician, nurse or whoever it may be to give at least a tentative answer to the question, 'Is this child abnormal?' If the answer is no, the anxious mother is reassured; if yes, further steps are taken to eradicate or minimize the abnormality, and to remove, if possible, its source. But this question is not quite as simple as may appear at first sight. . . . In practice we usually do not know the distribution of the unhealthy population and we lay down arbitrary 'limits of normality'. It is essential to recognize that these are arbitrary, and to understand what they imply.
>
> (Tanner 1952: 11)

Here, announcing his auxological proficiency to the world, he systematised the foundational theoretical framework of contemporary growth standards. Following D'Arcy Thomson, he insisted on the need for velocity standards.[2] He just couldn't as yet overcome the computational troubles brought by the spurt into the precise construction of velocity centile curves. Three decades later, in his history of growth science, Tanner (1981a: 395) spoke to this event (and himself) as follows: 'The true nature of what was necessary seems only to have dawned on him several years later, perhaps because of rereading Boas' papers for his contribution to the Boas centennial volume (Tanner 1959)'.

Bluntly put, the curves had to be constructed in such way so as to show 'individual' growth velocity at all ages – even if 'individual' corresponds to an average – rather than the mean yearly increments of a population as obtained through the conventional cross-sectional system. Hence, the curves should be drawn from longitudinal data and, as Boas had recommended, individually aligned by the point of peak growth velocity at puberty (be it the curves for height, chest circumference, or other measurements). By the mid-1960s, Tanner, Whitehouse, and Takaishi (1966) introduced a set of such curves for height and weight at adolescence in the British population. These 'longitudinal-type standards' (Tanner 1981a: 329) were the first major output of the famous Harpenden Growth Study.

Staging the Scale

In the 1960s, Tanner's research project at the Harpenden Children's Home became a well-established powerhouse of growth and maturational norms. The enterprise had started in 1948 in collaboration with Reginald H. Whitehouse, 'a man with a military training as background' (Tanner 1981a: 225). The Harpenden Growth Study ended in 1971. During the years of 1949–70,

260 girls and 450 boys were routinely measured, 85 boys and 48 girls over 10 or more years. Starting between ages 3 and 4, the measurements were taken every six months as a rule, and every three months during the pubertal years. Tanner was the architect, Whitehouse the data collector.[3]

> Height, sitting height, hip, shoulder, elbow and knee widths, circumferences of upper arms, calf and thigh, foot length, weight and four skinfolds were taken. Every measurement on every child on every occasion was done by Whitehouse, a robust man.
>
> (Tanner 1981a: 350)

In total, as Tanner (cf. 225) proudly wrote, Whitehouse took 15 measurements on about 9,000 'child-occasions'. These encounters also included taking photogrammetric pictures of children's naked bodies and radiological data collection. Finally, ratings were given for the shape and size of penises and testicles, or breasts in girls' case, and pubic hair. The examinations involved palpation techniques but also paraphernalia such as the skinfold calliper (to measure the thickness of skinfolds) and the orchidometer (to measure testicular volume).[4] All ratings were conducted by Tanner.

Besides providing the longitudinal data for the growth standards mentioned above, the Harpenden research also allowed for the construction of the famous Tanner Scale (or Staging). The Scale comprises 'pictorial standards' (Tanner 1981a: 354) for the rating of breast, male genitalia, and pubic hair growth, each of these being graphically displayed in a five-stage sequence – from Tanner Stage 1 to 5, as frequently termed nowadays. Proposed by Tanner in 1962, it became an internationally adopted tool in paediatric practice and research.[5] Later in that decade, in collaboration with experimental physiologist W. A. Marshall, Tanner used the Harpenden data on 228 boys and 192 girls 'to define the range of variation seen in the development of pubic hair, genitalia and breasts' (Tanner 1981a: 354). This led to their well-known publication of pubertal standards, showing significant variation within 'normal' sequences and stages of development (Marshall and Tanner 1969, 1970).

Together with illustrations of the pictorial standards used for ratings – composed of real photographs by then – Tanner and Marshall offered a number of diagrams showing the 'normal' temporal ranges for the onset and unfolding of pubertal changes. The results demonstrated that children undergo each pubertal sequence at different ages and complete each sequence at different speeds. As their studies also illustrated, such standards permitted the testing of temporal links between a particular maturational event or sequence (e.g. menarche or breast enlargement) and adolescent growth phenomena (e.g. acceleration in height velocity).

In delimiting 'the extent of normal individual variation in the events of puberty' (Marshall and Tanner 1970: 14), they incidentally uncovered a multiplicity of growth-maturational patterns in 'normal' developing bodies. From an auxological angle, 'normal' sexual maturation had never looked so complex, and thus so hard to standardise. Paradoxically, 'normal' ages and sequences of pubertal development had never been so tangible, precise, and implicitly *desirable*. The statistical results drawn from the Harpenden data were widely adopted as a reference for clinical practice, and their usefulness only recently challenged in the paediatric field (see Chapter 1).

Tanner was a passionate scholar of great academic ingenuity. But he embodied the spirit, and uncritically inherited the methodological rationale, of a truly *modern* auxologist, that is to say, of a late 1800s growth scientist. Without second thoughts, and with no obligatory research consent existing when his study started, he recruited a substantial number of institutionalised children – orphan, abandoned, or otherwise vulnerable. After having followed these children's physical development for a record-deserving period of time, he couldn't hide some jealousy concerning the 123 measurements made by Godin himself on 'about 1,000 boy-occasions', but 'at least Whitehouse had time to put down his instruments' (Tanner 1981a: 225). Indeed, alongside Galton and Boas, Godin was one of Tanner's greatest heroes, 'a man after the heart of anyone who has personally undertaken longitudinal studies on children' (p. 224). Tanner was clearly a most knowledgeable child measurer when it came to genetic or endocrinal mechanisms; but his 'heart' still belonged to Galton's biometrics.

Perhaps his most creative (and controversial) contribution to puberty science was none of the above. In the 1960s, Tanner came up with technology which, in the history of puberty science, was as successful as his Scale: the famous 'Trend towards Earlier Physical Maturation' (Tanner 1965; see also 1962). Though both have continually shaped experiences of 'the human body' and infused the social worlds constructed around it, they were founded by two different *personae*, as it were, or upon two distinctive rationalities. The Scale was made by Tanner, the growth scientist with a clinical mission; the Trend was championed by Tanner, the medical historian with an epidemiological agenda.

Staging the Trend

In October 1964, the British Eugenics Society held a symposium on *Biological Aspects of Social Problems* at the College University, London, where Tanner (1965: 49) delivered a paper on a 'trend towards earlier maturing during the last hundred years'.[6] He had gathered all the historical sources on menarcheal ages available to him, the data being from Denmark, Finland, Germany, Great Britain, Norway, Sweden, and the US. For each country, he calculated the median age of menarche for all calendar years that could be estimated using each national data-series. The data were somewhat meagre: for example, there were no 1800s samples for the US. Also, many of the collections were biased or unsound (by Tanner's own standards), and the overall data only permitted him to cover relatively sparse points over time. He anyway found it sufficient to make his case for the trend, which he depicted in a suggestive diagram. It showed one line per country descending across averaged points, each time indicating a significant fall in the median age. Curiously, he included none of the 1800s British samples in the graph; the line for Britain only start in the 20th century, just like the US line.[7]

'Most of the pre-1920 data', he cautiously acknowledged, 'concern hospital patients, who may be a biased sample of the population at large. Worse, these data concern entirely . . . the age at which menarche was remembered to have occurred by women interrogated five, ten or even twenty years after the event' (p. 50). Furthermore, since many of the 1800s authors didn't indicate the ages of the women at the time of inquiries, Tanner couldn't know the exact calendar years when the first menstruations had occurred in such cases. Therefore, he could but give an approximate estimation of an average year corresponding to a median age of menarche.[8]

Yet, in the same breath, he described the data as 'impressively consistent' and proceeded to state: 'Evidently menarche in Europe has been getting earlier during the last hundred years by between three and four months per decade' (p. 50). The trend, he argued, seemed consistent with Norwegian growth statistics on boys suggesting a fall in the average age of the adolescent spurt from 1825 to the 1930s (cf. 48). As for causes, notwithstanding genetic influences, he hypothesised that the trend essentially reflected the increasing improvement of socioeconomic conditions over time, most notably nutrition, especially among the less privileged populations of the industrialised world.[9]

A few months later, *The Sociological Review* published a scholarly critique of the eugenics symposium in which Tanner's contribution was described in the following terms: 'His attempt . . . to deduce the historical timing of the menarche from meagre literary evidence and his consequent bland statement that "it seems fairly likely then that in the towns of Europe the rate of maturation was slowed down during the late eighteenth and early nineteenth centuries" should not appear in a scientific publication' (Baines 1966: 96). The methodological issues of Tanner's argument were seldom noticed, though, and the 'trend' was happily established as a fact.

This 'fact' led the author of an excellent historical monograph on medical views of young people's masturbation in the 1800s to propose an absurd hypothesis: the rise of anti-masturbation campaigns in that century 'was in part a confused response to the earlier onset of puberty in Western Europe' (Neuman 1975: 1). The insight seemed supported by 'some evidence of a decline in the age of menarche and the onset of puberty since at least the 1840s' – as suggested in Tanner's 1965 paper, cited by the author (p. 6). Clearly, Neuman didn't think his logic through: in the 19th century, no doctor or parent could have noticed a 'decline in the age of menarche', something retrospectively estimated only in the following century. There was, of course, a whole host of fabulous fears concerning sexual development in the 1800s. But the problem of age 'decline' was not as yet one of them. The 'trend' and accompanying diagram would be reiterated until the 1970s (e.g. Tanner 1973; Eveleth and Tanner

1976), subsequently inciting to a stream of citations, follow-ups, corrections, and more academic contestation.

Troubling the Trend

One of Tanner's main sources covering the 19th century (all of which were from Europe) was hospital data for Norway. They gave median ages of menarche of about 17 and 16 years in 1844 and 1881, respectively, the ages then falling to slightly over 14 in 1928 and slightly over 13 in 1952.

In 1976, after re-examining those data, two Norwegian scholars concluded 'that there was no fall at all during the nineteenth century, and that the age at menarche was constant at approximately 16.0 years for the lower social classes throughout this period. It is also suggested that the age at menarche was constant at approximately 14 years for the higher social classes' (Brundtland and Walløe 1976: 363, abstract). Their results did indicate a sudden fall, but only starting in the early 1900s, which they attributed to the betterment of nutrition. Thus, their analysis contradicted 'Tanner's hypothesis of a steady fall. Preliminary investigations have convinced us that similar hypotheses also are supported by the historical sources for all the other Scandinavian countries' (p. 372).

Within the following few years, a new and extensive volume of medical records was found inside the cellar of the old Oslo's maternity clinic, allowing for another team of Norwegian researchers (including Walløe from the above study) to follow the ages of menarche of all women attending Oslo public clinics for delivery since about 1840. Unlike the previous study, their analysis suggested a fall in menarcheal ages from about 15.6 years around 1840 to about 13.3 years for patients born a hundred years later. Anyway, it was significantly less pronounced than Tanner had reported:

> Data from Norwegian investigations have been made much use of to illustrate the secular trend. In the manner these data have previously been interpreted, an almost linear fall has been shown from about 17 years for girls born around 1830 to just over 13 years for girls born after 1935 (Tanner 1962). These former interpretations deviate sharply form our result.
>
> (Brudevoll, Liestøl and Walløe 1979: 413)

By the start of the 1980s, two decades after Tanner's introduction of the 'trend', a fierce letter contesting it was addressed to the journal *Science* by Vern Bullough. He clarified what triggered his explosion upfront:

> Until recently, historical data about the age of menarche were probably of interest only to a few specialists. Much of the current publicity about the historical age of menarche has to do with the belief that in American girls menarcheal age has dropped from 17 years in the 19th century to 12.5 years today. This supposed trend has been regarded as the most significant factor

> in increasing teenage sexuality and the "growing problem of teenage pregnancy". Stories about it have appeared in almost every kind of popular journal from Newsweek to The Nation, and in scholarly literature of anthropology, psychology, child development, nursing, and other fields.
>
> (Bullough 1981a: 365)

These statements are interesting in that they document the continual dissemination of the 'trend' within a network of disciplines, especially in combination with anxieties around teenage pregnancy and the increasingly 'dangerous' sexuality of adolescents. Such articulations were getting the mainstream media's attention and making for striking news-headlines – as they still do today (see Roberts 2013a).

Bullough proceeded to show that nowhere in a number of historical sources was '17' given as an average menarcheal age. That was, however, the median age corresponding to the earliest point in Tanner's diagram (i.e. 1844). Rebelling against what clearly seemed to him an abusive stance entangled with increasingly exalted social fears, Bullough blamed the messenger:

> Where, then, does the age of 17 become established as the age of menarche in the 19th century? The source of this statement turns out to be an authority on physical development, J. M. Tanner. In 1962 Tanner wrote that "age at menarche has been getting earlier by some 4 months per decade in Western Europe over the period 1830–1960". . . . For the 19th century the graph shows data only from Norway, Finland, and Sweden, and some of that from a very small sampling.[10] It does not show any 19th-century data from American and English or other sources that Tanner cites. The American, Danish, Dutch, and British data in the graph begin with the 1940's. If the Dutch, British, German, or other available data were graphed from 1840 onward, the decline would be seen to be from between 14 and 15 years to between 12 and 13. Only one of Tanner's sources reports menarche at 17, and that is for Norway in 1844. . . . Since there is much individual variation, and menarche is dependent on diet, skeletal maturation, heredity, and perhaps other factors, a small, isolated Norwegian sample might not represent all of Norway.
>
> (Bullough 1981a: 366)

A short exchange followed. Tanner's (1981b: 604) response was as charming and pedagogical as it was evasive. Bullough, he said, 'is right to emphasize that generalizations about the secular trend of age at menarche based on European data should not be extrapolated to the United States'. Yet, Tanner contended, there were 'mistakes' in Bullough's assertions about ages. But, rather than reaffirming the validity of his original sample, Tanner referred his critic to the far more extensive compilation of menarcheal statistics offered in his freshly published *History* – where the controversial statement and diagram no longer appear (see Tanner 1981a: 286–8).[11] In other words, some of Bullough's readings of Tanner's *old* work were mistaken according to Tanner's *new* data. Bullough (1981b: 604) counter-argued as follows:

> Tanner's reply ignores my point. As I pointed out, Tanner's data does not document the graph or the statement about the drop in menarche of 4 months every decade since 1840. They didn't when they were first published, nor did they in subsequent editions of his work until 1981.

Bullough didn't care for Tanner's present corrections and revisions. He wanted him to give some explanation about having sustained such claims despite all the methodological quirks and limitations evident to himself. He wanted Tanner to account for his past decisions as the great maker of the 'trend'. Tanner never responded.

In taking up Bullough's disquiet, our point is not to search for Tanner's own ideological leanings and deep-rooted world views. Tanner's initial discourse on earlier development, and growth research overall, should be critically considered within a context of important disciplinary transitions in the human sciences. In the following, we look at the concerns around which the 'trend' emerged – what Tanner did actually say about its medical and social implications – and the type of discourses by which it has been framed as a health problematic since then. In short, under what biopolitical trends has the 'trend' been produced?

Puberty is in crisis!

Back to the 1964 symposium held by the Eugenics Society, it should be noted that Tanner did not present the trend towards early maturing as an index of the effects of social progress, or to demonstrate the influence of nutrition on development. Rather, the 'trend' permitted him to speak to the medical and social risks of earlier puberty from 'a demographer's point of view':

> It is unnecessary to detail the implications of the trend toward earlier maturation. The chief ones lie in the field of education and social behaviour. The trend may perhaps contribute to the earlier age of marriage and the increased fertility rate, in that so far as we know the menopause has become later rather than earlier, thus increasing the total reproductive span, or, from a demographer's point of view, the woman's time at risk.
>
> (Tanner 1965: 60)

Psychosocial challenges, early pregnancies, dilemmas around marital norms, girls' earlier exposure to health dangers: all certainly very appealing to the Eugenics Society. To be fair, these were by and large the concerns expressed since the 19th century in clinical cases of early and very early puberty. Just like

Novak's 'constitutional precocity', the 'trend' incited pedagogical and socio-political forms of action. However, Tanner wasn't speaking about a relatively rare condition, about the exceptional. He was naming a threat concerning the entire industrialised world, especially under the assumption that female reproductive subjects are 'at risk' by default. As such, the 'trend' reenergised old gendered anxieties (as Bullough's complaints suggested years later). It reasserted them from a unique bio-historical standpoint, one by which the temporality of maturation can be mathematically projected on to the plane of human history, that is to say, on to the evolutional plane of the species.

Before the 'trend', one could scientifically say "puberty, and female puberty in particular, is dangerous in itself". Such a statement was basically produced by the medical-psychiatric technology of abnormality. From the 'trend' onwards, one can say "not only is puberty a crisis, pubertal timing itself is *in* crisis!" The latter discourse is produced by a bio-historical technology of risk which ultimately dispenses with both abnormality and disease.

"Puberty in crisis" doesn't mean that populations are becoming abnormal or pathological. It means that there is a good chance that entire populations are starting pubescence increasingly earlier, eventually transgressing the culturally constructed limits of 'nature' and 'society' – and consequently the norms instituted within, and by reference to, those limits. Ultimately, this crisis speaks to somewhat uncertain yet alarming dimensions of collective disorder, to a future state of cultural monstrosity. The crisis of pubertal timing is not about the separation of normality and abnormality because the question, strictly speaking, no longer makes sense in the puberty-in-crisis discourse. Or rather, once the secular trend is scientifically accepted, established age norms cease to be valid and no longer allow for that clinical distinction; as such, their power to act as an instrument of sexual and social normativity is also compromised. "Puberty in crisis" is after all the crisis of normalness, that is to say, the alarming anticipation of its ending.

With Tanner's 'trend', the old eugenic wonderings about the evolutionary meaning of history rose around puberty. If changing life conditions are actually pushing sexual maturity to younger ages, what is the lower temporal threshold of sexual development in the species? How are we to manage this phenomenon in the best interest to society? Were Galton still alive, he would certainly have enjoyed the dilemmas suggested in Tanner's points:

> There is at present little sign that the trend shown in Figure 5 [his diagram] has stopped, or that girls are now maturing at something like the earliest possible age. It seems that these lines may be extrapolated onwards for at least another decade or two. Extrapolation backwards, however, is clearly an impossibility: if the trend we see between 1840 and 1960 had been going on equally before 1840, menarche in medieval times would have occurred, absurdly, after the age of thirty.
>
> (Tanner 1965: 51)

In a sense, while the whole question around unnaturalness had been abandoned in medical discourses on early development, that question resurged in the background of Tanner's speculations: when is this trend to stop? Is it really *natural*?[12]

From the 1980s onwards, searching for secular trends in sexual maturation became a fashionable multidisciplinary activity, most notably among Chinese, European, and US populations. A great many studies have provided statistical evidence of a fall in pubertal ages over the 20th century (e.g. Wyshak and Frisch 1982; Rosenberg 1991; Huen et al. 1997; Herman-Giddens, Wang and Koch 2001; Karlberg 2002; Euling et al. 2008). Some of the more recent studies suggest the prevalence of downward trends in the early 2000s (e.g. Aksglaede et al. 2009; Ma et al. 2009; Morris et al. 2011; Herman-Giddens et al. 2012).[13]

As described in the introduction to this book, Marcia Herman-Giddens and colleagues' controversial 1997 article gave this scholarship a new boost, provoking a whole new stream of critical commentary and research. According to their findings, US girls were not only maturing at younger ages but also during a longer period (i.e. at a slower tempo), which was similarly reported in that year for the urban Chinese population (Huen et al. 1997). Moreover, the US African-American girls were reaching puberty about a year earlier than the white girls. These results led Kaplowitz and Oberfield (1999) to propose the lowering of the age limits of 'normal' breast and pubic hair growth accordingly. Herman-Giddens and other paediatricians promptly supported the initiative (see Chapter 1).

Yet, the question of how prevalent and statistically significant these trends are has not been settled (see Walvoord 2010). For example, the Chinese research referenced above suggests a significant age decrease since the 1960s among Chinese girls, although 'the trend appears to be diminishing and may be coming into a halt with respect to pubic hair development and menarche age' (Huen et al. 1997: 1124). In the US, Shumei Sun et al. (2005: 354) find 'no persuasive evidence that sexual maturation for U.S. children has become earlier [between 1966 and 1994], but some evidence of earlier sexual maturation was found in non-Hispanic white boys and Mexican-American boys and girls'. In their important review study on secular trends in pubertal timing worldwide, Anne-Simone Parent et al. (2003) found no accentuated or generalised reduction in average onset-ages of puberty from the 1960s onwards. In several Western European countries, furthermore, the perceived trend towards earlier menarche seems now to be advancing at a much slower rate or might even have stopped (see Ong, Ahmed and Dunger 2006). In France, the authors of a study on menarcheal ages have contested the transposition of data from leading US research to the French context – while others have attempted to do so 'with little critical sense' (cf. Cozzi and Vinel 2015: 290).

Amid these debates, Tanner's view of the secular trend's longevity seems left behind – or otherwise simply offered as a given. As we illustrate next, the discussion is now focused on whether the phenomenon is really ongoing, and if so, where it's going to take us all.

Explaining the Trend

As Tanner had already proposed, a host of health researchers consistently suggest that epigenetic (environmental, social, and nutritional) as well as genetic factors can produce the variations in pubertal timing perceived globally (e.g. Karlberg 2002; Parent et al. 2003; Ong, Ahmed and Dunger 2006; Gajdos et al. 2010; Ellis 2013). Alongside the role of exogenous stimuli in phenotypic changes, the existence of genetic determinants of sexual development is widely accepted, and the 'racial'/'ethnic' differences found in downward maturational trends arguably support it (Parent et al. 2003; Gluckman and Hansen 2006a; Gajdos et al. 2010). This is certainly not to say that such research is seeking *the* genes accountable for early puberty – even though some specialists have endorsed that quest on clinical (preventive) grounds.[14] What this scholarship is overall concerned with is the multiplicity of ways in which genetics and environment interact so that pubertal timing varies across populations and changes over time. What is at stake, thus, is a virtually endless combination of cumulative conditions, factors, and causes. This is to say, modern pubertal knowledge is now subsumed under a new episteme wherein life processes are construed as 'unlimited-finite', as Paul Rabinow (1996: 92) defines it after Gilles Deleuze.

In this regime of 'unlimited-finite' reasoning, Tanner's (1981a: 298) pondering about a universal 'biological limit' of pubertal timing appears theoretically questionable. Ken Ong and colleagues signal this in their review article on European secular trends in pubertal tempo and timing. They call into question 'whether all these trends are leading towards a common target, or so-called genetic limit, beyond which age at menarche will no longer reduce further' (Ong, Ahmed and Dunger 2006: 9). While restoring Tanner's old statement – 'data have shown marked trends towards younger age at menarche over the last 150 years' (p. 8) – they contend:

> [T]he concept of a single lower genetic limit of puberty is inappropriate, as the distribution of age at menarche suggests that timing of puberty is determined by a large number of genetic factors, each contributing to a small degree. . . . Furthermore, if we consider the large normal range of puberty within each population, a significant proportion of South European girls maybe have menarche at ages 8–10 year old simply according to their genetic predisposition. This has obvious implications for clinical interpretation of early pubertal development, and the likelihood or pathological causes of early puberty (Kaplowitz and Oberfield, 1999; Viner, 2002), which will likely vary according to the child's population, socioeconomic and genetic backgrounds.
>
> (Ong, Ahmed and Dunger 2006: 9–10)

On the one hand, the different 'genetic predispositions' and biosocial 'backgrounds' of populations – what Galton and Darwin called 'races' – render the idea of a unique maturational threshold obsolete. On the other hand, the epidemiological mappings as well as the perceived biosocial causes of these trends have re-established 'racial'/'ethnic' and 'sex' differences in maturational timing. This is to say, while troubling the fixity of the age norms on which clinical interventions are decided, such findings also surface the old dilemmas around nature/nurture and biological determination. 'In this picture', as Cozzi and Vinel (2015: 294) point out, 'gender and race remain a conundrum. it is a cause *in se* (earlier puberty as gender and race dependent, in the dogma of genetic determinism), or an effect of inequality that stereotypes vulnerable groups such as poor minorities, poor immigrants, adopted children, and so on: let alone girls, which makes that inequality a gendered one'. These questions have remained at the margins of paediatric and epidemiologic research on the topic.

Yet, though the current genetic-environmental accounts of earlier puberty incidentally bring 'races' and sex differences into existence, that does not mean a return to old scientific forms of racism or sexism. Since its inception, the 'trend' serves the bio-historical purpose of contrasting, not the abnormal against the normal, not some population with another, but the human race against itself. Despite Tanner's initial dressing of the 'trend' with a great spoon of eugenic sauce, its primary function has never been that of reinforcing views of sexual abnormality, and even less the reassertion of racial differences in a Galtonian, eugenic fashion. The very fact that Tanner insisted on rehabilitating Galton as a 'humane' scientist in his retrospective portrayals of growth science (see an example below) is evidence of the discursive discontinuity between them. Instead of promoting a Galtonian style of eugenics concerned with racial enhancement, the 'trend' has foremost served to assert that practically every child population is at risk of growing into unnatural social bodies.

The 'trend' equally has nothing to do with the kind of scientific racism championed by John Roberton in the 1840s, and which historically anticipates eugenic discourse – a racism against what he saw as cultural monstrosities causing natural distortions within an entire nation (see Chapter 5). For Tanner, rather, although the age decrease is ultimately due to social factors acting upon biology (such as generalised better nutrition), the matter is obviously not about 'us' and 'them': it is about nature transforming itself, changing its order, and turning against maturational laws, against the social good. Quite simply, it is about the paradoxical combination of natural and unnatural forces producing social chaos: and, in that sense, Tanner's 'trend' still reflects fears of the monstrous.

After Tanner's 1965 talk, to be sure, his 'positive' eugenic approach would quickly recede as an embarrassing memory. By the late 1900s, it had become highly inappropriate to talk about genetic 'potentialities' in ways that could evoke Galton's science of heredity and its techniques of 'racial enhancement'. Virtually no scientist would want (or dare) to address the issues raised by earlier pubescence with the same kind of verbosity employed by Tanner in the 1960s to speak to the future of growth surveillance:

> Zygote and environment interact, develop together. Galton was, *perhaps*, more aware of this than the generation of geneticists immediately following him.[15] So in commemorating this very wise, humane and attractive man I want to draw your attention to this interaction. . . . The positive eugenist's attention, I believe, should be increasingly directed at providing the environmental stimuli most appropriate to evoke and derive from each zygote those potentialities which would best enrich and humanize our present culture.
>
> (Tanner 1966: 122, our emphasis)

The *Eugenics Review*, where the above was published, ended in 1968. The *Annals of Eugenics* (founded by Galton's disciple, Karl Pierson) had already changed its name for the more palatable *Annals of Human Genetics* in 1954.[16] Over the late 20th century, after having taken on the ways of the so-called sociobiology and its metaphorical enactments of society as a 'body' (see Rabinow 1996), Darwinism kept reinventing itself. New 'bio-psycho-social' approaches were introduced to evolutionary thought, as outstandingly reflected by the relatively recent Life History Theory (LHT).[17]

LHT proposes that adaptive life strategies of the individual organism, particularly those involving sexual reproduction, play an important role in the emergence of biological and behavioural differences in human development. As such, this framework pays special attention to the familial as well as ecological conditions contributing to variations in pubertal timing (Ellis 2013). Peter Gluckman and Mark Hanson (2006b: 7) importantly highlight how LTH approaches 'place early-onset menarche in perspective, challenge the concept that it is necessarily pathological and suggest a need for a greater societal awareness of the biological inevitability of early menarche in the 21st century'. Offering evolutionary arguments for understanding this trend as a recent phenomenon in human history, they make a key point:

> Our social structures are largely based on the belief that biological puberty is matched to psychosocial maturation. This is no longer the case, and might never be so again. The challenge is for society to adjust its structures to this biology; adjusting the biology to society is impracticable, unethical and potentially dangerous.
>
> (Gluckman and Hanson 2006b: 11)

In short, no more eugenics, please. But their warning is a reminder that in today's paediatric science, the impulse to adjust biology to society, to terminate all perceived dangers of developing earlier at their point of origin – the child's flesh – is still condoned. Conversely, where pubertal development is concerned, adjusting society to biology has often meant a restrictive type of sexual health politics under the banner of risk prevention. Unsurprisingly, LHT has also been a site for the dissemination of alarms about young people's sexual-reproductive choices and for re-articulations of puberty and risk behaviour (e.g. Kogan et al. 2013).

This tension between the recognition of new reconfigurations of life itself and the inability to accept it without expecting social decay is endemic to the current state of sexual paediatric discourse. In a 2013 commentary, the same paediatrician who has famously advocated new pubertal age norms for US girls, Herman-Giddens, also cautions against 'the new normal':

> Given that the exact trigger for pubertal initiation is still unknown, we hardly can fully understand the interactions of factors known to affect puberty, even with current sophisticated statistical modeling. We may have to live with uncertainty for a long time. Furthermore, because early puberty and menarche are associated with many detrimental health and psychosocial issues, we must not accept this premature development as the "new normal." Data may appropriately alter clinical decisions . . . but they should not alter forward movement on creating a healthier environment for our children. . . . With each new study in the past 2 decades, we hope the age of "early puberty" has bottomed out. When each "new study" has been published, however, we find the trend toward early puberty has continued. Fortunately, we have moved beyond controversy about the data and are responding to the wakeup call.
>
> (Herman-Giddens 2013: 1126)

Alas, herewith the difficult position of the contemporary paediatrician: let's not start invasive assessments and treatments without first remaking 'normal' pubertal timing and respective clinical guidelines (especially considering the limitations of our knowledge). But, paradoxically, these new norms should not accommodate a 'new normal', for earlier puberty carries a range of psychosocial risks and *might* actually be unhealthy. While the trend towards earlier development is ongoing, therefore, let's not lose sight of whatever 'normal' was or should be. Fundamentally speaking, Herman-Giddens' concerns do not fall short of Tanner's preoccupation with a 'biological limit'. This is to say, they suggest a similar sense of crisis regarding nature itself, or what we would call the deep fear of the unnatural. In her environmental hypotheses of early puberty, nature figures dangerously distorted and distorting; it is getting too *artificial*. Any corresponding set of pubertal norms is thus compromised. Ultimately, those new norms are not *normal*, in the sense that they are based upon natural circumstances which are deemed neither proper nor desirable. Accordingly, while new knowledge is yet to come to tame 'uncertainty', the scientific debate must now focus on 'creating a healthier environment for our children', rather than promoting more polemics around data. Over half a century after the its birth, the movement that the trend incites – 'the wakeup call' – is still foremost to act upon 'this premature development', as Herman-Giddens calls it, without truly reassessing the whole notion of normality, the politics of its medical uses, and the meanings of 'nature' embedding them.

Treating for what? The precocious body as a 'risk factor'

In the 1960s, to sum up, Tanner introduced the 'trend' to the scientific world. As a bio-historical technology of 'natural' sexual development, it produces a distinctive risk: social monstrosities spreading across the species. Its construction was a key event in the transposition of early puberty's epidemiological risks into the general clinical assessment of pubescent subjects. If the secular trend is ongoing, the children of tomorrow might be maturing even earlier than children *already* do at present. In this way, the 'trend' provided the framework by which early development came to concern virtually the whole world population. Thus, Tanner incidentally gave yet another reason to keep parents and clinicians attentive to the young bodies under their care.

In 1944, as previously shown, most cases of precocity were declared 'constitutional'. By then, doctors had no technology that could prevent children from maturing, and arguably avoid health risks such as final height reduction. No specialist could give parents anything better than placatory advice: "you will find a bunch of troubles to deal with, but please don't despair – your child is not a monster!" Under the good guidance of their families and educators, such children, the majority being girls, would grow into 'normal' adults of a 'normal' physical appearance, although predictably not as tall as they otherwise would have been. Quite paradoxically, this 'problem' was diametrically opposed to another for which clinical treatment was put in place in that same decade: girls considered too tall for their age were submitted to oestrogen therapy for the *reduction* of their stature.

Joyce M. Lee and Joel D. Howell (2006) offer an excellent historical rendition and critique of this paediatric drift. In the 1940s, it was known that pituitary disorders entailing insufficient steroid production prolong the period of growth by delaying epiphyseal closure, thus making children grow taller (i.e. opposite to what happens in early development). Oestrogen treatment was subsequently found to be effective in preventing excessive height in pathological instances. The first recipients of such therapy were children with acromegaly, which is caused by pituitary tumours and associated with several growth disorders, including abnormal height increase. In no time, the treatment's main target would turn to 'abnormally' tall girls otherwise in perfect health.

For over three decades, following a clinical case series reported in 1946, the use of oestrogen in girls considered at risk of getting 'too' tall as adults was consistently portrayed as successful in important paediatric literature (Lee and Howell 2006). By the late 1960s, while boys were seldom mentioned in review articles and expert commentary on the therapy, treating girls for excessive height figured as a medical imperative. In slowing girls' growth, it was presumed, the treatment would save them from more immediate psychosocial issues such as lacking self-esteem, social withdrawal, or depression. In the long run, their sexual attractiveness and mating success would not be jeopardised: oestrogen helped them fitting in a society where the wife shall be shorter than the husband.

At the time of such claims – i.e. in the 1960s–70s – alternative views of gender and bodies were gaining the day, partly as an important result of feminist activism and scholarship, partly due to systematic changes in the scientific normalisation of bodies. From the 1980s onwards, girls' excessive height was increasingly put into question as a 'problem' within the paediatric profession; medical calls for its treatment have faded since then (Lee and Howell 2006).

In the 1960s, when steroid therapy for girls' tallness had become a reality in medical history, another game-changing event took place: medroxyprogesterone-acetate (MPA) was introduced as treatment for constitutional (or idiopathic) early pubescence (cf. Kaplowitz 2004: 136, 145–6). The drug postponed pubertal changes, hence arguably preventing psychosocial problems. However, contrary to what was still suggested in the late 1970s, it did not solve the issue of final adult height.[18] At all events, from the moment the pharmaceutical control of pubertal timing became possible, the prevention of any threats posed by early puberty entered a whole new plane. It shifted from the management of abnormality into a modality by which healthy children are corrected on behalf of what may be summed up as the uncertain.

This technological shift was completed in 1981, when a team of researchers first reported the use of gonadotropin-releasing hormone (GnRH) analogues to delay puberty (Comite et al. 1981). Based on a preliminary trial with five girls diagnosed with idiopathic precocity, the authors suggested that the treatment potentially increased adult stature by delaying bone fusion, and would also avert detrimental psychosocial outcomes (see Hayes 2016). This is about where the diagnostic power of the doctor and the epidemiological rationality of risk become inextricably bound to each other in the history of puberty science, producing a new clinical stance on the precocious child: "I must treat you regardless of your actual health, not because you are necessarily 'abnormal', but quite simply because you are at risk". From the preventive treatment of girls' tallness to the preventive treatment of early developers' shortness, within this sequence of both contiguous and contradictory events, paediatric practice has opened itself up to a new set of power-knowledge relations with inescapable dead-ends and a great deal of ethical costs.

Since then, as viewed in Chapter 1, criticisms have seldom been voiced in specialised literature as to the 'medical' need to increase height, or to deal with behavioural issues through medication. Doctors have more frequently cautioned against possible over-prescription. This preoccupation is logically shared by the proponents of new age norms, such as Kaplowitz and Herman-Giddens, but also by Robert Rosenfield (1994), one of the leading experts who frantically fought the initiative. Yet, although agreeing that early puberty at age 6 or later 'generally does not have a serious cause or require treatment', Rosenfield and colleagues contend:

> Indeed, evidence is emerging that premature thelarche and premature pubarche *may on occasion be risk factors* for subsequent reproductive endocrine system dysfunction. When breasts or pubic hair appear before 8 or 9 years of age, respectively, regardless of race, we are of the opinion that a diagnostic evaluation should be initiated with evaluation of bone age and *height prediction*.
>
> (Rosenfield et al. 2000: 622, our emphasis)

However medically reasonable their warning is, these experts' reminder of timely diagnosis inescapably conflates the 'premature' onset of pubertal characteristics with health *risks*, among which the question of adult height appears as a self-evident 'clinical' issue.

Some doctors argue "not so fast with treatment evaluations!"; others argue "not so fast with changing age norms!" Doubtless, all these doctors are genuinely striving to protect the health of early developers. For the time being, nevertheless, children aged from 8 to 11 diagnosed with early puberty are treated, not for actual health complaints, but for risks associated with the condition (Hayes 2016), most of which are perceived as risks of sexual development alone.

Treating for the future. But what future?

Cozzi and Vinel (2015) have conducted an insightful mixed-method study (documental and ethnographic) on medical discourses on early development, and 'true precocious puberty' in particular (quoted in Chapter 1). Drawing on interviews with 61 doctors and other health staff members working in France and Italy, they highlight links as well as dissonances between the discourses circulating in published work and views from the field:

> What these health professionals state follows the mainstream of medical research, in that they focus nearly exclusively on girls and because such precocity is compared with a gap between the expected body at a certain age and the real body – as well as with the risks generated by this gap. They also refer to a prognostic medicine forecasting the size in the adult age correcting any future size considered as incapacitating before society. But the major difference is that, unlike the writing in medical literature, they do not see a large-scale advance in age at onset of puberty in girls – whatever the form, peripheral or central.
>
> (Cozzi and Vinel 2015: 293)

Whereas a global trend of earlier puberty raises eyebrows among these professionals, their talk and practices remain anchored in the paediatric promises of risk surveillance and management, transposing social fears directly onto early developers' bodies. In this type of discourse, as Cozzi and Vinel point out, 'risk is embodied and latent, and may be revealed if trigged by environmental factors' (p. 292).

In the meantime, after more than three decades of pharmaceutical research, apparently no one has managed to demonstrate that GnRH treatments indeed increase final height. Amid the ongoing debate around age norms, no one has explained why healthy children should be safeguarded from psychosocial issues by means of therapeutic programmes with inevitable implications for their subjectivities (Roberts 2014). Furthermore, the iatrogenic effects of the treatment have not been seriously considered and properly investigated. Possible IQ reduction, in particular, was disturbingly glossed-over when reported upon in 2001 and poorly addressed ever since (Hayes 2016, 2017).

Yet, the use of the drug to treat healthy early developers – i.e. girls, in most cases, entering puberty at or before age 8 – has widely been adopted as a gold standard in European and North American medical practice, and has exponentially spread globally over the last years, most notably in China and India (Cozzi and Vinel 2015; Hayes 2016). The treatment is also recommended for both girls and boys in medical online sites, and in prominent gynaecologic textbooks (namely the latest editions of the *Berek and Novak's Gynecology*, founded by Emile Novak in the 1940s).

In this clinical-disciplinary setting, early maturing children are to be corrected at the outset since their symptoms of precocity are construed as the very dangers that hormonal treatments are said to avert. Risks themselves – e.g. early sexual activity, social maladjustment, conflicting self-image, early pregnancies, illegal drug-taking – no longer represent mere probabilities but are rather deployed by the clinician as real, present threats located in the child's body. Pubertal signs, in short, become the risk factors that epidemiology seeks to predict within populations, and which, as it turns out, are impossible to measure where a single individual is concerned.

To be clinically 'at risk' means to be neither ill nor healthy, neither normal nor abnormal. It means to be in-between those terms and to embody all them at the same time. When clinicians say that early puberty is dangerous since it puts children at risk in some way, they are speaking of a probability, a future outcome which they can attempt to estimate but about which they can never be certain until it happens – if it happens.

However, precisely because no person or numerical science can ascertain the perceived possible outcomes of the condition regarding this or that particular child, power relations are inflated: 'the greater the indeterminism, the greater the control' (Hacking 1990: 2). Surveillance and intervention on the body, therefore, are the immediate answer. In this way, the doctor's diagnostic role is almost entirely colonised by this peculiar power of treating future outcomes that are statistically real and yet clinically incommensurable.[19]

Since at least the mid-1800s, puberty is not so much a 'state of health' as a 'state of risk'. But, to be sure, the pubertal 'crisis' of the 19th and 20th centuries meant a medical fight against abnormality on behalf of nature, even when the combat was ultimately between children and their own sexual instincts (see Chapter 7). Now, puberty science has discovered that nature itself has changed; it has become somewhat antagonistic to what 'normal' maturation was said to be. Nature is 'in crisis' and rebels against the old 'normal', consequently undermining current ideas of what a 'desirable' timing of sexualisation is. In other words, a new 'normal' has been found which not only threatens the orderly workings of society but also disrupts the standardised functioning of paediatric sexual science. In the pharmacological, bio-historical, and risk-oriented apparatus formed around pubescent bodies, clinicians find themselves in the position of combating nature – an altered, disordered nature, as it were – for the sake of individual and collective futures.

In fact, we would say that this medical regime has reached its threshold: Tanner's 'trend' does exist (at least in the minds of many), pubertal ages have continued to decrease, and doctors can effectively treat early developing children so as to avoid behavioural disorder and, ultimately, social decay. And yet, these 'facts' eventually led puberty science to bump against its own ethical and epistemic crisis once more. As Hermen-Gidden's frustration crystallises, there has been a paradox haunting the field for more than a century: 'we hardly can fully understand the interactions of factors known to affect puberty' (2013: 1126). Ever since our knowledge about puberty has become modern – i.e. based on truth-demonstration through positive methods – nobody has yet showed what triggers sexual development. What's more, 'normal' pubertal timing – either 'desirable' or simply 'average' – remains controversial. The dilemmas currently facing puberty science, as shown throughout this book, are not new. Yet, the field seems to have reached a point of philosophical and technical conundrum in which experts find themselves at odds with normative classifications and interventions while attempting to ease public concerns. Ultimately, not only is puberty perceived as being risky and itself at risk, or 'in crisis', the tectonics sustaining the medical normalisation of pubertal development are collapsing – if they haven't already.

Notes

1 By the 1930s, for instance, rather than asking for parents to inspect the bedsheets of the precocious pubescent boy for traces of semen, a routine prostate massage at the hospital would do (see Chapter 8).

2 As D'Arcy Thompson had written years before, 'to say that children of a given age vary in the *rate* at which they are growing would seem to be a more fundamental statement than that they vary in the *size* to which they have grown' (1945: 128, our emphasis). In other words, whereas standards for height or weight show whether a child has grown to

a normal *size* up until now, velocity standards show whether the child's growth is (and predictably will be) taking place at a normal *rate*. 'Hence for clinical use velocity standards are desirable, as well as distance ones' (Tanner 1981a: 395).

3 Their partnership has widely been portrayed as an example of excellence in paediatric research. Tanner passed away in 2010. An obituary by Noël Cameron was published in the *Annals of Human Biology* (formerly *The Eugenics Review*) which painted Tanner and Whitehouse's legacy as follows: 'The team of "Tanner and Whitehouse" were to become as synonymous to research in child growth as "bacon and eggs" are to an English breakfast' (Cameron 2011: 245).

4 See Noël Cameron (1978) for a detailed description of the methods and instruments employed in auxological anthropometry (with important references to the Harpenden Study).

5 Celia Roberts (2015: 61–90, 2016) offers a detailed history and critique of the Scale where she explores the methodological and ethical issues involved in its development (particularly with regard to the employment of child participants and the uses of medical photography in paediatric research).

6 The 'trend' was first offered in a historical review of statistical data on the age of menarche in several European countries, published in German in 1848 (see Brundtland and Walløe 1976), which provided Tanner with a few sources for his own study. The original author was Swedish anatomist and vocal proponent of eugenics, Gaston Backman, who had actively supported the Swedish pro-Nazi movement (see Felder 2013: 120–3).

7 The diagram had first been introduced in the 1962 edition of his *Growth at Adolescence*, and would continue to be published in slightly different versions until the 1970s (see below).

8 Let alone the assumption, 'from longitudinal studies', that the onset-age of menarche will always assume a Normal distribution in any given population (Tanner 1965: 49).

9 Accordingly, Tanner (1965: 55) cited a couple of findings: 'Menarche occurred in the 1940s some eight months earlier in well-off negroes in New York than in negroes in the Southern States . . . and some six months earlier in well-off Indians in Durban [South Africa] than in poorly off ones'.

10 Bullough referred to the diagram's later version (now representing data for Holland) which had recently appeared in the influential *Worldwide Variation in Human Growth* (cf. Eveleth and Tanner 1976: 218).

11 A scholar from Harvard University came to Tanner's defence: the criticism was no longer opportune, he suggested, for it was 'well-known' that Norwegian data had been recently reassessed and the average age corrected (Ellison 1981: 604).

12 In his *History*, concluding on a general decline in menarcheal ages around the globe, Tanner still entertained the question of a temporal limit of reproductive maturation. Speaking about the differences between North European and Mediterranean populations over a century, he wrote: 'The geographical difference has reduced to four to six months, presumably as girls in Mediterranean countries reach a biological limit beyond which earliness can go no further' (1981a: 298).

13 Most contemporary studies draw on data on menarcheal ages (usually averaged by probit analysis) and/or bodily ratings according to the Tanner Scale (often assessed through visual inspection).

14 Roberts (2015: 134) contests the scientific pertinence of such calls, noting as follows: 'Philip and Lazar (2005: 56) for example assert that "detection of these genes will provide a tool for identification of children at risk of developing CPP [central precocious puberty], enabling early intervention with the aim of preventing its distressing outcomes". Here genes become markers indicating future risk'.

15 Perhaps. But what we know for sure is that Galton spoke of the possible effects of environment on the shaping of people as 'petty influences', as opposed to the sovereign

mathematical evolutionary laws of heredity that he so inventively and brilliantly demonstrated to his audiences (cf. Hacking 1990: 185).

16 In 2011, addressing the elephant in the room, the journal made its complete archives available and published an insightful special issue on eugenics and its ramifications for contemporary genetics (see *Annals of Human Genetics* 2011).

17 See Roberts's (2013b, 2015: 150–60) critical engagements with the 'evolutionary theory of socialisation' advanced by Jay Belsky, Laurence Steinberg, and Patricia Draper in 1991. Put briefly, they propose that disrupted attachments in early life – due to 'inadequate' parenting or 'father absence', for example – may lead to earlier puberty (as an adaptive bodily response to stress, trauma, or loss). Notwithstanding its implicit endorsement of a heteronormative family model and its limited focus on parent-child relationships, Roberts argues, their 'socialisation' theory represents a ground-breaking step towards non-biologically determinist accounts of sexual development. For a thorough description of the main analytical models developed in the LHT field, see Stearns (1992).

18 By the end of that decade, for example, a Chilean team reported on a clinical trial with 16 children (aged 12 months to 9.5 years) diagnosed with true precocious puberty, concluding that MPA injections had been successful in improving the prognosis of final adult height in 14 of those cases (Abodovsky et al. 1979).

19 In her outstanding genealogy of the contemporary biopolitics of pregnancy, Lorna Weir (cf. 2006: 107) elaborates very similar points on the transposition of an epidemiological conception of risk into clinical (diagnostic) practice and discourse.

References

[Unless otherwise noted, all translations are the first author's responsibility.]

Abodovsky, N., Matos-de-la-Parra, A., Vivanco, X. and Onetto, E. (1979) 'Tratamiento de la pubertad precoz verdadera con acetato de medroxiprogesterona', *Boletín Médico del Hospital Infantil de México* 36(4): 581–97.

Aksglaede, L., Sørensen, K., Petersen, J.H., Skakkebaek, N.E. and Juul, A. (2009) 'Recent decline in age at breast development: the Copenhagen Puberty Study', *Pediatrics* 123(5): e932–9.

The American Journal of the Medical Sciences [author unknown] (1834) 'Case of puberty and pregnancy in a girl of ten years of age', 15: 266.

The American Journal of the Medical Sciences [author unknown] (1844) 'Age of puberty in girls', 7(14): 438–9.

The American Journal of the Medical Sciences [author unknown] (1904) 'On the albuminuria of puberty', 128: 167–8.

Anderson, S.E., Dallal, G.E. and Must, A. (2003) 'Relative weight and race influence average age at menarche: results from two nationally representative surveys of US girls studied 25 years apart', *Pediatrics* 111: 844–50.

Annals of Human Genetics (2011) 'Special issue: annals online archive 1925–1954', 75(3): 313–445.

Arribas-Aylon, M. and Walkerdine, V. (2008) 'Foucauldian discourse analysis', in C. Willig and W. Stainton-Rogers (eds.) *The SAGE handbook of qualitative research*. London: Sage, pp. 91–108.

Attwood, F. and Smith, C. (2011) 'Investigating young people's sexual cultures: an introduction', *Sex Education: Sexuality, Society and Learning* 11(3): 235–42.

Baines, D.E. (1966) 'Biological aspects of social problems' [book review], *The Sociological Review* 14(1): 95–7.

Baldwin, B.T. (1921) 'The physical growth of children from birth to maturity', *University of Iowa Studies in Child Welfare* 1(1): 411.

Belkin, L. (2000) 'The making of an 8-year-old woman', *The New York Times Magazine* 24 December [https://www.nytimes.com/2000/12/24/magazine/the-making-of-an-8-year-old-woman.html].

Benedict, F. (1919) 'Energy requirements of children from birth to puberty', *The Boston Medical and Surgical Journal* 181: 107–39.

Bethencourt, F. (2013) *Racisms: from the Crusades to the twentieth century*. Princeton: Princeton University Press.

Biro, F.M., Greenspan, L.C., Galvez, M.P., Pinney, S.M., Teitelbaum, S., Windham, G.C., Deardorff, J., Herrick, R.L., Succop, P.A., Hiatt, R.A., Kushi, L.H. and Wolff, M.S. (2013) 'Onset of breast development in a longitudinal cohort', *Pediatrics* 132(6): 1019–27.

Boismont, A.B. (1842) *De la menstruation considérée dans ses rapports physiologiques et pathologiques*. Paris: Germer Baillière.

Boismont, A.B. (1856) *Du suicide et de la folie suicide, considérés dans leurs rapports avec la statistique, la médecine et la philosophie*. Paris: Germer Baillière.

Bolin-Hort, P. (1996) *Bringing in the inspector: the framing and enforcement of the early factory legislation in Britain, 1825–1900*. Linköping: Linköping University.

The Boston Medical and Surgical Journal [author unknown] (1872) 'Comparative rate of growth in the two sexes', 10(25): 434–5.

Bowditch, H.P. (1877) *The growth of children: from the Eighth Annual Report of the State Board of Health of Massachusetts*. Boston: Albert J. Wright.

Breschet, G. (1821) 'Appendix II: account of a child of three years of age, in whom there appeared signs of puberty: abstracted from a paper communicated to the Society, by Gilbert Breschet, M.D. Superintendent of the anatomical department of the faculty of medicine in Paris, dated December 1820', *Medico-Chirurgical Transactions* 11(2): 446–7.

The British and Foreign Medical Review [author unknown] (1843) 'On the influence of manufactures on health', 15: 285–314.

The British Medical Journal [author unknown] (1886) 'Early puberty', 1(1310): 263.

The British Medical Journal [author unknown] (1911) 'Puberty and the neuro-psychic system', 1(2631): 1337–8.

The British Medical Journal [author unknown] (1924) 'Internal secretions of sex glands', 2(3330): 769.

The British Medical Journal [author unknown] (1945) 'Precocious female puberty', 1(4390): 268–9.

Brown, J.D., Halpern, C.T. and L'Engle, K.L. (2005) 'Mass media as a sexual super peer for early maturing girls', *Journal of Adolescent Health* 36: 420–7.

Bruch, H. (1941) 'Obesity in relation to puberty', *The Journal of Pediatrics* 19(3): 365–75.

Brudevoll, G.E., Liestøl, K. and Walløe, L. (1979) 'Menarcheal age in Oslo during the last 140 years', *Annals of Human Biology* 6(5): 407–16.

Brundtland, G.H., Liestøl, K. and Walløe, L. (1980) 'Height, weight, and menarcheal age of Olso schoolchildren during the last 60 years', *Annals of Human Biology* 7(4): 307–22.

Brundtland, G.H. and Walløe, L. (1976) 'Menarcheal age in Norway in the 19th century: a re-evaluation of the historical sources', *Annals of Human Biology* 3(4): 363–74.

Bullough, V.L. (1981a) 'Age at menarche: a misunderstanding', *Science* 213(4505): 365–6.

Bullough, V.L. (1981b) 'Menarcheal age', *Science* 214(4521): 604–6.

Burk, F. (1898) 'Growth of children in height and weight', *The American Journal of Psychology* 9(3): 253–326.

Burman, E. (1994) *Deconstructing developmental psychology*. London: Routledge.

Cameron, N. (1978) 'The methods of auxological anthropometry', in F. Falkner and J.M. Tanner (eds.) *Human growth (vol. 2): postnatal growth*. New York: Plenum Press, pp. 35–90.

Cameron, N. (2011) 'James Mourilyan Tanner 1920–2010', *Annals of Human Biology* 38(3): 243–6.

Castel, R. (1991) 'From dangerousness to risk', in G. Burchell, C. Gordon and P. Miller (eds.) *The Foucault effect: studies in governmentality*. Chicago: The University of Chicago Press, pp. 281–98.

Chalumeau, M., Chemaitilly, W., Trivin, C., Adan, L., Bréart, G. and Brauner, R. (2002) 'Central precocious puberty in girls: an evidence-based diagnosis tree to predict central nervous system abnormalities', *Pediatrics* 109(1): 61–7.

Christensen, J.F. (1947) 'Pubertas praecox: account of a case of the constitutional type in a three year-old girl', *Acta Paediatrica* 34(1–2): 157–63.
Christopher, W.S. (1900) 'Measurements of Chicago school children', *The Journal of the American Medical Association* 35(10): 618–23.
Christopher, W.S. (1901) 'The relation of unbalanced physical development to pubertal morbidity as shown by physical measurements', *The Journal of the American Medical Association* 37(11): 691–700.
Christopher, W.S. (1904) 'Types of children', *The Journal of the American Medical Association* 43(22–23): 1619–23, 1696–700.
Chumlea, W.C., Schubert, C.M., Roche, A.F., Kulin, H.E., Lee, P.A., Himes, J.H. and Guo, S.S. (2003) 'Age at menarche and racial comparisons in U.S. girls', *Pediatrics* 111: 110–13.
Cisternino, M., Arrigo, T., Pasquino, A.M., Tinelli, C., Antoniazzi, F., Beduschi, L., Bindi, G., Borrelli, P., De Sanctis, V., Farello, G., Galluzzi, F., Gargantini, L., Lo Presti, D., Sposito, M. and Tatò, L. (2000) 'Etiology and age incidence of precocious puberty in girls: a multicentric study', *Journal of Pediatric Endocrinology and Metabolism* 13: 695–701.
Clark, A. (1890a) 'Remarks on the barking cough of puberty (cynobex hebetis)', *The Lancet* 136(3512): 1319–21.
Clark, A. (1890b) 'Remarks on the barking cough of puberty (cynobex hebetis)', *The British Medical Journal* 2(1564): 1416–8.
Clouston, T.S. (1890) *The neuroses of development, being the Morison Lectures for 1890*. Edinburgh: Oliver and Boyd.
Cole, T.J. (2012) 'The development of growth references and growth charts', *Annals of Human Biology* 39(5): 382–94.
Comite, F., Cutler, G.B., Rivier, J.E.F., Vale, W.W., Loriaux, D.L. and Crowley, W.F. (1981) 'Short-term treatment of idiopathic precocious puberty with a long-acting analogue of luteinizing hormone-releasing hormone: a preliminary report', *New England Journal of Medicine* 305(26): 1546–50.
Cookston, W.C. (1948) 'Precocious puberty without a demonstrable tumor', *The Journal of Pediatrics* 33(1): 90–2.
Cooper, A. (1813) 'History of a case of premature puberty', *Medico-Chirurgical Transactions* 4: 207–9.
Cosgrave, E.M. (1888) 'The etiology and classification of the anaemia of puberty', *The British Medical Journal* 1(1422): 688–90.
Cozzi, D. and Vinel, V. (2015) 'Risky, early, controversial: puberty in medical discourses', *Social Science & Medicine* 143: 287–96.
Cunningham, H. (1990) 'The employment and unemployment of children in England c.1680–1851', *Past & Present* 126: 115–50.
Cunningham, H. (1991) *The children of the poor: representations of childhood since the seventeenth century*. Cambridge: Blackwell.
Curran, F.J. (1939) 'Psychotherapeutic problems of puberty', *The American Journal of Orthopsychiatry* 10(3): 510–21.
Darnall, W.M.E. (1904) 'The gynecological aspect of mental overstrain at puberty, and its influence on development', *The Boston Medical and Surgical Journal* 151(11): 291–4.
Darwin, C. (1871) *The descent of man, and selection in relation to sex*. London: John Murray.
Dennis, W. (1941) 'Effect of pubertas praecox on the age at which onset of walking occurs', *American Journal of Diseases of Children* 61(5): 951–7.
D'Espine, M. (1835a) 'Recherches sur des quelques-unes des causes qui hâtent ou retardent la puberté', *Archives Générales de Médecine* 2(9): 5–18.

D'Espine, M. (1835b) 'Recherches sur des quelques-unes des causes qui hâtent ou retardent la puberté', *Archives Générales de Médecine* 2(9): 303–18.

Diamond, I. and Quinby, L. (eds.) (1988) *Feminism & Foucault: reflections on resistance*. Boston: Northeastern University Press.

Dreyfus, H.L. and Rabinow, P. (1983) *Michel Foucault: beyond structuralism and hermeneutics*. Chicago: The University of Chicago Press.

Egan, R.D. and Hawkes, G.L. (2008) 'Endangered girls and incendiary objects: unpacking the discourse on sexualization', *Sexuality & Culture* 12(4): 291–311.

Elders, M.J., Scott, C.R., Frindik, J.P. and Kemp, S.F. (1997) 'Clinical workup for precocious puberty', *The Lancet* 350(9076): 457–8.

Ellis, B.J. (2013) 'The hypothalamic-pituitary-gonadal axis: a switch-controlled, condition-sensitive system in the regulation of life history strategies', *Hormones and Behavior* 64(2): 215–25.

Ellis, H. (1905) *Studies in the psychology of sex: the evolution of modesty, the phenomena of periodicity, auto-erotism*. Philadelphia: F.A. Davis Company.

Ellis, R.W.B. (1934) 'Precocious puberty in a boy aged 5', *Proceedings of the Royal Society of Medicine* 27(10): 1328–9.

Ellis, R.W.B. (1935) 'Precocious puberty and pseudohermaphroditism', *Proceedings of the Royal Society of Medicine* 28(8): 1071–3.

Ellis, R.W.B. (1937) 'Precocious puberty in a female infant', *Proceedings of the Royal Society of Medicine* 31(1): 13–14.

Ellis, R.W.B. (1945) 'Growth and health of Belgian children during and after the German Occupation (1940–44)', *Archives of Disease in Childhood* 20(103): 97–109.

Ellis, R.W.B. (1946) 'Height and weight in relation to onset of puberty in boys', *Archives of Disease in Childhood* 21(108): 181–9.

Ellis, R.W.B. (1947) 'Growth in relation to maturity', *Edinburgh Medical Journal* 54: 269–83.

Ellis, R.W.B. (1948a) 'Growth and physical performance of children in relation to maturity', *Proceedings of the Royal Society of Medicine* 41(6): 343–8.

Ellis, R.W.B. (1948b) 'Puberty growth of boys', *Archives of Disease in Childhood* 23(113): 17–26.

Ellis, R.W.B. (1950) 'Age of puberty in the Tropics', *British Medical Journal* 1(4645): 85–9.

Ellison, P.T. (1981) 'Menarcheal age', *Science* 214(4521): 604.

Euling, S.Y., Herman-Giddens, M.E., Lee, P.A., Selevan, S.G., Juul, A., Sørensen, T.I.A., Himes, J.H., Teilman, G. and Swan, S.H. (2008) 'Examination of US puberty-timing data from 1940 to 1994 for secular trends: panel findings', *Pediatrics* 121(Supp. 3): S172–91.

Eveleth, P.B. and Tanner, J.M. (1976) *Worldwide variation in human growth*. Cambridge: Cambridge University Press.

Fausto-Sterling, A. (1993) 'The five sexes: why male and female are not enough', *The Sciences* (March/April): 20–5.

Fausto-Sterling, A. (1995) 'How to build a man', in M. Berger, B. Wallace and S. Watson (eds.) *Constructing masculinity*. New York: Routledge, pp. 127–34.

Fausto-Sterling, A. (2000) *Sexing the body: gender politics and the construction of sexuality*. New York: Basic Books.

Felder, B.M. (2013) '"God forgives-but nature never will": racial identity, racial anthropology, and eugenics in Latvia 1918–1940', in M.F. Björn and P.J. Weindling (eds.) *Baltic eugenics: bio-politics, race and nation in interwar Estonia, Latvia and Lithuania 1918–1940*. Amsterdam: Rodopi B.V., pp. 115–46.

Fothergill, W.E. (1912) 'A note on some developmental errors of puberty', *The British Medical Journal* 2(2704): 1120–2.

Foucault, M. (1978) *The history of sexuality, vol. 1: an introduction*. Translated by Robert Hurley. New York: Pantheon Books.

Foucault, M. (1980a) 'Truth and power', in C. Gordon (ed.) *Power/knowledge: selected interviews and other writings 1972–1977*. Translated by Colin Gordon. New York: Pantheon Books, pp. 109–33.

Foucault, M. (1980b) 'The politics of health in the eighteenth century', in C. Gordon (ed.) *Power/knowledge: selected interviews and other writings 1972–1977*. Translated by Colin Gordon. New York: Pantheon Books, pp. 166–82.

Foucault, M. (1980c) 'The confession of the flesh', in C. Gordon (ed.) *Power/knowledge: selected interviews and other writings 1972–1977*. Translated by Colin Gordon. New York: Pantheon Books, pp. 194–228.

Foucault, M. (1982) 'Subject and power', *Critical Inquiry* 8: 777–95.

Foucault, M. (1988) 'On power', in L.D. Kritzman (ed.) *Politics, philosophy, culture: interviews and other writings of Michel Foucault, 1977–1984*. Translated by Alan Sheridan. New York: Routledge, pp. 96–109.

Foucault, M. (1995) *Discipline and punish: the birth of the prison*. Translated by Alan Sheridan. New York: Vintage.

Foucault, M. (2000) 'The ethics of the concern of the self as a practice of freedom', in P. Rabinow (ed.) *Michel Foucault ethics: subjectivity and truth (vol. 1, essential works of Foucault 1954–1984)*. Translated by Robert Hurley. London: Penguin, pp. 281–301.

Foucault, M. (2001a) 'Foucault', in D. Defert and F. Ewald (eds.) *Michel Foucault: dits et écrits (vol. II, 1976–1988)*. Paris: Gallimard, pp. 1450–5.

Foucault, M. (2001b) 'Michel Foucault explique son dernier livre', in D. Defert and F. Ewald (eds.) *Michel Foucault: dits et écrits (vol. I, 1954–1975)*. Paris: Gallimard, pp. 799–807.

Foucault, M. (2001c) 'Réponse à une question', in D. Defert and F. Ewald (eds.) *Michel Foucault: dits et écrits (vol. I, 1954–1975)*. Paris: Gallimard, pp. 701–23.

Foucault, M. (2001d) '"Qui êtres vous, Professeur Foucault?"', in D. Defert and F. Ewald (eds.) *Michel Foucault: dits et écrits (vol. I, 1954–1975)*. Paris: Gallimard, pp. 629–48.

Foucault, M. (2001e) 'Crise de la médecine ou crise de l'anti-médecine?', in D. Defert and F. Ewald (eds.) *Michel Foucault: dits et écrits (vol. II, 1976–1988)*. Paris: Gallimard, pp. 40–58.

Foucault, M. (2001f) 'Non au sexe roi', in D. Defert and F. Ewald (eds.) *Michel Foucault: dits et écrits (vol. II, 1976–1988)*. Paris: Gallimard, pp. 256–69.

Foucault, M. (2002) *The order of things: an archaeology of the human sciences*. Translated by Alan Sheridan. London: Routledge.

Foucault, M. (2003a) *"Society must be defended": lectures at the Collège de France, 1975–1976*. Translated by David Macey. New York: Picador.

Foucault, M. (2003b) *Abnormal: lectures at the Collège de France, 1974–1975*. Translated by Graham Burchell. New York: Picador.

Foucault, M. (2006) *Psychiatric power: lectures at the Collège de France, 1973–1974*. Translated by Graham Burchell. New York: Picador.

Frank, L.K. (1941) 'General considerations: certain problems of puberty and adolescence', *The Journal of Pediatrics* 19(3): 294–301.

Freedman, D.S., Khan, L.K., Serdula, M.K., Dietz, W.H., Srinivasan, S.R. and Berenson, G.S. (2002) 'Relation of age at menarche to race, time period, and anthropometric dimensions: the Bogalusa Heart Study', *Pediatrics* 110(4) [http://pediatrics.aappublications.org/content/110/4/e43].

Gajdos, Z.K.Z., Henderson, K.D., Hirschhorn, J.N. and Palmert, M.R. (2010) 'Genetic determinants of pubertal timing in the general population', *Molecular and Cellular Endocrinology* 324(1–2): 21–9.

Gibbs, C.E. (1923) 'Relation of puberty to behavior and personality in patients with dementia praecox', *The American Journal of Psychiatry* 80(1): 121–9.

Gluckman, P.D. and Hansen, M.A. (2006a) 'Changing times: the evolution of puberty', *Molecular and Cellular Endocrinology* 254–255: 26–31.

Gluckman, P.D. and Hansen, M.A. (2006b) 'Evolution, development and timing of puberty', *Trends in Endocrinology & Metabolism* 17(1): 7–12.

Godin, P. (1920) *Growth during school age: its application to education*. Boston: Richard G. Badger.

Gordon, A. (1923) 'Neurologic manifestations of puberty', *The Journal of Nervous and Mental Disease* 57(1): 74–5.

Gordon, A. (1933) 'Convulsive disorders of two opposite periods of life: puberty and climacterium', *The American Journal of Psychiatry* 89(5): 929–38.

Gould, S.J. (1977) *Ontogeny and phylogeny*. Cambridge: The Belknap Press of Harvard University Press.

Graves, T.C. (1920) 'Commentary on a case of hystero-epilepsy with delayed puberty', *The Lancet* 196(5075): 1134–5.

Guy, W.A. (1845) 'On the first and last appearance of the menses, and the relation existing between the two periods', *The Medical Times* 12: 363–4.

Hacking, I. (1990) *The taming of chance*. Cambridge: Cambridge University Press.

Hall, G.S. (1904) *Adolescence and its psychology and its relation to physiology, anthropology, sociology, sex, crime, religion and education*. Vol. 1. New York: D. Appleton and Company.

Hammond, T.E. (1926) 'The function of the testes after puberty', *Proceedings of the Royal Society of Medicine* 19(Sect Urol): 53–6.

Harre, E.H. (1962) 'Masturbatory insanity: the history of an idea', *The Journal of Mental Science* 452(108): 1–25.

Hausman, B.L. (1995) *Changing sex: transsexualism, technology, and the idea of gender*. Durham and London: Duke University Press.

Hawkes, G. and Egan, R.D. (2008) 'Landscapes of erotophobia: the sexual(ized) child in the postmodern anglophone west', *Sexuality & Culture* 12(4): 193–203.

Hayes, P. (2013) 'International adoption, "early" puberty, and underrecorded age', *Pediatrics* 131(6): 1029–31.

Hayes, P. (2016) 'Early puberty, medicalisation and the ideology of normality', *Women's Studies International Forum* 56: 9–18.

Hayes, P. (2017) 'Commentary: cognitive, emotional, and psychological functioning of girls treated with pharmacological puberty blockage for idiopathic central precocious puberty', *Frontiers in Psychology: Psychology for Clinical Settings* 8(44) [https://doi.org/10.3389/fpsyg.2017.00044].

Herman-Giddens, M.E. (2006) 'Recent data on pubertal milestones in United States children: the secular trend toward earlier development', *International Journal of Andrology* 29: 241–6.

Herman-Giddens, M.E. (2013) 'The enigmatic pursuit of puberty in girls', *Pediatrics* 132(6): 1125–6.

Herman-Giddens, M.E., Kaplowitz, P.B. and Wasserman, R. (2004) 'Navigating the recent articles on girls' puberty in *Pediatrics*: what do we know and where do we go from here?', *Pediatrics* 113(4): 911–17.

Herman-Giddens, M.E., Slora, E. and Wasserman, R.C. (2000) 'Current age of onset of puberty: in reply', *Pediatrics* 106: 622–3.

Herman-Giddens, M.E., Slora, E.J., Wasserman, R.C., Bourdony, C.J., Bhapkar, M.V., Koch, G.G. and Hasemeier, C.M. (1997) 'Secondary sexual characteristics and menses in young girls seen in office practice: a study from the Pediatric Research in Office Settings Network', *Pediatrics* 99(4): 505–12.

Herman-Giddens, M.E., Steffes, J., Harris, D., Slora, E., Hussey, M., Dowshen, S.A., Wasserman, R., Serwint, J.R., Smitherman, L. and Reiter, E.O. (2012) 'Secondary sexual characteristics in boys: data from the Pediatric Research in Office Settings Network', *Pediatrics* 130(5): e1058–68.

Herman-Giddens, M.E., Wang, L. and Koch, G. (2001) 'Secondary sexual characteristics in boys: estimates from the National Health and Nutrition Examination Survey III, 1988–1994', *Archives of Pediatric and Adolescent Medicine* 155(9): 1022–8.

Hertel, A. (1885) *Overpressure in high schools in Denmark*. London: Macmillan.

Huen, K.F., Leung, S.S.F., Lau, J.T.F., Cheung, A.Y.K., Leung, N.K. and Chiu, M.C. (1997) 'Secular trend in the sexual maturation of Southern Chinese girls', *Acta Paediatrica* 86: 1121–4.

Huffer, L. (2009) *Mad for Foucault: rethinking the foundations of queer theory*. New York: Columbia University Press.

Hutchison, R. (1924) 'Case of precocious puberty', *Proceedings of the Royal Society of Medicine* 17(Sect Study Dis Child): 8–9.

Ito, P.K. (1942) 'Comparative biometrical study of physique of Japanese women born and reared under different environments', *Human Biology* 14(3): 279–351.

Jackson, S. (2015) 'Girls' embodied experiences of media images', in J. Wyn and H. Cahill (eds.) *Handbook of children and youth studies*. Singapore: Springer, pp. 229–42.

Jacobson, J.D., Midyett, L.K. and Moore, W.V. (2004) 'Navigating recent articles on girls' puberty: where should our patients go for evaluation?', *Pediatrics* 115(1): 194–5.

Johnston, J.A. (1940) 'Puberty in the normal girl and in the girl with the minimal reinfection type of tuberculosis', *American Journal of Diseases of Children* 59(2): 287–309.

The Journal of the American Medical Association [author unknown] (1936) 'Endocrine tumours, and other essays' [book review], 106(26): 2259.

The Journal of Nervous and Mental Disease [author unknown] (1889) 'Mania of puberty', 14(12): 774–7.

The Journal of Nervous and Mental Disease [author unknown] (1905) 'Insanity at puberty', 32(11): 752.

Kaplowitz, P. (2004) *Early puberty in girls*. New York: Random House.

Kaplowitz, P.B., Herman-Giddens, M. and Wasserman, R. (2004) 'Navigating recent articles on girls' puberty: where should our patients go for evaluation? in reply', *Pediatrics* 115(1): 195.

Kaplowitz, P.B. and Oberfield, S.E. (1999) 'Re-examination of the age limit for defining when puberty is precocious in girls in the United States: implications for evaluation and treatment: drug and therapeutics and executive committees of the Lawson Wilkins pediatric endocrine society', *Pediatrics* 104(4): 936–41.

Kaplowitz, P.B., Slora, E.J., Wasserman, R.C., Pedlow, S.E. and Herman-Giddens, M.E. (2001) 'Earlier onset of puberty in girls: relation to increased body mass index and race', *Pediatrics* 108(2): 347–53.

Kark, E. (1943) 'Menarche in South African Bantu girls', *South African Journal of Medical Sciences* 8(1): 35–40.

Karlberg, J. (2002) 'Secular trends in pubertal development', *Hormone Research in Paediatrics* 57(Supp. 2): 19–30.

Kendle, F.W. (1905) 'Case of precocious puberty in a female cretin', *The British Medical Journal* 1(2301): 246.

Kessler, S.J. (1990) 'The medical construction of gender: case management of intersexed children', *Signs: Journal of Women in Culture and Society* 16(1): 3–26.

Kessler, S.J. (1998) *Lessons from the intersexed.* New Brunswick: Rutgers University Press.

Kogan, S.M., Cho, J., Simons, L.G., Allen, K.A., Beach, S.R.H., Simons, R.L. and Gibbons, F.X. (2013) 'Pubertal timing and sexual risk behaviors among rural African American male youth: testing a model based on Life History Theory', *Archives of Sexual Behavior* 44(3): 609–18.

Lallemand, C.F. (1836) *Des pertes séminales involontaires.* Paris: Béchat Jeune.

The Lancet [author unknown] (1827) 'Instance of early puberty: By Doctor Gedike, Berlin', 7(176): 468.

The Lancet [author unknown] (1833) 'Premature puberty', 19(496): 709.

The Lancet [author unknown] (1901) 'The period of puberty in relation to disorders and anomalies of development', 158(4075): 928.

The Lancet [author unknown] (1905) 'Pyromania, a psychosis of puberty', 165(4253): 583–4.

The Lancet [author unknown] (1936) 'Physiological changes during puberty', 227(5866): 269.

Lander, J. (1942) 'The pubertal struggle against the instincts', *The American Journal of Orthopsychiatry* 12(3): 456–61.

Laqueur, T.W. (2003) *Solitary sex: a cultural history of masturbation.* New York: Zone Books.

Le Beau, J. (1832) 'Case of premature puberty', *The American Journal of the Medical Sciences* 11: 42–3.

Lee, J.M. and Howell, J.D. (2006) 'Tall girls: the social shaping of a medical therapy', *Archives of Pediatrics and Adolescent Medicine* 160(10): 1035–9.

Lloyd, C.W., Lobotsky, J. and Morley, M. (1950) 'Precocious puberty', *Pediatrics* 6(3): 343–50.

Longrigg, J. (1998) *Greek medicine from the Heroic to the Hellenistic Age: a source book.* New York: Routledge.

Lucas, R.C. (1884) 'On the association of flat-foot, weak ankle, etc., of puberty, with albuminuria', *The British Medical Journal* 1(1218): 852–3.

Ma, H.M., Du, M.L., Luo, X.P., Chen, S.K., Liu, L., Chen, R.M., Zhu, C., Xiong, F., Tang, L., Wang, W. and Liu, G.L. (2009) 'Onset of breast and pubic hair development and menses in urban Chinese girls', *Pediatrics* 124(2): 269–77.

Macnaughton-Jones, H. (1913) 'The relation of puberty and menopause to neurasthenia', *The Lancet* 181(4674): 879–81.

Mahon, M. (1992) *Foucault's Nietzschean genealogy: truth, power, and the subject.* New York: State University of New York Press.

Marr, H. (1910) 'The psychology of puberty [La psychologie de la puberté]. Marro, A.', *The British Journal of Psychiatry* 56(232): 132–5.

Marshall, W.A. and Tanner, J.M. (1969) 'Variation in the pattern of pubertal changes in girls', *Archives of Disease in Childhood* 44(235): 291–303.

Marshall, W.A. and Tanner, J.M. (1970) 'Variation in the pattern of pubertal changes in boys', *Archives of Disease in Childhood* 45(239): 13–23.

Mason, L.W. (1949) 'Precocious puberty', *The Journal of Pediatrics* 34(6): 730–40.

McNay, L. (1992) *Foucault and feminism: power, gender, and the self*. Cambridge: Polity Press.

Meng, X., Li, S., Duan, W., Sun, Y. and Jia, C. (2017) 'Secular trend of age at menarche in Chinese adolescents born from 1973 to 2004', *Pediatrics* 140(2) [https://doi.org/10.1542/peds.2017-0085].

Midyett, L.K., Moore, W.V. and Jacobson, J.D. (2003) 'Are pubertal changes in girls before age 8 benign?', *Pediatrics* 111(1): 47–51.

Mills, C.A. (1937) 'Geographic and time variations in body growth and age at menarche', *Human Biology* 9(1): 43–56.

Morris, D.H., Jones, M.E., Schoemaker, M.J., Ashworth, A. and Swerdlow, A.J. (2011) 'Secular trends in age at menarche in women in the UK born 1908–93: results from the Breakthrough Generations Study', *Paediatric and Perinatal Epidemiology* 25(4): 394–400.

Mott, F. (1921) 'The psychopathology of puberty and adolescence', *The British Journal of Psychiatry* 67(278): 279–318.

Nakagawa, I. (1937) 'Changes in the basal metabolism of children during puberty', *American Journal of Diseases of Children* 53(4): 991–9.

Neale, A.V. (1938) 'Precocious puberty with a report on a case of pineal syndrome', *Archives of Disease in Childhood* 13: 241–8.

Neuman, R.P. (1975) 'Masturbation, madness, and the modern concepts of childhood and adolescence', *Journal of Social History* 8(3): 1–27.

Novak, E. (1944) 'Constitutional type of female precocious puberty with report of nine cases', *American Journal of Obstetrics & Gynecology* 47(1): 20–42.

Ong, K.K., Ahmed, M.L. and Dunger, D.B. (2006) 'Lessons from large population studies on timing and tempo of puberty (secular trends and relation to body size): the European trend', *Molecular and Cellular Endocrinology* 254–255: 8–12.

Oudshoorn, N. (1994) *Beyond the natural body: an archaeology of sex hormones*. New York: Routledge.

Parent, A.S., Teilmann, G., Juul, A., Sakkebaek, N., Toopari, J. and Bourguignon, J.P. (2003) 'The timing of normal puberty and the age limits of sexual precocity: variations around the world, secular trends and changes after migration', *Endocrine Reviews* 24(5): 668–93.

Parker, I. (2002) *Critical discursive psychology*. London: Palgrave Macmillan.

Pinchbeck, J. and Hewitt, M. (1973) *Children in English society, volume II: from the eighteenth century to the Children Act 1948*. London: Routledge and Kegan Paul.

Philip, M. and Lazar, L. (2005) 'Precocious puberty: growth and genetics', *Hormone Research in Paediatrics* 64(Suppl.2): 56–61.

Pitt, G.N. (1886) 'On cardiac dilatation at puberty, and its frequent occurrence in girls', *The British Medical Journal* 2(1352): 1028–9.

Playfair, W.S. (1895) 'Remarks on the education and training of girls of the easy classes at and about the period of puberty', *The British Medical Journal* 2(1823): 1408–10.

Polinière, M. (1820) 'Puberté', *Dictionnaire des Sciences Médicales* 46: 32–64.

Porter, R. (1998) *The greatest benefit to mankind: a medical history of humanity*. New York: W.W. Norton & Company.

Pritchard, J.C. (1836) *Researches into the physical history of mankind*. Vol. 1. London: Sherwood, Gilbert, and Piper.

Quetelet, A. (1835) *Sur l'homme et le développement de ses facultés, ou essai de physique sociale*. 2 vols. Paris: Bachelier.

Quetelet, A. (1842) *A Treatise on man and the development of his faculties*. Edinburgh: William and Robert Chambers.

Quetelet, A. (1869) 'Sur le tome XIX des Annales de l'Observatoire Royal de Bruxelles et sur le tome second de la nouvelle édition de la Physique Sociale', *Bulletins de l'Académie Royale des Sciences, des Lettres et des Beaux-Arts de Belgique* 28(8): 149–68.

Rabinow, P. (1996) 'Artificiality and Enlightenment: from sociobiology to biosociality', in S.B. Ortner, N.B. Dirks and G. Eley (eds.) *Essays on the anthropology of reason*. Princeton: Princeton University Press, pp. 91–111.

Raciborski, A. (1844) *La puberté, l'âge critique et la ponte chez la femme et les mammifères*. Paris: J.B. Baillière.

Raciborski, A. (1868) *Traité de la menstruation*. Paris: J.B. Baillière et Fils.

Reiter, E.O. and Lee, P.A. (2001) 'Have the onset and tempo of puberty changed?', *Archives of Pediatrics and Adolescent Medicine* 155: 988–9.

Renold, E. and Ringrose, J. (2011) 'Schizoid subjectivities? Re-theorizing teen girls' sexual cultures in an era of "sexualization"', *Journal of Sociology* 47: 389–409.

Renold, E., Ringrose, J. and Egan, D. (eds.) (2015) *Children, sexuality and sexualization*. Basingstoke: Palgrave Macmillan.

Richey, H.G. (1931) 'The blood pressure of boys and girls before and after puberty', *American Journal of Diseases of Children* 42(6): 1281–330.

Roberton, J. (1830) 'Period of puberty in women', *The Boston Medical and Surgical Journal* 3(42): 669–70.

Roberton, J. (1832) 'An inquiry into the natural history of the menstrual function', *The Edinburgh Medical and Surgical Journal* 38(113): 227–54.

Roberton, J. (1842) 'On the period of puberty in Negro women', *The London Medical Gazette* 2: 677–82.

Roberton, J. (1845a) 'On the period of puberty in Hindu women', *The Edinburgh Medical and Surgical Journal* 64(164): 156–69.

Roberton, J. (1845b) 'Supplement to Mr Roberton's paper on the period of puberty in Hindu women', *The Edinburgh Medical and Surgical Journal* 64(164): 257–64.

Roberton, J. (1845c) 'On the period of puberty in Esquimaux women', *The Edinburgh Medical and Surgical Journal* 62(162): 55–67.

Roberton, J. (1846a) 'On the period of puberty in Hindu women', *The Edinburgh Medical and Surgical Journal* 66(168): 56–64.

Roberton, J. (1846b) 'On the age of puberty in the island of Madeira', *The Edinburgh Medical and Surgical Journal* 66(169): 281–5.

Roberton, J. (1846c) 'On Hindu midwifery', *The Edinburgh Medical and Surgical Journal* 65(167): 308–19.

Roberton, J. (1848) 'On the period of puberty in the Negro', *The Edinburgh Medical and Surgical Journal* 69(174): 69–77.

Roberton, J. (1851) *Essays and notes on the physiology of women, and on practical midwifery*. London: John Churchill.

Roberts, C. (2010) 'Early puberty and public health: a social scientific pinboard', *Critical Public Health* 20(4): 429–38.

Roberts, C. (2013a) 'Early puberty, "sexualization" and feminism', *European Journal of Women's Studies* 20(2): 138–54.

Roberts, C. (2013b) 'Evolutionary psychology, feminism and early sexual development', *Feminist Theory* 14(3): 295–304.

Roberts, C. (2014) 'The entanglement of sexed bodies and pharmaceuticals: a feminist analysis of early onset puberty and puberty-blocking medications', *Subjectivity* 7(4): 321–41.

Roberts, C. (2015) *Puberty in crisis: the sociology of early sexual development*. Cambridge: Cambridge University Press.

Roberts, C. (2016) 'Tanner's puberty scale: exploring the historical entanglements of children, scientific photography and sex', *Sexualities* 19(3): 328–46.

Rodgers, T.S. (1935) 'Precocious puberty and overgrowth', *Proceedings of the Royal Society of Medicine* 28(6): 659–61.

Rose, N. (1994) 'Medicine, history and the present', in C. Jones and R. Porter (eds.) *Reassessing Foucault: power, medicine and the body*. London: Routledge, pp. 48–72.

Rosenberg, M. (1991) 'Menarcheal age for Norwegian women born 1830–1960', *Annals of Human Biology* 18(3): 207–19.

Rosenfield, R.L. (1994) 'Selection of children with precocious puberty for treatment with gonadotropin releasing hormone analogs', *Journal of Pediatrics* 124: 989–91.

Rosenfield, R.L., Bachrach, L.K., Chernausek, S.D., Gertner, J.M., Gottschalk, M., Hardin, D.S., Pescovitz, O.H. and Saenger, P. (2000) 'Current age of onset of puberty', *Pediatrics* 106: 622.

Ryan, M. (1834) 'Professor Thomson's lectures on medical jurisprudence', *The London Medical and Surgical Journal* 6(141): 435.

Schiebinger, L. (2004) *Nature's body: gender in the making of modern science*. New Jersey: Rutgers University Press.

Schlutz, F.W. (1941) 'What to do about the fat child at puberty?', *The Journal of Pediatrics* 19(3): 376–81.

Shuttleworth, F.K. (1937) 'Sexual maturation and the physical growth of girls aged six to nineteen', *Monographs of the Society for Research in Child Development* 2(5): 253.

Smart, R.B. (1858) 'On a case of premature puberty', *Medico-Chirurgical Transactions* 41: 455–62.

Smith, R.E. (1939) 'Observations on the descent of the testicle with special reference to spontaneous descent at puberty', *Archives of Disease in Childhood* 14(77): 1–13.

South, J.F. (1823) 'History of a case of premature puberty', *Medico-Chirurgical Transactions* 12(1): 76–85.

Spurzheim, J. (1825a) 'Lectures on phrenology by Dr. Spurzheim', *The Lancet* 4(81): 41–6.

Spurzheim, J. (1825b) 'Lectures on phrenology by Dr. Spurzheim: lecture 3', *The Lancet* 4(83): 102–8.

Stainton-Rogers, R. and Stainton-Rogers, W. (1992) *Stories of childhood: shifting agendas of child concern*. Toronto: University of Toronto Press.

Stearns, S.C. (1992) *The evolution of life histories*. Oxford: Oxford University Press.

Stepan, N. (1982) *The idea of race in Science: Great Britain 1800–1960*. London: Macmillan.

Stotijn, C.P.J. and Nauta, W.J.H. (1950) 'Precocious puberty and tumor of the hypothalamus: with report of a case, and a consideration of hypothalamo-hypophyseal connections', *The Journal of Mental and Nervous Disease* 111(3): 207–24.

Strange, J.M. (2000) 'Menstrual fictions: languages of medicine and menstruation, c. 1850–1930', *Women's History Review* 9(3): 607–28.

Sullivan, W.C. (1912) 'Automatic parricidal impulse in puberty', *The British Journal of Psychiatry* 58(242): 525.

Sun, S.S., Schubert, C.M., Liang, R., Roche, A.F., Kulin, H.E., Lee, P.A., Himes, J.H. and Chumlea, W.C. (2005) 'Is sexual maturity occurring earlier among U.S. children?', *Journal of Adolescent Health* 37(5): 345–55.

Talbot, F.B. (1919) 'The caloric requirements of normal infants and children from birth to puberty', *American Journal of Diseases of Children* 18(4): 229–37.

Tamboukou, M. (2003) *Women, education and the self: a Foucauldian perspective*. Basingstoke: Palgrave Macmillan.

Tanner, J.M. (1952) 'The assessment of growth and development in children', *Archives of Disease in Childhood* 27(131): 10–33.

Tanner, J. M. (1959). 'Boas' contributions to knowledge of human growth and form', in W. Goldschmidt (ed.) *The anthropology of Franz Boas: essays on the centennial of his birth*. San Francisco: Howard Chandler, pp. 76–111.

Tanner, J.M. (1962) *Growth at adolescence*. 2nd edn. Oxford: Blackwell.

Tanner, J.M. (1965) 'The trend towards physical maturation', in J.E. Meade and A.S. Parkes (eds.) *Biological aspects of social problems: a symposium held by the Eugenics Society in October 1964*. Edinburgh and London: Oliver & Boyd Ltd., pp. 40–65.

Tanner, J.M. (1966) 'Galtonian eugenics and the study of growth: the relation of body size, intelligence test score, and social circumstances in children and adults', *The Eugenics Review* 58(3): 122–35.

Tanner, J.M. (1973) 'Trend towards earlier menarche in London, Oslo, Copenhagen, the Netherlands and Hungary', *Nature* 243(5402): 95–6.

Tanner, J.M. (1981a) *A History of the study of human growth*. Cambridge: Cambridge University Press.

Tanner, J.M. (1981b) 'Menarcheal age', *Science* 214(4521): 604.

Tanner, J.M., Whitehouse, R.H. and Takaishi, M. (1966) 'Standards from birth to maturity for height, weight, height velocity and weight velocity: British children, 1965', *Archives of Disease in Childhood* 41(219–220): 454–71, 613–35.

Terman, L.M. (1905) 'A study in precocity and prematuration', *The American Journal of Psychology* 16(2): 145–83.

Thompson, D'A.W. (1945) *On growth and form*. 4th edn. Cambridge: Cambridge University Press.

Thomson, A.T. (1834a) 'Lectures on medical jurisprudence: lecture V', *The London Medical and Surgical Journal* 6(146): 481–7.

Thomson, A.T. (1834b) 'Lectures on medical jurisprudence: lecture VI', *The London Medical and Surgical Journal* 6(147): 513–19.

Thomson, A.T. (1834c) 'Lectures on medical jurisprudence: lecture IX', *The London Medical and Surgical Journal* 6(150): 609–15.

Thomson, A.T. (1834d) 'Lectures on medical jurisprudence: lecture X', *The London Medical and Surgical Journal* 6(151): 641–8.

Thomson, A.T. (1834e) 'Lectures on medical jurisprudence: lecture XIV', *The London Medical and Surgical Journal* 6(155): 769–76.

Thomson, A.T. (1834f) 'Lectures on medical jurisprudence: lecture XI', *The London Medical and Surgical Journal* 6(152): 673–8.

Topper, A. and Mulier, H. (1932) 'Basal metabolism of normal children: the puberty reaction', *American Journal of Diseases of Children* 43(2): 327–36.

Uddenberg, G. (1944) 'On pubertas praecox', *Acta Paediatrica* 31(3): 310–29.

Valverde, M. (1998) *Diseases of the will: alcohol and the dilemmas of freedom*. Cambridge: Cambridge University Press.

Vares, T., Jackson, S. and Gill, R. (2011) 'Preteen girls read "tween" popular culture: diversity, complexity and contradiction', *International Journal of Media & Cultural Politics* 7(2): 139–54.

Veeder, B.S. and Rholfing, E.H. (1927) 'Studies in pubescent growth with special reference to periodic gain', *American Journal of Diseases of Children* 34(2): 211–17.

Villermé, L.R. (1829) 'Mémoire sur la taille de l'homme en France', *Annales d'Hygiène Publique* 1: 551–99.

Virey, J.J. (1815a) 'Fécondation', *Dictionnaire des Sciences Médicales* 14: 463–80.

Virey, J.J. (1815b) 'Femme', *Dictionnaire des Sciences Médicales* 14: 503–72.

Virey, J.J. (1816) 'Géant', *Dictionnaire des Sciences Médicales* 17: 546–68.

Virey, J.J. (1817) 'Génération', *Dictionnaire des Sciences Médicales* 18: 1–68.

Virey, J.J. (1824a) *Histoire naurelle du genre human, tome premier*. Paris: Crochard.

Virey, J.J. (1824b) *Histoire naurelle du genre human, tome deuxième*. Paris: Crochard.

Walvoord, E.C. (2010) 'The timing of puberty: is it changing? Does it matter?', *Journal of Adolescent Health* 47: 433–9.

Wang, Y. (2002) 'Is obesity associated with early sexual maturation? A comparison of the association in American boys versus girls', *Pediatrics* 110: 903–10.

Weir, L. (2006) *Pregnancy, risk and biopolitics: on the threshold of the living subject*. New York: Routledge.

White, A. (1809) 'Historical account of Phillip Howorth, a boy, in whom Signs of puberty commenced at an early age', *Medico-Chirurgical Transactions* 1: 278–87.

Whitehead, J. (1848a) *On the causes and treatment of abortion and sterility*. Philadelphia: Lea & Blanchard.

Whitehead, J. (1848b) 'Period of puberty', *Provincial Medical and Surgical Journal* 12(2): 52.

Whitehead, J. (1848c) 'Age of puberty in England: Mr. Whitehead and Mr. Roberton', *Provincial Medical and Surgical Journal* 12(3): 83.

Wiegman, R. (1995) *American anatomies: theorizing race and gender*. Durham: Duke University Press.

Wiglesworth, J. (1893a) 'General paralysis occurring about the period of puberty', *The British Journal of Psychiatry* 39: 355–67.

Wiglesworth, J. (1893b) 'General paralysis occurring about the period of puberty', *The British Medical Journal* 1(1682): 635.

Wilson, D.C. and Sutherland, I. (1950) 'Further observations on the age of the menarche', *British Medical Journal* 2(4684): 862–6.

Wilson, D.S.P. (1939) 'The treatment of the incompletely descended testis', *Proceedings of the Royal Society of Medicine* 32(8): 969–86.

Wu, T., Mendola, P. and Buck, G. (2002) 'Ethnic differences in the presence of secondary sex characteristics and menarche among US girls: the Third National Health and Nutrition Examination Survey, 1988–1994', *Pediatrics* 110(4): 752–7.

Wyshak, G. and Frisch, R.E. (1982) 'Evidence for a secular trend in age of menarche', *The New England Journal of Medicine* 306(17): 1033–5.

Index

For Product Safety Concerns and Information please contact our
EU representative GPSR@taylorandfrancis.com Taylor & Francis
Verlag GmbH, Kaufingerstraße 24, 80331 München, Germany